America's Ten Greatest Presidents

America's
Ten
Greatest
Presidents

Edited by

MORTON BORDEN
Montana State University

RAND McNALLY & COMPANY
CHICAGO

Rand McNally HISTORY SERIES

FRED HARVEY HARRINGTON, *Consulting Editor*

Borden, ed., *America's Ten Greatest Presidents*

Freidel and Pollack, eds., *Builders of American Institutions*

Gatzke, *The Present in Perspective*, 2nd edition

Jones, *Ancient Civilization*

Mosse, *The Culture of Western Europe;
The Nineteenth and Twentieth Centuries*

Mosse, Cameron, Hill, and Petrovich, eds., *Europe in Review*

Palmer, ed., *Atlas of World History*

Palmer, ed., *Historical Atlas of the World*

Sellers, ed., *Berkeley Series in American History*

Shannon, *Twentieth Century America*

Starr, Nowell, Lyon, Stearns, and Hamerow,
A History of the World (2 Vols.)

Treadgold, *Twentieth Century Russia*

Williams, *The Shaping of American Diplomacy*

Wright, *France in Modern Times; 1760 to the Present*

Contents

INTRODUCTION

"The office of President," Alexander Hamilton predicted in 1788, "will never fall to the lot of any man who is not in an eminent degree endowed with the requisite qualifications. . . . It will not be too strong to say, that there will be a constant probability of seeing the station filled by characters preëminent for ability and virtue." None of America's presidents can properly be described as evil; indeed, it is a remarkable tribute to this country's political sagacity that while many demagogues have aspired to that office, none has yet succeeded. On the other hand, it is also unquestionably true that most presidents have not possessed the stature envisioned by Hamilton.

Hamilton, in fact, would not have approved of several presidents included in this volume; nor will every reader. All such selections are comparative; tastes differ, values change, and measuring rods come in assorted sizes and colors. If public popularity were an important basis for deciding America's greatest presidents, Dwight Eisenhower would rate higher than Lincoln who was convinced he could not win a second term in 1864. If courage, devotion, or hard work were the sole criteria, John Quincy Adams would be outranked by few. If creativity or brilliance were the prime indices, Washington would fail to qualify. If a sense of moderation and an ability to compromise were crucial, Andrew Jackson must be struck from the list. If the projection of a favorable image were instrumental, Polk failed. If political leadership were

1

the ultimate test, Cleveland was lucky and Wilson was inept in his second term. Finally, if the use of democratic means and a regard for legal and constitutional scruples were considered as *sine qua non*'s for presidential greatness, half the men included in this volume—and the better half—would not belong.

A decade ago Professor Arthur M. Schlesinger, Sr., conducted a poll of fifty-five prominent scholars of American history and government. He asked them to rate the performance of America's presidents according to these categories: Great, Near Great, Average, Below Average, and Failures (*Life*, November 1, 1948). Two presidents, Grant and Harding, were judged failures; seventeen were considered middling to poor; ten passed with flying colors. The results were, in part, as follows: (Great) 1., Lincoln; 2., Washington; 3., F. D. Roosevelt; 4., Wilson; 5., Jefferson; 6., Jackson; (Near Great) 7., T. Roosevelt; 8., Cleveland; 9., J. Adams; 10., Polk. Most provocative—since rating America's presidents is as personal and as difficult as handicapping thoroughbreds—was Professor Schlesinger's finding a "large measure of agreement among the 'experts' within the important categories of great, near great, and failures." For this reason the editor decided to employ the results of Professor Schlesinger's consensus.

More important than the question *who*, however, is the question *why*. The pendulum of historiography has swung from nineteenth century pietism to contemporary ultracriticism. Both are distortions. Too many modern historians see only the clay toenails of these allegedly great men. Abraham Lincoln, as a state representative and congressman, was a hack politician; he was inconsistent in his debates with Douglas; he freed no slaves; his actions against the Copperheads smacked of despotism; and so forth. Franklin D. Roosevelt wrecked the London Economic Conference; he was economically illiterate; he was not really responsible for most New Deal legislation. Theodore Roosevelt was a crude jingoist; Wilson was a foolish idealist; Cleveland was a strikebreaker; and Jefferson, as president, simply outfederalized the Federalists. Little wonder that the college student—conditioned to think of history in terms of TV westerns, heroes against villains—usually asks: If all this is so, then why do historians regard these ten men as great presidents?

The purpose of this volume is to strike the proper balance that will answer this question. Each contributor has enjoyed complete freedom regarding the content and organization of his essay. Aside from one significant reminder—that implicitly or explicitly, there must be an answer to the question *why*—ultimate responsibility rests squarely with the contributor.

MORTON BORDEN
Montana State University

George Washington

by J. A. CARROLL

C lose to ten o'clock on the morning of April 16, 1789, a tall man in his fifty-seventh year, dressed for travel in blue broadcloth and black boots and holding a tricorn hat in his hand, stood for a very brief moment on the piazza at Mount Vernon. From here on a clear day he could see some distance down the several miles of river that bordered his plantation, and the broad and quiet Potomac always rested his spirit. But there was no time left to contemplate the view. Makers of history, unlike those who study it, seldom are allowed the pleasures of retrospection.

General George Washington, soldier of the Revolution and Virginia's foremost farmer, was ready to make a journey that would put him into a new career. Two days earlier he had received notice of his elevation, by the vote of every elector, to the office of President of the United States—and now his carriage was waiting. "I bade adieu to Mount Vernon, to private life, and to domestic felicity," he wrote that night in his diary, "and, with a mind oppressed with more anxious and painful sensations than I have words to express, set out for New York . . . with the best disposition to render service to my country in obedience to its call. . . ." A few miles up the road at Wise's Tavern, the citizens of Alexandria honored their neighbor with a farewell dinner. "Go," Mayor Ramsay exhorted the President-elect, "and make a grateful people happy."

As it soon proved, the people of the United States were grateful indeed in 1789 that General Washington had consented to serve as chief magistrate of their new republic. His eight-day journey to New York, the first capital city, was in the manner of a triumphal procession of a Roman conqueror. At Baltimore, at Wilmington, at Philadelphia, at every town and coach stop along the route he was fêted with the pealing of bells, gun salutes, toasts and huzzas, gratulatory speeches and odes, parades and public banquets, and pyrotechnics through the night. The people of Trenton, eager to excel in their demonstration, provided a caparisoned white horse which Washington rode as ladies sung to him and children threw flowers in his path. Finally, after crossing Newark Bay in a festooned barge with a train of flag-flying small craft in his wake, the President-elect was met at the Battery by thousands of New Yorkers. The crowd was so dense, and so determined to applaud and admire, that it took Washington almost an hour to make his way from the wharf to the "Executive Mansion" nearby at No. 3 Cherry Street. If this was adulation in the extreme, if it was almost idolatry, it was something deeper also. Here, unmistakably, was a manifestation of the ebullient hopes of a people recently free and a nation freshly born.

Of the several presidents of the United States who have served their countrymen memorably in critical periods, none experienced so full a measure of public esteem in the hour of inauguration as George Washington. No chief executive has entered office better known to his contemporaries. From New England to Georgia in 1789 Washington was celebrated as the American Atlas, the American Fabius, the Cincinnatus of the Western Hemisphere; for almost a decade now he had heard references to himself as "Father of his Country." In 1783, upon retirement to his farm after eight years as Commander in Chief of the Continental Army, he was by all odds the most famous man in America. Even as proprietor of Mount Vernon he had been conspicuous, a kind of national host whose beautiful home on the Potomac became, as he said, a "well-resorted tavern" for unexpected and unannounced travelers of every type. His appearance at the Philadelphia Convention in 1787 brought him again into public view, and the architects and advertisers of the Constitution were quick to dramatize the fact that General Washington had presided at the rebuilding of the old Articles of Confederation into the "New Roof of Federalism." So familiar was his name by 1788 that no other could be mentioned seriously for the highest office in the new system of government. James Madison, major draftsman of the Constitution, visited Mount Vernon often and brought all his logic to bear against Washington's reluctance to leave retirement. From New York Alexander Hamilton sent urgent notes: "I take it for granted, Sir, you have concluded to comply with . . . the general call of your country in relation to the new government. You will permit me to say, that it is indispensable you should lend yourself to the first operation." The General still hesitated. "At my age and in my circumstance," he wrote, ". . . I have no wish which aspires beyond the humble and happy lot of living and dying a private citizen on my own farm." But his preference did not decide the matter. "We cannot, Sir, do without you," wrote Thomas Johnson of Maryland, adding that "thousands more" were in agreement. The first presidential election was a formality in the strictest sense, and unanimity was inevitable. The soldier-farmer from Virginia was the one American that his fellow-citizens, be they Federalists or "anti-Feds," knew best of all.

It is curious, then, that perhaps no president has proven more mysterious to posterity than the first. Historians have found it reasonably easy to chronicle the events of Washington's two administrations because the records and literary remains of the years 1789-97 are abundant. They have been able to dissect and to understand the opposite philosophies, social and economic, of the dominant personalities of the period, Alexander Hamilton and Thomas Jefferson. In detailed monographs they have shown how the clashing concepts of these two men ignited a political fire which, despite Washington's avowed determination to "walk on a straight line" and to act as "President of all the people," quickly divided the nation into sectional parties—Federalists following Hamilton northward and eastward, Republican-Democrats following Jefferson southward and westward. Scholars have identified party strife in the United States with the revolutionary upheavals that convulsed Europe in the 1790's, and possibly some have gone too far in ascribing "Anglomania" to Federalist leaders and "Gallomania" to Republicans. Washington's administrations, in any case, have been much discussed by modern historians. Their specialized studies fill a long shelf, and their conclusions are distilled accurately in many textboooks. Yet, to Americans in the twentieth century, President Washington presents something of an enigma.

Confident as we may be that we understand the period, we do not always understand the man.

For all the research and exposition and synthesis that scholars have lavished on the eight formative years that George Washington occupied the chair of state, the figure of the first president is remarkably vague. The American whom his contemporaries felt they knew so well in 1789 has become increasingly a puzzle to subsequent generations. Gilbert Stuart's "Landsdowne" portrait, representing Washington in presidential costume of black velvet, will always be familiar, but its subject does not stand today in clear relief. Vapors of obscurity surround Washington in his role as chief executive. While many historians have been careful to point out and to praise the qualities of statesmanship that he possessed in depth, still a vagueness persists. Still the question was heard: What kind of president, really, was George Washington?

This essay will not attempt to deliver a capsuled answer. Americans who desire to improve the qualities of their citizenship will profit vastly by investigating that question for themselves. Significant lessons may be learned, and great examples obtained, by moving patiently with Washington through the morass of mighty problems and myriad vexations that he met in eight years at the helm of the new republic. Sometimes singly, sometimes together, his controlling characteristics will appear: forthrightness, firmness, farsightedness, determination, decisiveness—each and all tempered by instinctive caution. "My political conduct," he wrote in 1789, "must be exceedingly circumspect . . . for the eyes of Argus are upon me." To this rule he remained constant, but at a cost neither to integrity nor to magnanimity. How he did so makes a story in statesmanship that is inspirational, and one that may be found fully as thrilling as tales of the battlefield.

Like a good poem, George Washington's character is perhaps better sensed than analyzed. It is better, in any case, to contemplate Washington in full size than to examine him by synthetic lens. Washington was not an architect in ideas; he was essentially a man of deeds. His thoughts do not array themselves in a convenient constellation that may be understood in outline; rather they form a massive milky way that must be considered from end to end. Washington does not emerge spontaneously in a pattern; he appears gradually in a procession of events. He is best portrayed not in composite overview, but by scrutiny of his thoughts and interpretation of his actions at climactic moments of his career. The cumulative method does not produce an image rapidly, but it has its delights. Douglas Southall Freeman, who studied Washington in this way for almost ten years while writing a large biography, regarded it an inestimable privilege to "live" so long in the company of a magnificent man. Others will find every hour they spend with Washington to be equally rewarding.

Reduced to enumeration, the achievements of Washington's administrations count to not less than ten. During his presidency the United States government gained its executive and legislative precedents, appended a bill of rights to the Constitution, established its credit at home and abroad, fostered manufacturing and encouraged commerce, survived a serious insurrection in the mountains of Pennsylvania, secured the transmontane frontier against Indian depredations, effected the removal of British troops from the Old Northwest, checked Spanish encroachments in the Old Southwest and obtained transit rights on the Mississippi, forged a policy for the disposition of public lands, and avoided involvement in the vortex of European wars. Analysis will reveal that Washington's hand was large in many of these accomplishments, and that in several his role was decisive. Proud of their record, Federalists were quick to acknowledge this: Washington's leadership was never nebulous to them. "Such a Chief Magistrate," said Fisher Ames, "appears like the pole star in a clear sky. . . . His Presidency will form an epoch and be distinguished as the Age of Washington." Ames was an orator who arranged his words nicely, but he was also as intuitive and straight-speaking a Federalist as there was in the party. However reluctantly, Republicans came to the same conclusion. In 1796 Jefferson expressed it simply: "One man outweighs them all in influence over the people."

Yet, by the eyes of posterity, Washington's role has not been seen in so sharp a light. It has long been a fashion to regard President Washington's administrations not so much his as Alexander Hamilton's. Critical research in the twentieth century has established beyond question that the genius and energy of Hamilton were responsible for much that the Federal government did—and, indeed, for much of what happened in the United States—between 1789 and 1797. As Senator William Maclay, dour Republican of Pennsylvania, remarked testily, "Mr. Hamilton is all powerful and fails in nothing he attempts." No student of the period would deny Hamilton's significance, but it may be that emphasis on the brilliance of the "Young Lothario" of the Federalists has worked to the disadvantage of a deeper consideration of the President's own part in the affairs of the new republic. In its business, great and small, the President was always there. He was neither listless nor dull, as sometimes he has been portrayed, and neither too old nor too deaf to participate fully. "He was an Aegis," Hamilton admitted, "very essential to me."

Surely it is not incorrect to think of the Federalist era as the heyday of Hamiltonian ideals. But it is quite wrong to suppose that Washington loved the pomp and ceremony with which his aides surrounded him, that his attitudes were more English than American, or that he concurred readily with Hamilton's extreme and often-quoted remark on the necessity of rule by the "rich and well-born." And it is altogether wrong to imagine that the President responded automatically to Hamilton's every suggestion, that he permitted a Svengali-like control to be exercised over him, or that he turned to Hamilton in helpless frustration when the pressures of office became too great.

Washington did none of these things. Instead, as chief executive, he developed to a remarkable degree the science of deliberate and responsible consultation. While Hamilton served as secretary of the treasury and Jefferson as secretary of state, Washington solicited advice from them almost equally. In 1789 and 1790 he consulted the "heads of departments" individually on specific matters, and made his decision largely on one officer's specific advice. By the end of 1791, however, he was calling them together for discussion of larger problems. The Cabinet met several times in 1792, and many times during Washington's second term. Washington's closest friend in the Cabinet was neither Hamilton nor Jefferson but rather his old military comrade, General Henry Knox, the secretary of war. It may be argued reasonably that Knox, who served until 1795, was a convenient mirror for Hamilton's views; but in these same years the President's thinking over a wide range of major problems more nearly approximated that of Edmund Randolph than of any other member of the Cabinet. This gifted Virginian was in no way a Hamiltonian Federalist—and, according to Jefferson, not very much of a Republican. Jefferson thought Randolph "indecisive" and a "chameleon." Washington thought him impartial and sound.

Randolph, one of the forgotten figures in American history, was Washington's protégé as a boy, then a Richmond lawyer and governor of Virginia, the first attorney general in 1789, and successor to Jefferson in the Department of State four years later. The President's faith in the judgment of Randolph was high, perhaps higher than historians have yet discovered, and the estrangement of the two men in 1795 amounted to a tragedy for each. For Randolph, who was accused of soliciting a French bribe and of defalcation in diplomatic funds, it meant disgrace and oblivion. For Washington, it meant the end of a treasured relationship. Only at this point, after the exit of the last member of his original Cabinet, did Hamilton's correspondence with Washington begin to reflect with startling vividity in the decisions of the President—and by now he was in the final year of his second term. No attempt is being made in these remarks to minimize the contributions of Hamilton to the policies and projects of Washington's government. They are meant only to underscore the central fact that, in the achievements of the Federalists between 1789 and 1797, the man who was President played a personal, an integral, and a most important part.

Of the ten enumerated achievements of Washington's administrations, the last in the list is perhaps the first in significance. Nothing that the Federalists did between 1789 and 1797 was of larger moment then, or deserves the larger gratitude of posterity, than their efforts to keep the United States out of the wars of the French Revolution. Whether their sympathies incline to the Federalists or to the Republicans, historians have been in general agreement that American participation in the wars which erupted in Europe in 1793 would have proven disastrous. The American Union, then just four years old, scarcely could have survived such an experience. No man in the United States saw this more clearly in 1793 than George Washington. And in no instance during his tenure as chief executive did Washington demonstrate his role in the government so abundantly, or his greatness in statecraft so dramatically, as in the decisions he made—and in the manner he made them—early in that year. The preservation of American neutrality was Washington's mightiest personal achievement as President of the United States. In February, March, and April of 1793 he forged the neutral rule in its fundamental form, and through the next four years his every policy was built on it. Of the several examples that might be used to indicate the active hand of Washington in the great affairs of government, this one has been chosen as much for its illustrative value as for its importance.

On March 4, 1793, in the Senate chamber at Philadelphia, Washington took the presidential oath for the second time. The first Federal administration, he could be sure, had accomplished much. Procedures had been established and many precedents set, the Constitution had been enlarged with the Bill of Rights, the stature of the central government had been assured, the machinery of national finance put into motion, and plans had been laid for a permanent capital city to be erected on the north bank of the Potomac. With these specifics and with the rapid rise of manufacturing and commerce that augured so well for the prosperity of the nation, Washington was immensely pleased. "A spirit of improvement displays itself in every quarter," he declared, "and principally in objects of the greatest public utility . . . things which seem eminently calculated to promote the advantage and accommodation of the people at large." The young republic had come far since 1789; further progress, the President felt, was certain if citizens would fix their minds and fasten their energies on such internal and immediate goals as inland navigation, road and bridge building, and settlement of the frontier. Then suddenly, in the opening weeks of his second term, the United States approached the precipice of war. The appeal of the French Revolution now threatened to draw the new American nation into a global conflict that would obliterate its fairest prospects.

Satisfied as he was with the results of his first administration, Washington entered his second term in a mood of apprehension. The national progress in which he took such pride had been gained, he knew, only at a very dear price. The bills on funding, assumption, residence, the excise, and the national bank—each one a device of Hamilton's to engross the prestige of the Federal government and multiply its powers under the Constitution—had loosened a torrent of opposition, criticism of Hamilton and Vice President Adams as "monocrats," and denunciation of all Federalists as "speculators" and "corruptionists." In Congress and in every city the Federalist followers of Hamilton and the Republican disciples of Jefferson were arguing vociferously, hurling epithets in their newspapers, and straining for advantage in what Fisher Ames now aptly styled "the pitched battle of parties." And, as political strife came to high tide in the vice-presidental contest of 1792 between the Federalist Adams and the candidate of the Republicans, Governor George Clinton of New York, Washington realized that the ebb of controversy soon would wash against his own door. No longer could he regard himself as "President of all the people," and he hardly could expect the same immunity in his second term that had shielded his office and his person from public censure in the first. "Convulsed as we are," Edmund Randolph warned him early in 1793, "I cannot but believe that there is scarcely a man in the Government whom party will not sooner or later destine for an attack."

Washington was past sixty, his health uncertain and his hearing impaired, and he longed for the shade of retirement at Mount Vernon more fervently now than ever. Still, because both Hamilton and Jefferson had urged him to do so—and because both Secretaries promised to remain in the Cabinet—he consented to a second term. "The motives which induced my acceptance," he wrote to a friend, "are the same which have ever ruled my decision, when the public desire (or, as my countrymen are pleased to denominate it, the *public good*) are placed in the scale against my personal enjoyment or private interest." But now, he might have added, Hamilton and Jefferson seemed farther than ever from agreement on just what constituted the "public good," and at this moment his countrymen were exhibiting a "public desire" that alarmed and dismayed him. The anxiety of Americans for news of the French Revolution was so intense as to be frightening. Did the people of the United States feel such communion with the cause of France that they might actually wish to plunge into the European conflagration?

For almost a year no news, not even the details of the vice-presidential contest, had been so epidemic from New England to Georgia as the "interesting advices" from abroad. Nine months prior to Washington's second inauguration the American diplomat in France, Gouverneur Morris, reported from his Paris station: "We stand on a vast volcano. We feel it tremble. We hear it roar." Throughout the autumn of 1792 Americans waited in high and rapturous suspense for echoes of the eruption. Already it was known that the French experiment in constitutional monarchy, born in the Revolution of 1789, was disintegrating, and that a new system was rising in its place. In April, 1792, the French ministry had ordered its armies—under America's old friend, Lafayette, and other commanders—into the field against the monarchies of Austria and Prussia; and the failures of this campaign shook Paris violently in July and August. The Girondists clung to power, yet

13

lost control as mass demonstrations by Robespierre's Jacobins threw the city into tumult; the Tuileries fell, King Louis XVI was imprisoned, Lafayette fled the vengeance of the mob and was taken by the Austrians, the Assembly was disbanded and the Constitution of 1791 set aside, a mammoth National Convention was elected and empowered, and thousands died in the streets in the first week of September. It was evident to Morris that the climax had come. "The middle party, prime movers of the Revolution," he predicted in a dispatch to Jefferson, "must fall to the ground. . . . Matters are now brought to a simple question between absolute monarchy and a republic, for all middle terms are done away."

Of this there could be little doubt. "Those mad and corrupt people in France have destroyed their government," wrote William Short in disgust from The Hague, adding that the instruments of all authority now resided with "the most mad, wicked, and atrocious assembly that was ever collected in any country." In their love of order and dread of anarchy, Federalists in the United States might take this estimate at its face. But Jefferson would not. "Our monocrats here," he mused, might sit miserably in silence, but true Republicans gloried in the progress of the French Revolution because they were able to recognize that "the liberty of the whole earth" depended on its success. To the Secretary of State, who had spent five years as American minister at Paris during a period when men talked much of overturning tyranny and overcoming poverty, recent developments in France were the inevitable outcome of that nation's "beautiful revolution." The French Jacobins, he thought, were merely "republican patriots" who had given every chance to constitutional monarchy, had found it unsatisfactory, and now of necessity had to employ "the arm of the people, a machine . . . blind to a certain degree." And, after all, the French were following the example of Americans in rising against a king and condemning all his works. For Jefferson, the author of the Declaration of Independence, there could be nothing so noble, so worthwhile as such an effort. "Was ever such a prize," he asked, "won with so little innocent blood? . . . Rather than it should have failed, I would have seen half the earth desolated. Were there but an Adam and an Eve left in every country, and left free, it would be better than it now is."

Jefferson did not exaggerate the enthusiasm of Americans for the French Revolution. At Philadelphia in mid-December, 1792, a "grand exultation prevailed" when word came that a reorganized French army had routed Austro-Prussian forces at Valmy and that the National Convention had declared France to be a republic. Soon rumors were circulating that the French were 600,000 strong and that they meant to turn their fury against the major monarchies of Europe, England and Spain. From Boston to Savannah the effect was electric. Led by Philip Freneau's *National Gazette* at Philadelphia, the Republican press took up the chant of *Ça Ira!* and applauded all Jacobins, damned all Tories and aristocrats, and made fun of the Senate because portraits of Louis XVI and Marie Antoinette still hung in its hall. Men and women alike now adorned their garments with the French cockade, spoke of "liberty, equality, fraternity" to all who would listen, addressed each other as "citizen" and "citess," sang the Marseillaise in the streets, and danced the Carmagnole with joyous abandon. In New York, in Baltimore, in Richmond, in Charleston, it was the same. Liberty poles and liberty caps were visible everywhere, and "civic feasts" were staged at the slightest excuse. Indeed, as Jefferson reminded William Short in his next instruction, "99 in 100 Americans" sympathized fully with the cause of the French. And, he added pointedly, President Washington regarded France "the sheet anchor of this country and its friendship a first object."

Washington scarcely would have denied that the good will of the French was precious to him. His personal gratitude to the soldiers of France for their unstinting aid in the war of American independence could never be dimmed. Without quibble he approved Jefferson's official reply to formal notification of the establishment of the French Republic: "The Government and the citizens of the United States . . . consider the union of principles and pursuits between our two countries as a link which binds still closer their interests and affections." But beyond this the President would not go. He did not agree with Jefferson that America's experiment in representative government was tied irrevocably to the French Revolution. As Washington walked alone in High Street, taking his exercise in the early mornings of March, he saw the tricolor on display in Philadelphia windows and knew that his nation was drifting into a storm of difficulties, a tempest of diplomatic problems blowing together with domestic ones, that would put to an ultimate test his wisdom and skill as national helmsman. If Washington was the "indispensable" leader, as his admirers had insisted in 1789 and again recently, this was the crisis that would show it. If his first term had been disfigured somewhat by conflicting attitudes in his Cabinet and the subsequent rise of parties, factionalism would now thicken and spread under new stimuli from abroad. The questions of policy would be large, complex, fraught with peril. Anticipating them, the President let the whole business filter through his mind time and again. Finally he was resolved on two points: Whatever developed in Europe, the United States must remain strictly neutral; whatever developed in the Cabinet or in the public temper, the President must remain impartial and dispassionate. The pilot must steer a safe and constant course.

Even before his second administration had officially begun, problems of diplomacy were pressing him hard. On February 8, 1793, the French minister, Ternant, presented to the Secretary of State an urgent request for an advance of $554,500 so that foodstuffs might be purchased for immediate shipment to France, where famine now was threatening. Regular installments on the French debt had been suspended the previous autumn in the absence of an established government at Paris, and Hamilton computed that $318,000 was still owing for 1792. Since the 1793 installment of $628,000 soon would fall due, Jefferson advised that Ternant's application be approved at once and in the full amount. Hamilton, on the other hand, argued that no more than the sum in arrears—$318,000—should be made available. Attorney General Randolph tried to see both sides. The nations at war with France, he told Washington, would have good reason to object strenuously to "a voluntary payment of what is not yet due"; yet, he pointed out, a denial of the request certainly would agitate "the zealous partizans of French politics in America." Washington deliberated for a week, then approved Ternant's request in full. Jefferson was jubilant. "Urged by the strongest attachments to France," he wrote Gouverneur Morris, "and thinking it even providential that monies lent to us in distress could be repaid under like circumstances, we had no hesitation to comply. . . . We shall certainly . . . omit no opportunity of convincing that nation how cordially we wish to serve them." But it had not happened exactly this way.

Then, on February 20, Jefferson was visited by Colonel William S. Smith, son-in-law of Vice President Adams, who had just arrived from France with a commission as confidential agent of the Girondist party. The Gironde, said Smith, had organized a ministry under Brissot de Warville, and meant to fulfill the spirit of the Revolution by waging war on all monarchies. Toward this end the Gironde had engaged the soldier-adventurer Francisco de Miranda for an attack on Spanish Louisiana; and, Smith hinted, the new French government would hardly object if the United States decided to move against Spanish Florida. Finally, Smith reported, the Gironde was sending a young intellectual named Genêt—who had been expelled from his diplomatic post in Russia because of revolutionary enthusiasms and antimonarchical declarations—to Philadelphia to replace the aristocratic Ternant; and, in turn, the Gironde hoped that the aristocratic Morris would be succeeded at Paris by an envoy more sympathetic to the objectives of the Revolution.

That evening the Secretary of State hurried to the President's house with a memorandum on Colonel Smith's conversation. The idea of an American assault on the Floridas, to coincide with Miranda's project against Louisiana, was dismissed by Washington as preposterous—and Jefferson agreed. But would not the United States be wise at this moment to avoid any pledge on her part to *defend* the colonies of Spain? Should Miranda actually attack New Orleans, Jefferson reasoned, the United States must be "free to act" in taking full advantage of Spain's distress. Washington concurred heartily; there might be found here a splendid opportunity to extort from the Spaniards those concessions and guarantees in the Southwest which had been sought in vain since 1784. The Secretary of State was instructed to write accordingly to William Carmichael, the American envoy in Madrid.

But what to do about Morris? Surely, said Jefferson, he had aroused "great disgust" in Paris and must be removed at once. Washington could understand this; he knew Morris well, and knew him to be as outspoken as he was competent. Jefferson advised that Thomas Pinckney, the American minister in England, be transferred to France, and that Morris be reassigned to London. This plan did not impress the President as sound; it might anger the French, he thought, if Morris was rewarded for his monarchial utterances with a choice post—and would not France have good reason for deep and continuing suspicions with a man of Morris' ability and connections just across the Channel? Washington wondered, then, if Jefferson himself might go to Paris. The Secretary of State said no, announced that he would soon retire from public office, repeated his suggestion of an exchange between Pinckney and Morris, and bade the President goodnight.

Washington went at once to Edmund Randolph and asked the

17

Attorney General to appeal earnestly to Jefferson, but Randolph soon reported that the Secretary of State was "immovable in the resolution he expressed to you the other day." Nor could Randolph persuade "the other gentleman" whom the President had mentioned—probably Congressman James Madison or Senator James Monroe—to take the Paris assignment. Randolph agreed that the "middle ground" of an exchange would be wrong because the French would fear Morris, "dangerous from his talents," in the London post. Also, the Attorney General predicted, American Republicans would assert immediately that Morris "is not only protected in his misconduct but that a partiality is discovered for his ideas on government, against which they are eminently inveterate from their real sympathy with the Revolution of France." There it rested. Washington recognized that Morris had become objectionable to the French, and that he ought to be replaced. Yet nothing could be done gracefully at the moment.

On March 16 came news that many Americans had been awaiting eagerly for weeks: the National Convention had found Louis XVI guilty of treasonable conspiracy against the people, and by a vote of 361 to 360 had sent him to the guillotine. The tempo of Republican excitement increased with each repetition of a crude quip, "Louis Capet has lost his caput!" and few Americans missed hearing it. Jefferson thought the execution of the king to be a useful warning to all monarchs and aristocrats; Washington was silent. Then, as speculation mounted on the probability of open war between France and England, Jefferson advanced the idea that the British must certainly be the aggressors. The Secretary of State anticipated that England, confident as ever in her control of the sea lanes, would soon decree against American shipment of foodstuffs to France, and probably would begin to impress American sailors into His Majesty's navy. Such outrages, Jefferson felt, would demand retaliation, and the President would have to summon Congress back into special session. "As the Executive cannot decide the question of war on the affirmative side," he wrote to Madison, "neither ought [he] to do so on the negative side by preventing the competent body from deliberating on the question." Jefferson would not urge actual hostilities with England, but he did hope that Congress would "instantly exclude" from the ports of the United States "all the manufactures, produce, vessels and subjects" of all nations at war with the Republic of France.

This may have been Jefferson's view late in March, but it was not the President's. As he prepared for a trip to Mount Vernon, he took time to draft long letters to Morris in France and David Humphreys in Portugal. Washington's statements reveal his thoughts on March 25: "I trust that we shall have too just a sense of our own interest to originate any cause that may involve us in it, and I ardently wish we may not be forced into it by the conduct of other nations. . . . If we are permitted to improve without interruption . . . many years will not revolve before we may be ranked not only among the most respectable but among the happiest people on this globe. . . ." And more: "Unwise should we be in the extreme to involve ourselves in the contests of European nations, where our weight could be but small though the loss to ourselves would be certain. . . . This country is not guided by such narrow and mistaken policy as will lead it to wish the destruction of any nation under an idea that our importance will be encreased [sic] in proportion as that of others is lessened." By March 27, when the President left for Virginia, no authenticated report of a general European war had yet reached Philadelphia. But fresh rumors were arriving with every vessel, and Washington instructed his mail to be held at Baltimore, Georgetown, and Alexandria.

On April 4 the post to Mount Vernon brought a note from Jefferson, who expressed his feeling that recent stories of Anglo-French hostilities were exaggerated—and that it was more probable that England faced a civil war. Eight days later the President opened a letter from Hamilton which could leave "no room for doubt" that a global conflagration was raging. Marie Antoinette had been executed, Hamilton wrote, and on February 1 the French Republic had formally declared war against the British Empire, the Spanish Empire, and The Netherlands. Hamilton's letter was sent on April 5; Jefferson wrote on the seventh that a general war was now "extremely probable" and the United States should "take every justifiable measure for preserving our neutrality" while providing France with "those necessaries for war which must be brought across the Atlantic." On the same day that he received Hamilton's communication, and before Jefferson's had arrived, the President penned his instructions. "It behooves the Government of this country," he wrote the Secretary of State, "to use every means in its power to prevent the citizens . . . from embroiling us with either [belligerent]"; would Jefferson, therefore, please give "mature consideration" to a plan which would insure "a strict neutrality"? In the same post he placed notes to Hamilton and Secretary of War Knox which made unmistakably clear the President's wish for "immediate precautionary measures." The next morning, April 13, his coach left for Philadelphia by the shortest possible route, and Washington was in High Street by late afternoon on the seventeenth.

When Jefferson appeared at the President's office early the next day, he had in hand four dispatches from Thomas Pinckney at London—each many weeks old and of trivial content. These the Secretary of State presented, but he had prepared no memorandum and could offer no plan to guarantee the nation a neutral role in the European war. If Washington's temper rose, he kept it in leash. Later the same day he saw Hamilton, and the Secretary of the Treasury spread before him the detailed draft of a program for "perfect" neutrality. Hamilton had a set of questions on paper, and the logic behind them in his mind; he even had ready a suggested "proclamation," the text of which Chief Justice John Jay had written hastily at his request. It was obvious that the Secretary of the Treasury had been feverishly occupied for some time in business that properly belonged to the Secretary of State; it was equally obvious that the two Cabinet officers had conferred not at all on the vital business in point. The President did not know the extent of Hamilton's dabbling in diplomatics; he was unaware of Hamilton's confidential assurances to the British envoy at Philadelphia, George Hammond, that the United States would maintain—as the Englishman reported to his superiors—"as strict a neutrality" as possible because "any event which might endanger the external tranquility . . . would be fatal to the systems he [Hamilton] has formed. . . ." Whatever the indiscretions of the Secretary of the Treasury, they would not blur the blueprint he advanced at this moment. The President had decided on neutrality. What he needed was a prescription for it. Hamilton had that in hand, and Jefferson did not.

No time was to be lost. Washington copied out Hamilton's interrogatories, labeled them "sundry questions . . . arising from the present posture of affairs in Europe," and sent identical lists to Jefferson, Knox, and Randolph with a request that the Cabinet meet at his house the next morning, April 19, at nine. The President's covering note did not indicate that Hamilton had originated the questions; but this is not to imply, as some historians have, that Washington was attempting to deceive his advisers. He could hardly have been able to conceal their authorship; nor would he have tried. Even before the President's return to Philadelphia, Hamilton had discussed with Randolph "the whole chain of reasoning" behind the questions. Still Jefferson was profoundly annoyed. "It was palpable from the style and from their ingenious tissue and suite," he complained in his diary, ". . . that they were raised upon a prepared chain of argument. . . . The language was Hamilton's and the doubts his alone." True as this was, the Secretary of State could blame only himself for failing to respond to a crisis that the President considered imminent and grave. Hamilton simply had stolen the moment from him.

The questions totaled to thirteen, but essentially the "doubts" were three. Should the President issue a proclamation to the American public, and should it include an explicit "declaration of neutrality"? Should Genêt, who would arrive soon as minister of the new French government, be formally accredited; and, if so, should his reception be "absolute" or "qualified"? Could and should the United States either disavow or suspend the Treaties of Alliance and Commerce made with France in 1778? The second and third points, Washington realized, would be highly antagonistic to Jefferson. They challenged the legitimacy of the Republic of France and suggested that the French Revolution ultimately would fail—as Hamilton plainly expected it would. Should the *de facto* government in France be recognized forthwith? Should the United States in 1793 be free to annul treaties concluded in 1778 with a monarchy that was now overturned, or were those treaties always to be valid because they existed between the *peoples* of nations rather than between the *governments* of nations? By their nature these considerations were central to the whole problem of erecting a permanent neutrality for the United States. Washington saw this and was grateful to Hamilton for raising pertinent points which soon would have to be discussed at length and in depth by the Cabinet. No precedent stood as a sure guide on the question of recognition, and likewise none on the validity of treaties. The President might anticipate long legalistic arguments and much heated opinion in his Cabinet before a decision could be wrought on either point.

There need be no delay, however, in adopting "immediate precautionary measures" against possible participation by Americans in the European war. To Washington this was the immediate issue, the paramount one. Questions of *de facto* recognition and the status of treaties could be, as they were, "postponed for further consideration" to "another day"; but the first question could not. What should the President do to prevent unneutral acts by Americans which might propel the United States into war? If American enthusiasm for the cause of the French Revolution was as intense as it appeared to be, a belligerent act might occur at any hour in any of a dozen seaports. The slightest unneutral gesture might be seized upon by the English, and America again might be fighting for her own freedom. It would be too late then to argue on the finer distinctions of international law, and Washington did not wish to debate them in detail until he had taken "immediate precautionary measures" to insure that no accident or irresponsible act would bring war to the shores of the American republic. This was the crisis of Friday, April 19, 1793—and George Washington did not mistake it.

Should the President, then, issue a public proclamation, and should it include a "declaration of neutrality"? Hamilton, Knox, and Randolph considered an immediate proclamation to be imperative. Jefferson acquiesced, but insisted that a "declaration of neutrality" would amount to "a declaration that there should be no war," and, he said, only Congress had the right to determine that question. "If on the one hand the Legislature have the right to declare war," Hamilton answered, "it is on the other the duty of the Executive to preserve peace till the declaration is made." But Jefferson had another argument, a compelling one, against any "premature declaration" that the United States would remain neutral. "It would be better," he reasoned, "to hold back the declaration of neutrality as a thing worth something" to each side. This was the same logic on which the Secretary of State had premised his opinion regarding Miranda's possible attack on Spanish Louisiana—that the United States must be "free to act" in pressing for diplomatic concessions—and now Jefferson wished to wring from the British "the broadest privileges" that American neutrality would buy. Redcoats of His Majesty's Canadian regiments still occupied seven forts on American soil in the Northwest; this might be a way to get them out. Washington liked the idea, and on his preference the decision of April 19 was made: the President would issue a proclamation immediately, but it would not contain an explicit "declaration of neutrality." It would serve as a positive warning to American citizens against "all acts and proceedings inconsistent with the duties of a friendly nation toward those at war," but it would avoid words and phrases that might negate the bargaining power of the United States in the market place of diplomacy.

The decision of April 19, 1793, established an important precedent in American history, but neither Hamilton nor Jefferson took particular satisfaction in the day's work. When the Secretary of State indicated that he did not care to prepare the proclamation, Washington assigned the task to the Attorney General. After showing his draft to Jefferson, who noticed only that "there was no such word as *neutrality* in it," Randolph delivered it to the Cabinet on April 22, and the President signed it that day. These are the significant sentences in the famous proclamation:

> . . . the duty and interest of the United States require that they should with sincerity and good faith adopt and pursue a conduct friendly and impartial toward the belligerent Powers. I have therefore thought fit by these presents to declare the disposition of the United States to observe the conduct aforesaid toward those Powers respectively; and to exhort and warn the citizens of the United States carefully to avoid all acts and proceedings whatsoever which may in any manner tend to contravene such disposition. . . .

Hamilton's friend, Senator Rufus King of New York, expressed the attitude of most Federalists in his reaction: "I could have wished to have seen in some part of it the word 'neutrality' which everyone would have understood and felt the force of. . . . We must not become entangled with this mad war." James Madison's response characterized that of ardent Republicans: "It wounds the popular feelings by a seeming indifference to the cause of liberty." And President Washington, a few hours after he had issued the proclamation, explained his decision in these words: "To administer justice and receive it from every power will, I hope, be always found the most prominent feature in the administration of this country; and I flatter myself that nothing short of imperious necessity can occasion a breach with any of them." It was, he said, "the sincere wish of the United States to . . . live in peace and amity with all the inhabitants of the earth."

The work of George Washington as a statesman has been obscured to posterity not only by Alexander Hamilton's ascendancy in the 1790's, but equally as much by the very legend that attaches to his name. That legend is essentially military, and has been so from its seeding. Myths have grown up around other Americans, but none is so old or heavily leafed as the legend which has enveloped Washington. It merits considerably more attention than it has received at the hands of historical writers. In their familiarity with it, they sometimes have forgotten that the saga of Washington was a potent factor in the intellectual growth of nineteenth-century America. Abraham Lincoln, for instance, fastened it in his memory as a child. And few Americans a hundred years ago grew to maturity without a mental picture of General Washington at the head of a long column, resplendent in regimentals and astride a fine horse.

What ought to be emphasized here, however, is that the legend of Washington has been largely military. This fact does much to explain why his achievements as president are not as obvious to posterity as they should be. Washington was a statesman fully as long as he was a soldier, and his achievements in council were fully as significant as those in the field. But he was first a soldier, and primacy is vital in legend-making. So is drama, and so also is an undisputed leading role. The campaigns of the Revolution can be rendered infinitely more interesting than the problems of statecraft in the formative period. And, as a soldier, Washington occupied the center of the stage. The eyes of the people were on him alone; no meteoric financier distracted their gaze. In its roots, then, the legend of Washington was military, and so has been much of its foliage. Washington's biographers, even to the most recent, have put their subject first in war and second in peace. They have preferred the General's tent to the President's table.

It has often been remarked, and with more simple truth than profundity, that the biographers of George Washington either have found him a paradox and made him a paragon, or found him a paragon and left him a paradox. Either they have unveiled a flawless piece of sculpture draped magnificently in the toga of a hero and wearing the halo of a saint, or they have passed along their conviction that Washington was so inscrutable and so complex a personality as to defy characterization. Surely a mountain of literature has accumulated to demonstrate that Washington was either paragon or paradox to many who have attempted to chronicle and interpret his life. In a century and a half the publishing houses of the United States have offered several hundred biographies of this man to a receptive public. The mountain of words on Washington stands imaginatively as high as the monument which bears his name, and this literary corpus will appear all the more massive when contrasted against the fact that there are many remarkable figures in American history whose careers have yet to be commemorated by one adequate biography.

Washington's popularity as a biographical subject is easily explained. He was America's first hero in war. John Adams, who was capable of descending to a certain level of bitterness during the years that he served inconspicuously as vice president in Washington's administrations, put it this way: "The history of our Revolution will be one continued lie from one end to the other. The essence of the whole will be that Dr. Franklin's electrical rod smote the earth and out sprang General Washington, that Franklin electrified him with his rod, and thence forward these two conducted all the policy, negotiations, legislatures, and war." Neither Benjamin Franklin's admirers nor Washington's have ever advanced this theory, but certainly the Commander in Chief of the Continental Army emerged from the war of independence with a major share of credit for its success. Then, as many Americans delighted in depicting it, the General followed the noble example of the Roman soldier Cincinnatus by retiring modestly to his farm and plow in the bright hour of victory—and this, above victory itself, emblazoned him with greatness in the eyes of the people.

When rumors were heard that Washington had been provoked to high anger by a suggestion of one of his officers that the Army use its power to establish a monarchy with the Commander in Chief as king, his fame was fixed. To the end of his days, however significant his later endeavors and achievements, he would remain the hero of the struggle for independence, America's first soldier, the Cincinnatus in whom all citizens of a free nation might take immeasurable pride. As Washington's contemporaries were wont to view him, so would posterity receive him: not at a desk with quill and scroll, but on horseback with sidearms and sword. In somber presidential dress he could be claimed only by Federalists. In Continental buff and blue he belonged to all Americans.

Like the flora of his Virginia, the legend of George Washington was early to blossom. Within a half dozen years of his death in 1799, American readers already had the choice of two biographies. One was a thin, simple book of eighty pages which presented the fiction of the cherry tree and the prayer in the snow at Valley Forge, and in the last paragraph ushered its subject through the Pearly Gates and into the Kingdom of the Angels. Few biographers of any hero have dared to go this far, but Mason Locke Weems was a self-styled clergyman and he was unfettered by footnotes. His *Life of General Washington* earned "Parson" Weems an emperor's ransom in royalties and a reputation as one of the most pleasant and plausible charlatans in American literature. Such success with Washington prompted Weems to consider the careers of other champions of the Revolution, and he did not lay down his prolific pen for many years.

The second biography was quite different. The overwritten, oversized, and overpriced work of Chief Justice John Marshall brought the author of these five volumes no return in dollars. Instead it gave him some nostalgic satisfaction of a political kind. With his party out of power, it pleased Marshall to recall that he and Washington had been Federalists together in the age of that giant race of patriots before the Republican flood of 1800. Marshall understood politics extremely well and had lived in high place during the years of Washington's presidency. Had he reduced his work to a convenient and inexpensive size and had he recorded the political developments of the years 1789-97 as he must have known them, Marshall could have done much to make a living president out of Washington. As it proved, however, Marshall's Washington was essentially a soldier and his chapters on politics amount to no more than a Federalist tract. The only historiographical distinction of the enterprise is that Marshall did some pioneering research in the vast collection of Washington's personal and public papers which are now deposited at the Library of Congress in 350 red morocco portfolios.

Weems by eccentricity and Marshall by ponderous reverence etched an image of George Washington which the next century of American readers contemplated lovingly and in full trust—and which subsequent biographers have done little to efface. Weems and Marshall put Washington in his saddle, gave him his buckles and blade, and erected a mighty myth in the enduring façade of folklore. Young America needed a hero in literature. Weems and Marshall produced the logical one.

A generation after Weems and Marshall came Jared Sparks, professional editor and tireless gatherer of historical documents. Sparks thought it would be well to present Washington to the reading public in the General's own words. But, as it happened, Harvard's first professor of history was more of an editor than anyone knew. In ten volumes Sparks proceeded to correct the spelling, the syntax, and even some explicit ideas in Washington's collected correspondence. Stranger in his tastes even than Sparks was a classical scholar, Francis Glass, whose notion it was that a proper life of the American Cincinnatus could be accomplished only in Latin prose! At mid-century the gifted novelist, Washington Irving, set himself to the scale of Marshall and produced a biography in five volumes which was a landmark at the time—and again, because it was widely read, did a disservice to Washington in that his military career was its central theme. And on it went for years, with professional and amateur writers alike trying their pens at twice-telling or venturing "new" interpretation that seldom was at variance with the verdict of Weems or very much deeper than the research of Marshall.

Long after Weems's little book had become a thing for children and Marshall's tomes were library relics, the concept of Washington created by them remained essentially unchanged. That first image of the soldier, for most Americans, has been the last and the best. Even trained scholars in the twentieth century have not been inclined to alter the basic approaches of the earliest writers. The most meticulous of Washington's biographers, Douglas Southall Freeman, probably never would have undertaken his multi-volume task if Washington had not been prominent in war. Freeman's first interest was military history—his notable studies of Robert E. Lee and Lee's commanders attest to this—and unquestionably he was drawn to Washington because of the challenge of a detailed recounting of the War of the Revolution.

While the legend of Washington has been heavy with the laurels of the soldier, it nonetheless has communicated a valid impression. For all the ardor of their researches, modern historians have not turned up evidence that Washington in life was appreciably less than the great American patriot imaginatively painted in words by Weems. Catch-penny debunkers appear occasionally, to be sure, but they are compensated for their efforts as much in ridicule as in royalties. This is as it should be. Washington's life and times have been rigorously researched, his silhouette has been exposed to different light by different scholars, and we may be certain today that he is quite deserving of the halo that has been his. Weems, so fictitious in detail, was authentic in spirit: George Washington was a great and good man, great in the largest sense and good in the deepest.

How was it that Weems, who consulted no other source than his fertile fancy, could be so accurate in basic portrayal? It happened naturally. Weems was not so much a grower as a reaper. He did not plant the legend of George Washington in the minds of Americans; he merely took in the first harvest. The legend was seeded by circumstance during the years of the Revolution, and cultivated continuously in the two decades that followed. The extravagances of the inaugural journey of 1789 give a hint, but nothing testifies so positively to the existence of an aura around Washington's person as the spectacle of mourning occasioned by his death ten years later. Other champions of American independence preceded Washington to the grave—Benjamin Franklin and Nathanael Greene were two such—but their passing had been virtually unnoticed. Washington's demise, on the other hand, produced a national phenomenon. Political affiliation played no significant part. "The whole United States," admitted a prominent Republican, "mourned for him as a father."

For six months after Washington's burial at Mount Vernon, black cloth was hard to find in American shops. Continuously for seven weeks the people of the United States voiced their bereavement in Congress, in state legislatures, in town meetings, and in the columns of their newspapers. This exhortation in the Senate set the pitch: "Let his countrymen consecrate the memory of the heroic General Washington. . . . Let them teach their children never to forget that the fruit of his labors and his example are their inheritance." Most remarkable among the features of the pageant of national grief were the funeral enactments, almost two hundred in number and each complete with procession and solemn oration, which were staged in towns from Maine to Georgia. Eulogists vied for the honor of speaking, then strained for the most appropriate adjectives and analogies. Washington was contrasted favorably against the military masters of Europe, Frederick of Prussia and Bonaparte of France, and his contributions compared with those of the soldier-statesmen of Greece and Rome. Some speakers, following a scriptural theme, likened the loss of Washington to the American people with the loss of Moses to the Israelites.

Few times in the history of the republic have Americans found themselves in such deep spiritual communion. Henry Knox predicted that these "testimonials of respect" would provide an "excellent stimulus to future patriotism." What Knox and other Federalists were hoping was that the legend of Washington would spring up stout enough to support the sagging structure of their regime, and in this they were to be disappointed. Not even Washington's name and fame could save the Federalists in 1800, but the collapse of the party in no way retarded the growth of the legend. Its roots were military, not political, and it was ready to bloom. Even before Weems had rushed into print with the first edition of his *Life*, several collections of funeral orations were available in book form and thousands of separate pamphlets had been distributed as far west as the Mississippi. By the time Weems's "cherry tree" edition was ready in 1806 and Marshall was completing the last of his volumes, the legend of Washington was entwined in every memory of the man.

However deep the roots of any legend, it will die in poor ground. The legend of George Washington did not wither because its soil was uniquely rich. In an oration at St. Paul's Church in New York, Gouverneur Morris spoke a sentence that goes far to explain its endurance. "Born to high destinies," said Morris, Washington was "fashioned for them by the hand of nature." Had this not been so perfectly true, it is doubtful that this legend would have flowered as it did. More than any personage of his time and more perhaps than any American who followed him to the national stage, Washington presented an ideal subject for adulation. In him, physically and psychologically, were the elements of heroism. In seeing Washington, in meeting him, Americans and Europeans alike received the same spontaneous impression. Many described it, but none better than Jefferson who saw him daily for several years. As the first Secretary of State appraised the first President, "His person was fine, his stature exactly what one would wish," and more:

> His mind was great and powerful, without being of the very first order; his penetration strong, though not so acute as that of a Newton, Bacon, or Locke; and as far as he saw, no judgment was ever sounder. It was slow in operation, being little aided by invention or imagination, but sure in conclusion. . . . Perhaps the strongest feature in his character was prudence, never acting until every circumstance, every consideration, was maturely weighed; refraining when he saw a doubt, but, when once decided, going through with his purpose whatever obstacles opposed. His integrity was most

pure, his justice the most inflexible I have ever known, no motives or interest or consanguinity of friendship or hatred being able to bias his decision. . . . On the whole, his character was in its mass perfect, in nothing bad, in few points indifferent; and it may truly be said that never did nature and fortune combine more perfectly to make a man great, and to place him in the same constellation with whatever worthies have merited from man an everlasting remembrance. . . .

John Adams

by STEPHEN G. KURTZ

John Adams was elected to succeed Washington by a margin of three electoral votes. The taunt that he was a "three-vote president" stung him, and Jefferson's victory in 1800 left him with the conviction that his best efforts had been misunderstood. By the pragmatic test of re-election he had failed. In spite of the Anglo-Saxon brevity of his name, John Adams remains one of the presidents most often forgotten by school children. Yet the list of his achievements distinguishes him among a group of remarkable contemporaries. Adams had risen from obscurity to a place of distinction at the bar before the Revolution and had launched a political career that was able to survive his defense of the villains of the Boston Massacre. He worked with such skill and vigor toward a declaration of independence that Jefferson hailed him as "the Great Colossus" of the Second Continental Congress. He was chosen to serve as a peace commissioner with Benjamin Franklin and John Jay at the end of the Revolution, and he held the post of minister to England at the time of his election as vice president.

Scholars know Adams as a distinguished student of politics, master of four foreign languages, and owner of one of the largest private libraries of his time. Vernon Parrington's judgment bears repetition: "In spite of his dogmatism and inconsistencies he remains the most notable political thinker—with the possible exception of John C. Calhoun—among American statesmen."

The picture of Adams that has been handed down to us, however, is not altogether a flattering one. More often than not, his presidency has been judged a reflection of his worst qualities as a man, a record of political ineptitude set off against one great decision. Adams is portrayed as vain and jealous, particularly of Franklin and Washington. His outburst to Benjamin Rush in 1790 may be cited as evidence and often is: "The history of our Revolution will be one continued lie from one end to the other. The essence of the whole will be that Dr. Franklin's electrical rod smote the earth and out sprang George Washington."

Adams was a stubborn fighter, probably the only American on record who has answered a single critical letter with three volumes of rebuttal. Turgot's famous letter to the English republican Price struck Adams in a tender spot, because it criticized the complex governments established by the American states. Certain that liberty was best preserved within a system that could hold democratic and aristocratic forces in balance, Adams was the architect of the Massachusetts constitution adopted in 1780. A comparison between the Massachusetts framework and the national constitution adopted eight years later reveals marked similarities. His direct reply to Turgot's strictures on mixed governments, *Defence of the Constitutions of Government of the United States of America*, was written in London in 1786 and 1787. Circulated among the delegates to the Philadelphia Convention, the work revealed Adams to be a conservative republican, devoted to the rule of law and an admirer of the British constitution which he regarded as the greatest bulwark to freedom ever erected. Unfortunately for Adams many Americans concluded that he had become an Anglophile and a partisan of aristocracy. It was probably not until the last year of his presidency that contemporaries realized how strong his commitment to republican government was and how thoroughly he believed in a foreign policy of neutrality. Adams demonstrated his independence of foreign loyalties convincingly but at the price of alienating the faction of his party led by Hamilton, a group that Adams believed to be pro-British.

In spite of a deep desire to be understood and to clear the acts of his administration from taints of irresponsibility or egotism, Adams was unable to write an autobiography. He attempted at least four times to write one but could not complete it, "so dull an employment that I cannot endure it," he complained. "I look so much like a small boy in my own eyes, that, with all my vanity, I cannot endure the sight of the picture."

His recorded conclusion about his administration was that he had accomplished one notable objective. He had been able to keep the United States from a civil conflagration that seemed more imminent to contemporaries than it has to many historians. Manning J. Dauer suggests a bold analogy: "In the next century the German liberals were overwhelmed in moulding the character of the rising German state by the policies pursued by Bismarck after 1862. Liberalism was defeated and a military character given to the new state. In the United States of 1798 there were many domestic forces in the direction of popular government. But the situation was fluid. What changes could be wrought in a period of military adventure? These Hamilton sought to experiment with."

Whether such a comparison is justified may be suggested by an examination of the events that transpired between the election of Adams and the Jeffersonian victory of 1800.

The United States was a small nation in terms of population, wealth, and military power at the end of the eighteenth century. While there were those like the poet Joel Barlow who were caught up in a vision of America's future, statesmen were made painfully aware of the new nation's weakness in a world at war. Caught between Britain's definition of contraband and French insistence that the United States fulfill her treaty obligations under the alliance of 1778, Washington had sent John Jay on a pacific mission to London in 1794. As the French and their American champions viewed the results Jay had surrendered American claims against England which dated back to the Revolution, and Federalists had compromised their moral integrity in ratifying the resulting treaty. The French government refused to admit that a treaty of amity and commerce with England was anything less than a disguised naval alliance, and they shaped their American policy accordingly. It was a foregone conclusion that Washington's successor would face a severe diplomatic crisis with France as well as continued naval harassment from Great Britain. Jefferson saw the political implications, rejoiced at escaping the presidency, and predicted the future with accuracy. "The President is fortunate to get off just as the bubble is bursting, leaving others to hold the bag. Yet, as his departure will mark the moment when the difficulties begin to work, you will see that they will be ascribed to the new administration. . . ."

The unpopularity of the Jay Treaty was woven tightly into

the fabric of politics in 1796. In a well-conceived plan the Virginia Republicans were able to transfer their determination to block the Treaty's operation into the House of Representatives where a two-month debate over foreign policy pointed to the virtues of a more conciliatory policy toward France. While Jefferson had no desire to be president, his friends were convinced that his reputation for republican orthodoxy and friendship for France would best serve the nation if he were chief executive. As Pennsylvanians went to the polls in November the French minister, Pierre Adet, announced the suspension of diplomatic intercourse between the two nations. He also hinted that a change of party control in America would ease strained relations. In spite of this bald interference voters elected men pledged to Jefferson and Aaron Burr in Pennsylvania, Federalists securing only one Adams elector.

On their part Federalists found their most potent weapon in the immense prestige of Washington. The suggestion that Republicans in the House aimed at an impeachment trial was made by Washington himself in a reply to their request for diplomatic papers. This was enough to galvanize the efforts of Federalists into vigorous efforts on behalf of Adams and his erstwhile running mate, Thomas Pinckney of South Carolina. Hamilton, who led the party and who shared an aversion for Adams with many of his friends, looked upon Pinckney as the more promising presidential candidate of the two and did his best to see that he was elected. Those Federalists who found Hamilton their spokesman were rarely at ease with Adams. They shared with Adams a mistrust of unchecked popular government but not his distaste for aristocracies of propertied men. At the same time that they may have agreed with his condemnation of the French Revolution, they were confused by his suspicion of banks and speculation. Adams had supported the establishment of the Bank of the United States and the constitutionality of Hamilton's funding and assumption plans, but he was fearful of inflation and had made it known that he believed speculative schemes arising out of Hamiltonian programs responsible for it. In economic terms Adams was no more safe than Jefferson in the eyes of Hamiltonians. Through private letters Hamilton and his closest friends suggested the virtues of Pinckney to men who shared their misgivings.

Adams could count on little, if any, support south of the Potomac. If New England electors could be convinced that only by supporting Adams and Pinckney equally would Jefferson be defeated, the result would be Pinckney's election since he was certain of Southern votes. The plan was plausible and drew many outstanding Federalist leaders within its orbit, but it did not gauge the depth of New England sentiment for Adams. Confused about the intentions of Southern Federalists, New England electors deserted Pinckney by scattering eighteen votes among favorite sons. South Carolina electors the same day cast their ballots for Pinckney and Jefferson. The result was that Adams and Jefferson, separated by only three votes, found themselves drawn together once more, each determined to block Hamiltonian designs for the United States.

"There is an active spirit in the Union who will fill it with his politics wherever he is," Adams concluded in writing to his wife. "He must be attended to, and not suffered to do too much." Hamilton's prestige among leading Federalists had been badly shaken. "We are broken to pieces," Fisher Ames of Massachusetts lamented to Hamilton. "Some able man of the first order of abilities and possessing the rare union of qualities that will fit him to lead a party is wanting."

In the two-month period between his election and inauguration Adams suggested by his actions that he was capable of completely overlooking the party structure. He made it known that he hoped for a united administration with his old friend Jefferson, and his warm words of praise and esteem were quickly forwarded to Virginia by their mutual friend, Dr. Benjamin Rush, who rejoiced at the prospect of peace between political parties. Jefferson, equally sanguine and pleased over Hamilton's blunder, repeated similar sentiments and appeared ready to join hands with Adams until Madison cautioned him to move slowly. When Jefferson arrived at Philadelphia at the end of February, 1797, and took rooms in the boarding house where Adams was living, it looked as if a new alliance had been formed. "If Mr. Adams has vanity," observed Hamilton, who had no doubts on that score, "t'is plain a plot has been laid to take hold of it."

Events occurring in France, however, soon put an end to all hopes for a coalition between Adams Federalists and Republicans. It was authoritatively reported that the French Directory had refused to recognize the new American minister, Charles Cotesworth Pinckney, who had replaced the Francophilic James Monroe at Paris. Accounts written by both Jefferson and Adams agree that their only consultation during this period concerned the possibility of sending Madison on a peace mission to France as a counterbalance to the Jay mission of Washington's administration. Jefferson, after talking with Madison, convinced Adams that such an appointment would be refused, while Adams confessed to having met with opposition from his Cabinet on the question. Secretary of the Treasury Oliver Wolcott, Jr., offered to resign rather than see the Virginian appointed, and Adams dropped the idea of naming any Republican. Here the rumored Adams-Jefferson coalition ended.

In his inaugural address Adams emphasized the warm feelings which he had entertained for the French people during his residence in France and pledged his efforts toward maintaining neutrality in European wars. Such sentiments together with his disavowal of both aristocratic and monarchical ideas of government, won the praise of the Republican press. "It is universally admitted that Mr. Adams is a man of incorruptible integrity, and that the resources of his mind are equal to the duties of his station," commented the Jeffersonian Philadelphia *Aurora*. "He declared himself the friend of France and of peace, the admirer of republicanism, the enemy of party, and he avows his determination to let no political creed interfere in his appointments. . . . How characteristic of a patriot."

The fears of Hamiltonians and the praise of Jefferson's supporters did not last long, however. Three weeks after the inauguration Adams issued a proclamation calling Congress into special session in order to take up what were termed "divers great and weighty problems." On the sixteenth of May Adams made it clear that the problems were weighty indeed. He announced that Pinckney had been ordered to leave France after being denied recognition, that France would receive no American envoy until grievances against the United States had been redressed, and that commercial relations between the two nations had been suspended. Adams recommended legislation allowing for the arming of merchant ships, the completion of frigates and the purchase of smaller vessels for convoy duty, the erection of harbor defenses, immediate additions to the cavalry and artillery of the regular army, and authority to recruit a larger army if and when the situation demanded it. A stunned joint session of Congress heard the President conclude by suggesting that the United States could best defend its neutral rights by threatening to join with other neutral states in a defensive naval alliance.

The message was directed primarily against France despite Adams' reiteration of desires for neutrality, and Federalists rejoiced. Within two days Jefferson noted that two Republicans from the Virginia congressional delegation had left for home. Many wondered what had turned Adams, previously considered conciliatory, toward armaments and defiance. Traditionally, the explanation has been that he fell under the influence of his predominantly Hamiltonian Cabinet. Adams, however, went further in his statements than Hamilton at first thought wise, and he was to show almost complete independence of the opinions of Cabinet officers in his conduct of foreign relations.

Events proved his Cabinet a poor instrument. Timothy Pickering, secretary of state, was the servant of Hamilton rather than Adams; Oliver Wolcott, Jr., secretary of the treasury, despite occasional displays of independent thinking, was a Hamiltonian stalwart; and James McHenry of the War Department almost worshipped Hamilton. The young attorney general, Charles Lee, held what was regarded as a part-time office and, although dependable, was without wide influence. Adams kept them, because he opposed the principle of rotation in office, because he knew what tortures of embarrassment Washington had suffered in trying to find advisers at the prevailing salary scale, and because he apparently regarded them as men who would serve him honorably. Contrary to his reputation for impatience, Adams proved almost unbelievably forebearing in his relations with the Cabinet. Years later McHenry stated the cause of much friction between President and advisers. "Three of the gentlemen who were heads of departments with Mr. Adams were also heads of departments with General Washington. These gentlemen could never for a moment depart from his maxims."

The diplomatic and political crisis that was announced by Adams in May, 1797, lasted unbroken until 1800 when Napoleon signed a convention which lifted the burden of the 1778 French alliance from the Administration's shoulders. In large measure, therefore, the Adams administration was a wartime administration. Armaments, fortifications, naval vessels, officers' commissions, tax increases and a doubled national budget produced severe strains. Each of these problems resulted in division; if Adams and the Hamiltonians were united, the Jeffersonians stood bitterly opposed; if the Republicans applauded Administration action, the Hamiltonians were scornful; and there were times when Adams was mistrusted by both groups. Only in terms of the difficulties involved in building retaliatory power as a means to peace can sense be made of the Adams record, a feat that may prove less difficult from the vantage point of the mid-twentieth century than before.

Hamilton sized up the situation that confronted the Government realistically. "The U. States have the strongest reason to avoid war," he told the Cabinet. "They may lose a great deal; they can gain nothing. . . . France in declining to receive Mr. Pinckney has not gone to the *ne plus ultra*. She has declined to receive a minister until grievances of which she complains are redressed." Hamilton's own plan was for the appointment of a bipartisan peace commission that might include Jefferson or Madison, but Pickering and Wolcott would not hear of it, and Adams knew that neither of the Republican leaders would accept. The matter had already been settled. It was, therefore, decided to nominate John Marshall of Virginia and Francis Dana of Massachusetts to join Pinckney in Europe. Their names were sent to the Senate on the same day that a request went to the House for defense appropriations. When Dana refused the appointment, Elbridge Gerry of Massachusetts took his place much to the disgust of most Federalist leaders. Like Adams, Gerry was not a party politician. He leaned toward the Republicans in his interpretation of the Constitution and was repeatedly sought as a Republican candidate for Governor of Massachusetts, but as an elector he had voted for Adams and not for Jefferson in 1796.

Adams in calling for armaments and in speaking of peace with honor became the toast of ardent Federalists. George Cabot of Boston described his May address to Congress as the best antidote to Jacobin poisons ever administered. "After reading it all Sunday afternoon at my home, a large company of good men all agreed that it was in every particular exactly what they would have wished." The most extreme Federalists concluded that war was hanging in the balance. "The theme of every man's inquiries is, are we going to war with France," Fisher Ames reported; and Representative Uriah Tracy of Connecticut had already concluded that war was a necessity. "Unless an alteration, either of men or measures, or both, takes place in France, we must have war with her," Tracy informed Oliver Wolcott, Jr.

Republicans found themselves as dispirited as Federalists were elated. John Dawson, who had taken Madison's seat in Congress, saw a young French general named Bonaparte holding the future of American republicanism in his hands. An enforced peace in Europe, thought Dawson, was the only way of averting an American declaration of war; and Jefferson momentarily viewed the survival of liberal institutions as dependent upon the remote possibility of a republican revolution in Britain. He could point to Virginia Republicans who had deserted principles and voted for war measures as the basis for his pessimism.

Both sides assumed that John Adams was as eager for war as the most hotheaded of his supporters. Many believed that he would seize the opportunity to lead the nation into war as the most direct road to personal ascendency and re-election. Adams bluffed his way through the French crisis, however, winning his point as a diplomatist but failing the final test as a politician in the process. Few could see that his belligerence had decided limits. While Federalists applauded his spirit and awaited his call to hold Congress in extra session over the summer, Adams packed his bags and returned to his New England farm. Men around him found such conduct erratic, and it remains a riddle unless his use of strategic withdrawal in conducting diplomacy is taken into consideration. One of his favorite tactics was silence, and he insisted that secrecy was essential to the intelligent conduct of foreign policy. There were Federalists who explained the President's behavior as due to whim and instability of purpose, but John Marshall in conversation with Adams prior to his departure for France found him "a sensible, plain, candid, good tempered man."

By the fall of 1797, however, the first effects of the French crisis showed signs of wearing thin. Despite the President's plea for defense measures in both his November message to Congress and in his December State of the Union address, the House carried a resolution to prepare a bill authorizing the arming of merchant ships only as a result of the Speaker's tie-breaking vote. Congressional moderates and Republicans were loath to raise taxes until further developments proved them necessary. Impatient Federalists became bitter over the ability of Congress to procrastinate as rumors of the peace mission's failure spread. An angry exchange between Vermont's Matthew Lyon and Connecticut's Roger Griswold led to spitting, brawling, and Lyon's expulsion from the House. Adams dismissed the Comptroller of the Treasury on the basis of anti-Federalist pamphleteering, and the Attorney General became engaged in a pamphlet war with James Monroe. Republican Congressman Albert Gallatin of Pennsylvania alleged that the president of the North American Insurance Company was removed from office by company directors simply for holding democratic convictions.

Perhaps it was only chance, but it was at this point that both Hamilton and Jefferson became the objects of scandal, Hamilton confessing to an adulterous relationship and Jefferson remaining silent under charges of libel. By mid-February partisan feeling had reached an intensity that led Senator James Ross of Pennsylvania to consider any legislation impossible unless one party or the other could win large majorities in both houses.

On partisan issues such as the expulsion of Congressman Lyon from the House, Federalists held a majority, but in terms of tax and defense measures Ross was right. A small group of moderates, nominally Federalist for the most part, held the balance. Adams, in announcing the failure of the peace mission on the fifth of March, 1798, broke a log jam of legislation; and when he revealed that the French Directory had refused even to recognize the official existence of the peace envoys two weeks later, patriotic resentment flamed up. His request for defense measures now took on the appearance of a call to a crusade. "Mr. Adams has immortalized himself," exulted Jonathan Mason, Jr., of the famous Essex Junto in Massachusetts. Republicans only added fuel to the fire by scoffing and by demanding that the full diplomatic record be made public.

The "X.Y.Z." papers, as these documents came to be known, were released on the fifth of April. Jefferson leaves some idea of the effect produced by noting that before the day was over he had heard himself accused of a criminal correspondence with members of the French government. Two weeks later he believed that Bache's anti-Administration paper, the *Aurora*, would be forced to close for lack of subscribers, and he was alarmed to note again that more Virginians had deserted their desks in Congress to return home.

Adams, by contrast, had not been so popular since 1776, and he took advantage of the situation by answering scores of spirited public resolutions that flooded into Philadelphia during the spring and summer of 1798 with exhortations to further excite public opinion. The number of these presidential letters cannot be estimated at less than a hundred, and they may have numbered twice as many. Writing them was a tremendous undertaking. There is little doubt that Adams was personally more responsible than any other man for the creation of what Jefferson called "the X.Y.Z. fever." Although Adams did not ask for alien or sedition laws, he alluded to both problems indirectly in several of his public letters. Referring to those who seemed to prefer French institutions to those of the United States he suggested conveying them within French lines in the event of invasion. He spoke pointedly of a "spirit of falsehood and malignity" that threatened to undermine loyalty to the Government, and he bluntly pointed to the French government as the most infamous example of corruption and falsehood in historical memory. In view of the time and effort which Adams spent in stirring up public sentiments it seems clear that he considered such a propaganda effort as essential to both defense measures and the success of his foreign policy.

The Republicans looked upon the President with a sense of horror. "The answers of Mr. Adams to his addressors," Madison declared, "form the most grotesque scene in the tragi-comedy acted by the government." But Federalists, gaining strength in spring elections and, convinced that Adams was correct in his view of revolutionary France, outdid themselves in praising his leadership. "A greater and better man than Pericles . . . will not be disappointed in the honorable opinion formed by his countrymen," read one extravagant comment. Hamilton understood Adams' objectives but was apprehensive, he told Secretary Wolcott, that the President would "run into indiscretion." He warned the Cabinet to check presidential enthusiasm.

France had assumed that her friends in America could be depended upon to defend her actions. The activities of her three ministers, Genêt, Fauchet, and Adet, in fitting out privateers, in encouraging the Whisky Rebellion of 1794, in intervening in the election of 1796, demonstrate how well established the opinion was that a pro-French government could be brought to power in America by means of maneuver and threat. The election of Adams was taken as an unfriendly act in itself. Open attacks upon American shipping and refusal to accept an avowed Federalist, Pinckney, in place of Monroe, a high-ranking Republican, were the immediate results. Britain, as Republicans were quick to point out and as Adams also admitted, continued to search American vessels, seize cargoes, and impress American seamen in spite of the Jay Treaty. Many Republicans regarded France as justified in fighting fire with fire. Monroe was one of them, and he was elected governor of the largest state in the Union after his return from

France. In order to demonstrate to France that Americans would not shape their policies in accord with the dictates of Paris, Adams gave himself to the task of unifying national sentiments. The immediate objective was to prepare public opinion for armaments and the high taxes that they would demand. Adams asserted repeatedly that a navy which would inevitably be ranged alongside the British Navy would have far more influence upon Talleyrand's conduct than months of negotiation and counter-threat. He was also convinced that the American Army must be modernized and plans adopted for the recruiting of a larger land force in the event of war. From start to finish, his aim was simply to force France to reverse her coercive policy and to accept the United States as a free and equal nation. He was not attempting to prepare public opinion for war.

Whether the response to his public addresses surprised him by its intensity or whether assurances of Talleyrand's willingness to negotiate came more quickly than he had anticipated, Adams made it apparent upon his return to Philadelphia in the fall of 1798 that his interest in propaganda had abated. Congress had authorized the purchase of munitions, the arming of merchantmen, the establishment of the Department of the Navy, and the building of frigates, but over the Army a basic split developed between the President and the Hamiltonians that gradually revealed wide divergencies in policy aims.

Adams wished to entrust the defense of American interests to an American navy and had called for only three thousand additional troops to be added to the standing army. He had asked for authority to recruit twenty thousand reserve troops if the situation called for them. What the Federalist majority in Congress provided, however, was authority to raise the standing army to twenty thousand and the reserve army to thirty thousand, the first good-sized pork barrel in America's national history. They saw little need for a powerful navy when British strength seemed obviously equal to the task of dealing with French commerce raiders. The dominant Federalist faction, therefore, pressed for a declaration of war that would seal an alliance between England and the United States in fact, if not in name. Adams refused to call for a declaration of war, however, and he became increasingly disturbed over the army and the uses to which such a force might be put.

In addition to armaments, the Federalists enacted the Sedition Act and four laws regulating aliens. Adams later insisted that it was Hamilton's influence that had produced these hated laws. He went so far as to suggest that Jefferson shared in the responsibility for them, since the Vice President had signed them in his role as presiding officer of the Senate. There is little doubt, however, that Adams approved the acts at the time. A year after they had been enacted he granted permission to the secretary of state to prosecute under the provisions of both Alien and Sedition Acts. "The Alien Law, I fear, will upon trial be found inadequate to the object intended," he commented, "but I am willing to try it in the case of [Victor] Collot." Collot was known to be a French agent on special mission for his government, and his activities had been watched since Washington's administration. Although Adams was severely criticized by Federalists for making too little use of these laws, he seems to have regarded them as essential to national security.

The program enacted by the Federalists in 1798 was also harsh in economic terms, at least by eighteenth-century standards. A land tax, a tax on houses or "window tax," and a stamp tax were passed, Republicans complaining that the burden had fallen unevenly upon the Southern states. The cost of the French crisis drove the Federal budget from six million dollars in 1797 to eight million dollars by 1798. In 1800 the cost of government rose to eleven and a half million dollars—double the budget of 1796.

Behind the Federalist program was the driving energy of self-righteous men. For more than five years they had been forced to submerge their deepest resentments against revolutionary France because of public enthusiasm. Striving to build the good life on foundations of stable laws, contractual obligations, commerce, and a sound currency, they were not prepared to surrender to what they regarded as a band of egalitarian fanatics. In their view the election of French partisans was tantamount to public debauchery; there was a positive need to prevent it; and like others who have desired to preserve liberty in a time of national jingoism, the Federalists of 1798 became trapped in the eternal ends-and-means dilemma. The X.Y.Z. dispatches confirmed their belief that French republicanism was corrupt in whatever constitutional form it appeared. Their last doubts about American Republicans were removed: Those who still persisted in defending France seemed beyond redemption.

Fisher Ames, the conscience of the prowar faction, was regarded as the most penetrating commentator and most powerful

43

voice of the party. Frequently ill, he could not serve in Congress after 1796, but in retirement at Dedham, Massachusetts, viewed his country with unrelieved dismay. Ames shared the fear of anarchy. He had shuddered at its proximity to Boston in 1786 when Shays's Rebellion threatened the security of his world; he had applauded the Government's vigorous action in 1794 when the Whiskey Rebellion was suppressed; and in 1796 he had condemned a government that feared reaction to a direct tax more than it respected strength. "Our proceedings smell of anarchy," he wrote Hamilton. "We rest our hopes on foolish and fanatical grounds . . . on human nature being different from what it is, and better here than anywhere else. . . . We want officers, courts, habits of acquiescence in our country, and the principles of Congress would hardly begin to form any of these. France is ready to hold Louisiana. The thread of connection is slender. . . . Yet we disband regiments."

In July, 1798, Ames warned Pickering that the moment to strike would pass quickly; Congress was not keeping pace with the President in its zeal for armaments, and what he termed "the Jacobins" were still alive. "They will soon rise from the mire where they now lie and attach themselves to any set of honest men, who in every question shall be for doing the least and the latest."

Theodore Sedgwick of western Massachusetts was a veteran congressman and a senator when he began to press for an immediate declaration of war. He confessed to Rufus King, American minister in London, his fear that the opposition might gain advantage with the people in posing as the party of peace. There was, he maintained, a majority in both houses prepared to vote for war in July, and Sedgwick considered it best to face the Republicans with the *fait accompli*. Stephen Higginson of Boston had similarly emphatic views. "Nothing but an open war can save us, and the more inveterate and deadly it shall be, the better will be our chance for security in the future," he told Secretary of the Treasury Wolcott.

Such war sentiment was not confined to the Bay State. Hamilton's father-in-law, Philip Schuyler of New York, was honestly distressed when Adams did not call for a declaration of war in the summer of 1798. He had heard rumors, he said in a letter to Hamilton, that France was disposed to make terms. He hoped them unfounded. "I feel that war with all its calamities, would be less injurious to my country than a peace which might be followed by the reintroduction of the destructive principles that prevail in France."

Hamilton himself could see little to be gained from a declaration of war, but he was, nonetheless, an aggressive advocate of military preparedness. He shared with other Federalist leaders their mistrust of popular government and considered large standing armies a necessity in any well-regulated society. In the period between the American Revolution and the overthrow of monarchy in France he had repeatedly declared himself a supporter of republican government. "As to my own political creed," he had written in 1792, "I give it to you with the utmost sincerity. I am affectionately attached to the republican theory. . . . On the whole, the only enemy which republicanism has to fear in this country is in the spirit of faction and anarchy. . . ." That spirit, he believed, had been unleashed in France. He had urged Washington to move with overwhelming force in suppressing the Whiskey Rebellion and had ridden with the President when the army moved into western Pennsylvania. When in the spring of 1799 a local outbreak of resentment against the window tax led to defiance of tax collectors in central portions of Pennsylvania, Hamilton's fear, as he expressed it to Secretary of War McHenry, was that too little force would be used in support of government. "Wherever the Government appears in arms, it ought to appear like a Hercules, and inspire respect by the display of strength."

John Adams, with memories of the Boston Massacre, detested standing armies, but Hamilton threw himself wholeheartedly into the creation of a new army in 1798 out of a conviction that the great crisis between local and national authority which he had long feared had arrived. "He well knew," wrote his friend Gouverneur Morris at the time of Hamilton's death, "that his favorite form [of government] was inadmissible, unless as the result of civil war; and I suspect that his belief in that which he called 'an approaching crisis' arose from a conviction that the kind of government most suited to this country could be established in no other way."

That the bloodletting of the French Revolution had modified Hamilton's convictions there can be little doubt. The phenomenon was common among men of the period. His dislike for the Republican party of Jefferson and Madison grew intense, so extreme that he was willing to contemplate military action against the Southern states. During the winter of 1798-99 the United States passed through a severe constitutional crisis that brought civil war perilously near. Contemporary political leaders were convinced that Virginia Republicans and their neighbors meant to carry their 1798 resolutions to a defiance of the law, and Hamilton, as field commander of the army, was prepared to put them "to the test," as he expressed it.

In three letters written during January and February, 1799, Hamilton outlined for powerful Federalist political leaders a program that would almost certainly have precipitated rebellion in the South. Two letters were addressed to Jonathan Dayton of New Jersey, retiring Speaker of the House, and the third was written to Theodore Sedgwick of Massachusetts, who was to be Speaker of the Sixth Congress. Virginia had already purchased five thousand small arms and had passed the famous Resolutions protesting the army, heavy taxes, and the constitutionality of the Alien and Sedition Acts. Commenting on these actions, Hamilton declared, "It is stated that the opposition party in Virginia, the headquarters of the faction, have followed up the hostile declarations which are to be found in the resolutions of their General Assembly by an actual preparation of the means of supporting them by force—that they have put the militia on a more efficient footing, are preparing considerable arsenals and magazines, and have gone so far as to lay new taxes on their citizens."

To meet these actions of Virginia, Hamilton advised the building of roads and canals through the South, laws that would strengthen the Federal courts, vigorous use of the Sedition Act, and "the subdivision of the great states." A few weeks later he repeated the same suggestions and criticized Adams in doing so. "What avail laws that are not executed? Renegade aliens conduct one or more incendiary presses in the United States. . . . Why are they not sent away. . . . If the President requires to be stimulated those who can approach him ought to do it."

Even more specific was the legislative program submitted to Sedgwick, who as the new Speaker was more important to the scheme than Dayton. First, Hamilton suggested that a committee of Congress should be appointed to study the Virginia Resolutions and inform the nation of "the full evidence which they afford of a regular conspiracy to overturn the government." Second, the alien and sedition laws should be strengthened; third, a pamphlet should be written and printed for distribution in the South that would contain evidence of the incipient Southern rebellion; and fourth, recruiting should be increased and an army moved toward Virginia. "Then," he concluded, "let measures be taken to act upon the laws and put Virginia to the test of resistance." While Federalists dreamed of permanently eclipsing the Republicans, Hamilton and his most trusted friends considered a provocative scheme that would have fomented armed rebellion. Simultaneously their imaginations were fired with the dream of adding vast stretches of Spanish territory to an American empire. The possibility that Spain's American provinces might be sprung loose by a French invasion of the Iberian Peninsula was considered real enough to involve Rufus King in secret talks with both William Pitt and the Venezuelan patriot, Francisco de Miranda. King felt sufficiently encouraged to collect maps and to urge the joint Anglo-American project upon the President, who showed little interest in it, thus adding one more crime to a growing list. Adams was discovering that if he were to succeed in his plan of arming for the purpose of forcing a change in French policy he would have to move independently. As he gained the support of men like Gerry and Marshall he became expert at throwing both parties off balance by the unexpectedness of his movements.

During the spring and summer of 1798 Adams used his position to bring public opinion to bear upon foreign policy. The President had been provided with powerful means of influencing this opinion in the Alien and Sedition Acts and in the provisional army, but Adams did very little with any of these weapons as Federalist leaders saw it. They complained constantly that he made too little use of the Sedition Act and no use at all of alien legislation. "We refused all the positive advantages that hostilities offered," Rufus King later declared, "and reserved only one negative right of excluding frenchmen and jacobinism, which right, however, we refrained from exercising."

When the large standing army was ordered by Congress, Adams could make no public protest that would not have undermined his strategy with regard to France. Instead, he quietly obstructed the creation of the army by refusing to issue recruiting orders. A year after the crisis had broken out with the release of the X.Y.Z. dispatches, Adams had done nothing to raise new troops. Sedgwick complained bitterly, "The conduct of the Executive has been astoundingly dilatory. As yet, not a single enlisting order has been issued." At the same time, however, Adams was hurrying the Navy toward completion and was lecturing Secretary of War McHenry about his impatience. McHenry was driven to distraction by his duties and Hamilton's constant goading. He was bluntly told by Adams that in a quarrel between Benjamin Stoddert, the newly appointed secretary of the navy, and the War Department the President would side with Stoddert. Not until peace negotiations had again been put in motion did Adams allow recruiting to begin, and by then it had become clearly ridiculous. As effective as any of Adams' actions against the army was his retention of McHenry in office. Both Washington and Hamilton testified to McHenry's incompetence.

Adams had made the original mistake of giving Washington, as commanding general, a free hand in selecting his general officers. Washington immediately chose Hamilton to be second in command, and only after a prolonged correspondence between Quincy and Philadelphia did Adams give in, dating Hamilton's commission ahead of those of Henry Knox and Benjamin Lincoln. It was not until the fall of 1798, however, that Hamilton was in uniform.

Although Adams could see no sense in recruiting thousands of enlisted men at Government expense, he saw advantages in signing commissions for officers whom he had no expectation of calling to active duty. He deliberately tried to bring moderate Republican leaders like Peter Muhlenberg and Aaron Burr into the military organization, but, as he put it, "I soon found that if I had not the previous consent of heads of departments and Mr. Hamilton, I ran the utmost risk of a dead negative in the Senate."

If the President aroused suspicion by fighting Hamilton's appointment while proposing Burr's, his worst display of independence concerned Elbridge Gerry, who had become anathema to Federalists by refusing to leave France and by continuing conversations with Talleyrand after both Marshall and Pinckney had returned to the United States. Whatever doubts Adams entertained concerning Gerry's discretion were gradually dispersed as the result of private talks which the two conducted at Quincy in the fall of 1798. Separated from the influence of his advisers, Adams moved much further from their position on French negotiations than they suspected. Gerry, Hamiltonians charged, had charmed Adams. Just prior to his departure for Philadelphia Adams posed a question to the Cabinet which alarmed the ultramontanes. He asked whether in his December message to Congress he should request a declaration of war or whether he should nominate a new peace envoy, and he even went so far as to suggest four names for consideration. The President also enclosed dispatches from the American minister to Holland, William Vans Murray, that testified to Talleyrand's increasing concern over American armaments and the possibility of an Anglo-American naval alliance. Adams declared himself much impressed with this indication of change at Paris.

If the Cabinet was playing a game with Adams, it is clear that he was also playing, but with stronger cards. His message to Congress of December 8, contrary to Pickering's advice, stated that he would reopen negotiations if and when he received assurances that an American mission would be received with dignity. Pickering, who saw Gerry's personal influence behind the sudden shift, became so alarmed that he had his movements watched and reported. What he learned, however, was that Gerry defended Adams on all occasions and that he had refused the Republican nomination for Governor of Massachusetts. Jefferson, on the other hand, could sense no sincere change in Adams' temper and saw the presidential message as simply one more call for defense measures.

Adams had privately determined to make peace. He released Gerry's notes to Congress on the eighteenth of January after receiving further evidence of good intentions at Paris in the form of a letter from Talleyrand to the French chargé at The Hague. American Minister Murray had forwarded it to Adams at once. Talleyrand expressed willingness to receive an American envoy with the dignity befitting "a free, powerful, and independent" nation, the exact phraseology that Adams had insisted upon. Indirect as this approach seemed, Adams was determined to accept it as sufficient basis for negotiation.

Without warning his advisers, Adams took the step that resulted in the overthrow of the war advocates. On February 15 he announced that France had suspended a decree authorizing the capture of American merchant ships, and three days later he astounded men of every faction by unceremoniously naming William Murray to be minister plenipotentiary to France. Jefferson was dumbfounded by the unexpectedness of the move, describing it as the "event of events," but Secretary of State Pickering, who had known nothing of the decision in advance, hurried to inform friends that he had had no part in the insane action. The Republican press was jubilant, for Murray's appointment presented the Hamiltonians with an obvious dilemma. If they accepted peace as a possibility their military dreams were ended, but if they admitted their preference for war or a continuation of the undeclared naval war they would split the Federalist party and allow Jefferson's friends to capitalize on the peace issue. They took the only alternative available, that of attempting to delay the new mission by haggling with Adams over Murray's inexperience and the need to name others to accompany him. Adams, however, refused to quarrel and immediately named Chief Justice Oliver Ellsworth and Governor William Davie of North Carolina, both respected Federalist leaders. What no one knew was that Adams viewed the peace mission as window dressing. The skill of negotiators would not force Talleyrand and Napoleon to reverse policy, but the American Navy could. The weeks of delay before the envoys sailed bothered him very little, for it allowed the completion of naval vessels essential to success.

Having broken with the extremists, Adams once more left for his farm at Quincy. While their anger and disappointment became a public spectacle, the President's isolation and apparent lack of concern for their situation pointed up the schism. The Hamiltonians had been warned for months by Rufus King in London that the Directory would move to reopen negotiations. What made Adams' action appear incredible was that he seemed to accept Talleyrand's assurances at face value. The militarists were also convinced that sustaining the crisis until the fall of 1800 would guarantee Federalist majorities in Congress and Adams' re-election. Entering into negotiations was certain to end the sweep of patriotic fervor which had served the party so well. Although Gilbert Chinard concluded that Adams was "the most realistic statesman of his generation," most students have concluded that Adams was inept as a political tactician.

Adams had become convinced as a result of Gerry's testimony and Murray's dispatches from Holland that Talleyrand wished to escape the consequences of his own blunder. Federalists condemned Gerry as guilty of treason and would not listen to the reports. Adams listened but was more impressed by private letters from John Quincy Adams at Berlin which confirmed Gerry's and Murray's reports. Adams would not wait until Talleyrand made the forthright apology that Pickering and his extremist friends demanded, because it was unreasonable to expect it. The main point at issue between Adams and the Hamiltonians, however, was whether to negotiate at all. Adams wished to end the deadlock; they did not. When a note from George Washington arrived expressing the belief that the people were deeply desirous of peace, Adams, as Washington's biographers have noted, took advantage of it, holding the letter as a trump card should the war party refuse to follow. By 1799 Adams had come to fear both Hamilton's power and ambition and the rumblings of civil conflict. He was also convinced that many Federalist leaders would attempt to block his re-election in 1800 and accepted at last the need to fight them openly.

George Cabot, who had been appointed by Boston Federalists to sound him out, found the President breathing fire. He denounced what he called "the dictatorial temper of high-minded [i.e., military-minded] Federalists." Adams defended Gerry and admitted that one of his own motives had been "to soothe Jacobin spirits." To Attorney General Charles Lee, who had approved his peace move, Adams wrote in a similar vein. He had struck, he said, against "combinations of Senators, generals, and heads of departments." To both Cabot and Lee he asserted that the peace policy would be supported by the voters, but few would believe this.

Federalists and their apologists have indulged in a great deal of nostalgia over the war that might have been and its probable heroes. The evidence suggests, however, that public opinion, as Washington noted, preferred peace to war and that widespread dislike of heavy taxes, a large army, and the Sedition Act had largely extinguished the patriotic sentiments of early 1798. Adams was fully aware of this change and told Theodore Sedgwick a week before appointing Murray that public opinion would tolerate the tax laws little longer. Jefferson was careful to direct attention to the tax issue during the political contests of 1799. As early as November of 1798 he had predicted an end to militarism. The disease would pass, he wrote to John Taylor of Virginia. "Indeed the doctor is now on his way to cure it, in the guise of a tax collector."

Massachusetts Federalists grew uneasy over the effects of direct taxes and the wave of speculation that Government contracts and bond issues had stimulated. "In the New England states the alien and sedition acts make less noise than the land tax," Joseph Hale of the Essex Junto informed Rufus King. Adams' former law student, Jonathan Mason, confessed to Congressman Harrison

Gray Otis in January, 1799, that the effect of taxation in the vicinity of Boston had been to double the number of peace advocates. A Pennsylvania Federalist testified in his memoirs that "the tax on real property was the fatal blow to Federalism in Pennsylvania."

Aside from its cost, the Army had proven a curse in countless ways. It was drawing the most disorderly elements into its ranks, and complaints of desertion were common. Adams, with no sympathy for his plight, told the Secretary of War that he could see no reason for men to enlist at five dollars a month when three times as much could be earned in the merchant marine. He added that there was better chance of seeing a French army in heaven than in America. Hamilton complained to Washington that the Army was short of clothing, barracks, and munitions. Adams' procrastination, McHenry's mismanagement, and Wolcott's opposition to further increases in the military budget had produced a situation that Hamilton found disgraceful.

The Philadelphia *Aurora's* Republican editor found evidence of enough violence and petty larceny committed by military personnel to publish a weekly newspaper entitled, *Cannibal's Progress,* and was rewarded in May, 1799, by being dragged from his office and beaten by a group of young officers. When in the gubernatorial contest of that year the Pennsylvania Federalists promoted the candidacy of a young man who could lead militia against an invading army, Republicans successfully ran the aged conservative, Thomas McKean, on a platform of opposition to the Army and the Sedition Act. "The zeal and enthusiasm which were excited by the publication of the X.Y.Z. dispatches . . . are evaporated," Washington declared.

Adams, in defending his peace decision, maintained that the program of 1798 had recoiled upon its creators and that a change of policy would prove a political blessing. Spring election in 1799 seemed to bear this out. In New York City Republicans were turned out of office for the first time in three years; while Massachusetts Republican votes increased by six thousand over the 1798 poll, the Federalist candidate for governor drew seven thousand more votes than in 1798; and the upsurge of Federalist strength in the South was generally admitted to be spectacular. Southern Federalists, however, were enthusiastic for the President's foreign policy and condemned the Sedition Act. Georgia elected its first Federalist to Congress; five of South Carolina's six Representatives were Federalists, as were seven of ten elected in North Carolina; and most significant, almost half the large Virginia delegation were Federalist. Washington considered Virginia's new senator, John Taylor, a Republican in name only. George Cabot admitted that to his surprise the President's actions had proven "much less pernicious than was feared."

To Jefferson the outcome was a distinct shock. "The Virginia congressional elections have astonished everyone," he wrote to Tench Coxe of Pennsylvania. John Taylor wrote Jefferson in the fall, "I give up all for lost." And at the end of the year Madison, back in politics after repeated urgings, saw Administration supporters in the Virginia legislature as almost equal in strength to his anti-Administration block—an unknown phenomenon up to that time.

Adams remained at Quincy while Pickering made every effort to delay the departure of the peace envoys. He was aware of Cabinet opposition to his policy, as his heated remarks to Cabot show, but it was a confidential letter from Secretary of the Navy Stoddert that revealed how determined Pickering was to sabotage the mission. Napoleon's sudden seizure of power led many Federalists to predict a Bourbon restoration and to urge upon Pickering further delay. While it is now apparent that Adams was alive to the machinations of his Hamiltonian advisers and willing to see negotiations delayed, he left immediately for Trenton, the temporary capital, when Stoddert told him that Pickering was urging the Cabinet to take a stand for indefinite delay.

Upon arrival Adams showed neither concern for the sailing of his envoys nor hostility toward Pickering. Suddenly, however, with what Pickering considered complete inconsistency, he wheeled about and issued orders for the departure of the two commissioners within two weeks. In anger and astonishment Pickering admitted to Cabot, "In most matters we are consulted and our ideas often adopted, but in this all important question from first to last, we have been absolutely excluded."

The shock of this action was almost as inexplicable to his enemies as Murray's appointment had been. The only explanation that made sense to them was that Adams and Jefferson had struck a political bargain. "God grant that all may end well," wrote Mrs. Otis to her husband in commenting on reaction at Boston; "The President stands high with the Jacobins, the Essex Junto decry him on all occasions." The orthodox Stephen Higginson that same week reported to Pickering that he had heard private talk of Adams' fury against members of the Cabinet, of his determination to punish their disloyalty, and of his resolve to carry as many Federalists with him as possible while seeking accord with the Republicans. Higginson admitted that Adams was popular with the people and that not a single Massachusetts elector could be chosen who would vote for anyone else as president.

Rumors of an Adams-Jefferson coalition persisted, and when the President refused to endorse the Federalist candidate for governor of Massachusetts in the spring of 1800 it seemed confirmation enough. The candidate of the Republican party, however, was Elbridge Gerry, who made it clear that he stood behind Administration policy. A writer for the Republican *Independent Chronicle* reflected the confusion that abounded by insisting that Gerry was not only a Republican but also a Federalist and a better one than Caleb Strong, his opponent. "It is true, an Essex Junto have censured his conduct while in France; but as these people live by war, and are maintained by a war establishment, we cannot wonder that they are opposed to Mr. Gerry. But let us inquire whether President Adams has censured him. On the contrary, he esteems him as the firm friend of prosperity for the country."

Adams was adopted by the Republicans for campaign purposes, and he would not disown Gerry. "Much has been done by holding up Gerry as the friend of Adams and of peace, as well as the people and the rights of man," Higginson reported to Pickering. "The President's patronage has been very efficacious, and his friends have been in favor of Gerry."

When the returns in Massachusetts revealed that Gerry had come within two thousand votes of defeating the Federalist machine it was looked upon as a staggering blow to the prestige of the party. Simultaneously, Hamilton's Federalist ticket in New York was defeated in an assembly election that would determine the electoral vote of the state in the ensuing presidential election. Despite the feelings of the Hamiltonian faction, it was at this critical point that a congressional caucus renominated Adams and named General Charles C. Pinckney as his running mate. Adams completed the divorce between himself and the Hamiltonians by a peremptory dismissal of both Pickering and McHenry from the

Cabinet. "Beyond a doubt there is a coalition between Mr. Adams and Mr. Jefferson," Pickering concluded.

There is no evidence of any such agreement, though Adams clearly had moved in the direction of bridging the gulf between his own and Jefferson's positions since the winter of 1798. It was correctly divined that he had attempted to separate himself from the harsh program of 1798 and to break the grip of Hamilton on the Federalist party by his direction of foreign affairs. His lack of faith in the success of his second peace mission points to the possibility that this was a very important motive for his actions. The number of Federalists whose private letters reveal loyalty to Adams in 1800 are a surprising tribute to his success on the political level: John Jay, Rufus King, Theophilus Parsons, Harrison Otis, Caleb Cushing, Samuel Dexter, Henry Knox, Thomas Johnson, Samuel Bayard, and John Marshall, to mention the best known of them. Hamilton, as Richard B. Morris has phrased it, was left "a party leader without a following."

Adams' disappointment over Jefferson's victory was deep and led him to the petty act of refusing to attend Jefferson's inaugural. He had acted like a candidate in the closing weeks of the campaign of 1800, giving as many public addresses as occasion presented opportunity for, raising toasts to independence and neutrality, condemning England as well as France for attacking American commerce. Possibly he had hopes that Jefferson would recognize the merits of his struggle against the "high-Federalists" by throwing electoral support to him rather than to Burr, a man mistrusted by politicians of both parties. If such disappointed hopes explain the bitterness he exhibited in 1801, they are evidence of Adams' place outside the American party tradition. His proud insistence later that he had never depended upon party, his independent conduct of foreign policy and unwillingness to seek accord with the dominant faction in the Federalist party, his hope for a united administration with Jefferson in the aftermath of 1796, are all indications of a spirit very different from that exhibited by Jefferson in placating Aaron Burr after the election of 1796.

The political strength behind John Adams was such, however, that men who would gladly have deserted him were forced to accept his candidacy twice. The electoral vote of 1800 is a tribute to his prestige among the rank-and-file of a badly-divided party.

Against constant intrigue and the opposition of powerful opponents he had kept the nation at peace, averting both war and domestic strife.

When questioned about his actions years later, he replied, "To dispatch all in a few words, a civil war was expected. The party committed suicide; they killed themselves and the national president (not their President) at one shot, and then foolishly or maliciously indicted me for the murder. My mission to France . . . I esteem the most splendid diamond in my crown."

Thomas Jefferson

by MORTON BORDEN

*F*or twelve years the Constitution worked, after a fashion.
From its inception the new document had been subjected
to severe trials and divisive strains. A rebellion in Pennsylvania,
a naval war with France, a demand for states' rights from Virginia and Kentucky, and various Western schemes of disunion—all
had been surmounted. Had it not been for the great prestige of
George Washington and the practical moderation of John Adams,
America's second attempt at a federal union might have failed like
the first. Partisan passions had run high in the 1790's, and any
single factor on which men disagreed—Hamilton's financial plans
or the French Revolution or the Sedition Act—might easily have
caused a stoppage of the nation's political machinery.

The two-party system emerged during this decade, and on
each important issue public opinion seemed to oscillate between
Federalist and Democratic-Republican. Perhaps this was to be
expected of a young nation politically adolescent. Year by year
Americans were becoming more politically alert and active; if
there was little room for middle ground between these two factions, yet opinions were hardly fixed and irrevocable. The cul-
mination of partisan controversy and the test of respective
strengths took place in the monumental election of 1800.

Jefferson was feared, honestly feared, by almost all Federalists.
Were he to win the election, so they predicted, all the hard constructive gains of those twelve years would be dissipated. Power

would be returned to the individual states; commerce would suffer; judicial power would be lessened; and the wonderful financial system of Hamilton would be dismantled and destroyed. Jefferson was an atheist, and he would attack the churches. Jefferson was a hypocrite, an aristocrat posing as democrat, appealing to the baser motives of human beings in order to obtain votes. Jefferson was a revolutionary, a Francophile and, after ruining the Army and Navy under the guise of economy measures, might very well involve the nation in a war with England. In short, it was doubtful if the Constitution could continue its successful course under such a president.

In like manner the Republicans feared another Federalist victory. To be sure, John Adams had split with Hamilton and had earned the enmity of the Essex Junto. But would he not continue Hamilton's "moneyed system"? Did not Adams share the guilt of every Federalist for the despicable Alien and Sedition Acts? Was it not true that "His Rotundity" so admired the British system that he was really a monarchist at heart? Republicans were not engaging in idle chatter, nor were they speaking solely for effect, when they predicted many dire consequences if Adams were elected. A typical rumor had Adams uniting "his house to that of his majesty of Britain" and "the bridegroom was to be king of America."

Throughout the country popular interest in the election was intense, an intensity sustained over months of balloting. When the Republicans carried New York City, Alexander Hamilton seriously suggested that the results be voided. And when the breach between Adams and Hamilton became public knowledge, Republicans nodded knowingly and quoted the maxim: "When thieves fall out, honest men come by their own."

The Federalists were narrowly defeated. But the decision was complicated by a result which many had predicted: a tied electoral vote between the two Republican candidates, Aaron Burr and Thomas Jefferson. (Indeed, the Twelfth Amendment was adopted in 1804 to avoid any such recurrence.) A choice between the two would be made by the House of Representatives. At this moment, February, 1801, the Constitution seemed on the verge of collapse. Federalist members of the lower house united in support of Burr; Republicans were just as adamant for Jefferson. After thirty-five ballots, neither side had yet obtained the necessary majority. The issue seemed hopelessly deadlocked. What would happen on March 4, inauguration day?

One representative from Maryland, sick with a high fever, was literally carried into Congress on a stretcher to maintain the tied vote of his state. The Republican governor of Pennsylvania, Thomas McKean, threatened to march on Washington with troops if the Federalists persisted in thwarting the will of the people. Hamilton was powerless; his advice that Jefferson was the lesser evil went unheeded. So great was their hatred of the Virginian that most Federalists in Congress would have opposed him regardless of the consequences. After all, they reasoned, Jefferson would dismantle the Federal government anyway. In the end, however, patriotism and common sense prevailed. For the choice was no longer Jefferson or Burr, but Jefferson or no president at all. A few Federalists, led by James A. Bayard of Delaware, could not accept the logic of their party, and threw the election to Jefferson.

What a shock it was, then, to read Jefferson's carefully chosen words in his inaugural address:

> But every difference of opinion is not a difference of principle. We have called by different names brethren of the same principle. We are all republicans—we are all federalists. If there be any among us who would wish to dissolve this Union or to change its republican form, let them stand undisturbed as monuments of the safety with which error of opinion may be tolerated where reason is left free to combat it. I know, indeed, that some honest men fear that a republican government cannot be strong; that this government is not strong enough. But would the honest patriot, in the full tide of successful experiment, abandon a government which has so far kept us free and firm, on the theoretic and visionary fear that this government, the world's best hope, may by possibility want energy to preserve itself? I trust not. I believe this, on the contrary, the strongest government on earth. I believe it is the only one where every man, at the call of the laws, would fly to the standard of the law, and would meet invasions of the public order as his own personal concern. Sometimes it is said that man cannot be trusted with the government of himself. Can he, then, be trusted with the government of others? Or have we found angels in the form of kings to govern him? Let history answer this question.

The words were greeted with applause—and confusion. It was obvious that Jefferson wanted to salve the wounds of bitter factionalism. While many Federalists remained distrustful and some even regarded it as hypocritical, most men approved the tone of their new president's message.

But what did Jefferson mean? Were there no economic principles at stake in his conflicts with Hamilton? Were there no political and constitutional principles implicit in the polar views of the respective parties? And, in the last analysis, did not these differences reflect a fundamental philosophical quarrel over the nature of human beings? Was not the election of 1800 indeed a revolution? If not, then what is the meaning of Jeffersonianism?

For two terms Jefferson tried, as best he could, to apply the standards of his inaugural address. Naturally, the Alien and Sedition Acts were allowed to lapse. The new secretary of the treasury, Albert Gallatin, was instructed to devise an easily understood program to erase the public debt gradually. Internal taxes were either abolished or reduced. Frugality and economy were emphasized to an extreme. Elegant and costly social functions were replaced by simple and informal receptions. The expense of maintaining ambassadors at the courts of Portugal, Holland, and Prussia was erased by withdrawing these missions. The Army and Navy were pared down to skeleton size. To be sure, Jefferson had to reverse himself on the matter of patronage for subordinate Government posts. Originally he planned to keep these replacements to a minimum, certainly not to permit an individual's partisan opinions to be a basis for dismissal unless the man manifestly used his office for partisan purposes. This position was politically untenable, according to Jefferson's lieutenants, and they pressed him to accept a moderate number of removals. Indeed, Jefferson's handling of patronage is symbolic of what Hamilton once called his "ineradicable duplicity."

The Federalist leaders cried out in anguish at every one of these policy changes. The lowering of the nation's military strength would increase the danger of invasion. It was a rather risky gamble to assume that peace could be maintained while European war was an almost constant factor, and the United States was the major neutral carrier. The abolition of the excises, especially on distilled spirits, would force the Government to rely on tariffs, an unpredictable source of revenue depending on the wind and waves. It was charged that several foreign ambassadors were offended by Jefferson's rather affected and ultrademocratic social simplicity. Most important, the ultimate payment of the public debt would reduce national power.

This time, however, the people did not respond to the Federalist lament of impending anarchy. After all, commerce prospered throughout most of Jefferson's administration. Somehow the churches remained standing. No blood baths took place. The Bank of the United States still operated. Peace was maintained. Certainly, some Federalist judges were under attack, but the judicial power passed through this ordeal to emerge unscathed and even enhanced. Every economic indicator—urban growth, westward expansion, agricultural production, the construction of canals, turnpikes and bridges—continued to rise, undisturbed by the political bickering in Washington.

At first the Federalists were confident that they would regain power. Alexander Hamilton's elaborate scheme for an organization to espouse Christianity and the Constitution, as the "principal engine" to restore Federalist power, was rejected out of hand. He was told that "our adversaries will soon demonstrate to the world the soundness of our doctrines and the imbecility and folly of their own." But hope changed to despair as the people no longer responded; no "vibration of opinion" took place as in the 1790's. Federalism was the party of the past, an antiquated and dying philosophy. "I will fatten my pigs, and prune my trees; nor will I any longer . . . trouble to govern this country," wrote Fisher Ames: "You federalists are only lookers-on." Jefferson swept the election of 1804, capturing every state except Connecticut and Delaware from the Federalist candidate, Charles C. Pinckney. "Federalism is dead," wrote Jefferson a few years later, "without even the hope of a day of resurrection. The quondam leaders indeed retain their rancour and principles; but their followers are amalgamated with us in sentiment, if not in name."

It is the fashion of some historians to explain the Federalist demise and Republican ascendancy in terms of a great change in Jefferson. A radical natural law philosopher when he fought as minority leader, he became a first-rate utilitarian politician as president. The Virginian became an American. Revolutionary theory was cast aside when Jefferson faced the prosaic problem of having to run the country. He began to adopt some of the techniques and policies of the Federalists. Indeed, it is often observed that Jefferson "outfederalized the Federalists." There is much to be said for this view. After all, less than three months after he assumed the presidency, Jefferson dispatched a naval squadron to the Mediterranean on a warlike mission, without asking the permission of Congress. Two members of his Cabinet, Levi Lincoln and Albert Gallatin, thought the action unconstitutional, and so advised the President. Almost from the moment of its birth the young nation had paid tribute, as did every European power, rather than risk a war with the Barbary pirates. But Jefferson could not abide such bribery. No constitutional scruples could delay for a moment his determination to force the issue. Later, Congress declared war, and in four years Barbary power was shattered. The United States under Jefferson accomplished an object that England, France, Spain, Portugal, and Holland had desired for more than a century—unfettered commerce in the Mediterranean. Here, then, in this episode, is a totally different Jefferson—not an exponent of states' rights and strict interpretation of the Constitution, but an American nationalist of the first order.

Perhaps the most frequently cited example of Jefferson's chameleon quality, however, was on the question of whether the United States should or should not purchase the Louisiana Territory from France. On this question the fundamental issue was squarely before Jefferson, and a choice could not be avoided. The purchase would more than double the size of the United States. Yet the Constitution did not specifically provide for such acquisition of foreign territory. Further, the treaty provided that this area would eventually be formed into states, full partners in the Union. Again, the Constitution did not specifically cover such incorporation. A broad interpretation of Article IV, Section III, however, might permit United States' ratification of the treaty. Should theory be sacrificed and an empire gained? Or were the means as important as the ends?

Broad or loose construction of the Constitution was the key to the growth of Federal power. Federalists had argued in this vein to justify most of their legislation in the 1790's. To Jefferson, individual liberty and governmental power were on opposite ends of a see-saw, which the Federalists had thrown off balance. He believed that government, especially the central government, must be restricted within rather narrow and essential limits. Only by continually and rigidly applying strict construction to the Constitution could this tendency to overweening power be controlled and individual liberty be safeguarded. As early as 1777, Jefferson, then governor of Virginia, had warned that constitutions must be explicit, "so as to exclude all possible doubt; . . . [lest] at some future day . . . power[s] should be assumed."

On the other hand, the purchase of Louisiana would fulfill a dream and solve a host of problems. Jefferson envisioned an American empire covering "the whole northern, if not the southern continent, with a people speaking the same language, governed in similar forms, and by similar laws." The purchase would be a giant step in the direction of democracy's inevitable growth. "Is it not better," asked Jefferson, "that the opposite bank of the Mississippi should be settled by our own brethren and children, than by strangers of another family?"

Of more immediate interest, Westerners would be able to ship their goods down the Mississippi without fear that New Orleans might be closed. Indian attacks undoubtedly would taper off without the Spanish to instigate them. Uppermost in Jefferson's mind, however, was the freedom from England that the purchase would assure. He did not fear Spanish ownership. A feeble, second-rate nation like Spain on the frontier offered little threat to America's future security. The continued possession of Louisiana by an imperialistic France led by the formidable Napoleon, however, might force the United States into an alliance with England. At first Jefferson thought a constitutional amendment specifically permitting the purchase might solve the dilemma. But Napoleon showed signs of wavering. The treaty had to be confirmed immediately, with no indication of constitutional doubt. Jefferson asked the Republican leaders in the Senate to ratify it "with as little debate as possible, and particularly so far as respects the constitutional difficulty."

In still other ways Jefferson's presidency was marked by Federalist policies which encouraged the growth of central power. Internal improvements loomed large in Jefferson's mind. While many turnpikes and canals were financed by private and state capital, he realized that Federal support would be necessary, especially in the western part of the nation. With the use of Federal money obtained from the sale of public lands, and (later) aided by direct congressional appropriations, the groundwork for the famous Cumberland road was established during Jefferson's administration. He enthusiastically supported Gallatin's plan to spend twenty million dollars of Federal funds on a network of national roads and canals. Other more pressing problems intervened, however, and it was left to later administrations to finance these local and interstate programs. If Hamilton had pressed for internal improvements in the 1790's (he suggested them in the *Report on Manufactures*), Jefferson probably would have raised constitutional objections.

Finally, is not Jefferson's change of tack further reflected in the political history of that era? Over the span of a few years it seemed as if each party had somehow reversed directions. In 1798-99 Jefferson and Madison penned the Virginia and Kentucky Resolutions as an answer to the Federalists' infamous Alien and Sedition Acts. In 1808-9 more radical but comparable rumblings of dissatisfaction emanated from some New England Federalists over Jefferson's Embargo Act. For the embargo, says one of Jefferson's biographers, was "the most arbitrary, inquisitorial, and confiscatory measure formulated in American legislation up to the period of the Civil War." Further, both parties splintered during Jefferson's administration. Many moderate Federalists, like John Quincy Adams, found themselves in closer harmony with Administration policy than with Essex Junto beliefs. And Jefferson's actions alienated old comrades, like John Randolph, Jr., whose supporters were called the Tertium Quids. It is interesting to note that there is no historical consensus of why, when, how, or what precipitated the break between Randolph and Jefferson. Randolph is always referred to as brilliant but erratic; and whatever immediate reason is alleged, the cause somehow has to do with Randolph's personality and Jefferson's betrayal of the true doctrines.

It is part of Jefferson's greatness that he could inspire a myth and project an image. But one must not confuse myth and reality, shadow and substance. Thomas Jefferson as he was, and Thomas Jefferson as people perceived him, are quite different. While both concepts of course, are of equal value in understanding our past, it is always the historian's task to make the distinction. Too often, in Jefferson's case, this has not been done. Too often the biographers have described the myth—have taken at face value the popular view of Jefferson and his enemies, contained in the vitriolic newspaper articles and pamphlets, the passionate debates and fiery speeches of that period—and missed or misconstrued the reality.

This is understandable. Even the principals inevitably became involved and helped to propagate the exaggerated images of the 1790's and thus misunderstood one another's aims and motives. Jefferson, according to his grandson, never considered Federalist fulminations "as abusing him; they had never known him. They had created an imaginary being clothed with odious attributes, to whom they gave his name; and it was against that creature of their imaginations they had levelled their anathemas." John Adams, reminiscing in a letter to Jefferson, wrote: "Both parties have excited artificial terrors and if I were summoned as a witness to say upon oath, which party had excited . . . the most terror, and which had really felt the most, I could not give a more sincere answer, than in the vulgar style 'Put them in a bag and shake them, and then see which comes out first.' "

On March 4, 1801, following a decade of verbal violence, many Americans were surprised to hear that "We are all republicans— we are all federalists." Some historians act as if they, too, are surprised. These historians then describe Jefferson's administration as if some great change took place in his thinking, and conclude that he "outfederalized the Federalists." This is a specious view, predicated on an ultraradical Jefferson of the 1790's in constant debate with an ultraconservative Hamilton. Certainly Jefferson as president had to change. Certainly at times he had to modify, compromise, and amend his previous views. To conclude, however, that he outfederalized the Federalists is to miss the enormous consistency of Jefferson's beliefs and practices.

Jefferson was ever a national patriot second to none, not even to Hamilton. He always conceived of the United States as a unique experiment, destined for greatness so long as a sharp line isolated American civilization from European infection. Thus he strongly advised our youth to receive their education at home rather than in European schools, lest they absorb ideas and traits he considered "alarming to me as an American." From "Notes on Virginia" to his advice at the time of Monroe's doctrine, Jefferson thought of America first. It matters not that Hamilton was the better prophet; Jefferson was the better American. The French minister Adet once reported: "Although Jefferson is the friend of liberty . . . although he is an admirer of the efforts we have made to cast off our shackles. . . . Jefferson, I say, is an American, and as such, he cannot sincerely be our friend. An American is the born enemy of all the peoples of Europe."

Jefferson's nature was always more practical than theoretical, more common-sensical than philosophical. Certainly the essence of his Declaration of Independence is a Lockean justification of revolution; but, said Jefferson, "It was . . . an expression of the American mind," meant "to place before mankind the common sense of the subject." Jefferson always preferred precision to "metaphysical subtleties." The Kentucky and Virginia Resolutions can be understood only as a specific rebuttal of the Sedition Act. "I can never fear that things will go far wrong," wrote Jefferson, "where common sense has fair play."

One must also remember that Hamilton's power lessened considerably in the last four years of Federalist rule. He had a strong coterie of admirers, but the vast body of Federalists sided with John Adams. Despite all Hamilton did to insure Adams' defeat, and despite the split in Federalist ranks, the fact that Jefferson's victory in 1801 was won by a narrow margin indicated Federalist approval of Adams' actions. Certainly the people at that time— Jefferson and Adams included—regarded 1801 as the year of revolution. But if historians must have a revolution, perhaps Adams' split with the Hamiltonians is a better date. "The mid-position which Adams desired to achieve," writes Manning Dauer, "was adopted, in the main, by Jefferson and his successors."

To be sure, the two men disagreed on many matters of basic importance. Jefferson placed his faith in the free election of a virtuous and talented natural aristocracy; Adams did not. Within the constitutional balance, Jefferson emphasized the power of the lower house; Adams would give greater weight to the executive and judiciary. Jefferson, as a general rule, favored a strict interpretation of the Constitution; Adams did not fear broad construction. Both believed that human beings enjoyed inalienable rights, but only Jefferson had faith in man's perfectability. Jefferson could say, "I like a little rebellion now and then. It is like a storm in the atmosphere"; Adams had grown more conservative since 1776. Jefferson always defended and befriended Thomas Paine; Adams found Edmund Burke's position on the French Revolution more palatable.

Yet, the sages of Quincy and Monticello were both moderate and practical men. Despite the obvious and basic contrasts, both Adams and Jefferson stood side by side on certain essentials: to avoid war, to quiet factionalism, to preserve republican government. Their warm friendship, renewed from 1812 to 1826 in a remarkable and masterful correspondence, was based on frankness, honesty, and respect. "About facts," Jefferson wrote, "you and I cannot differ, because truth is our mutual guide; And if any opinions you may express should be different from mine, I shall receive them with the liberality and indulgence which I ask for my own." Jefferson and Adams represent, respectively, the quintessence of the very best in American liberalism and conservatism. Their indestructible link, then, was "a keen sense of national consciousness," a realization that America's destiny was unique. This is the meaning of Jefferson's words: "We are all republicans—we are all federalists."

"I can say with truth," Jefferson confided to Abigail Adams in 1804, "that one act of Mr. Adams's life, and one only, ever gave me a moment's personal displeasure. I did consider his last appointments to office as personally unkind." Three weeks before Adams left the presidency, the Federalists passed a new judiciary law. This enactment lowered the number of Supreme Court justices from six to five following the next vacancy, raised the number of district courts from thirteen to sixteen, and created sixteen new circuit courts. Aside from the provision affecting the number of Supreme Court judges, which obviously was designed to preclude a Jeffersonian appointment in the case of a death or retirement, the remainder of the law was completely justified. Under the old system, Supreme Court justices traveled on circuit for part of the year. This was an extreme hardship, and it was jocularly remarked that physical qualifications for these judges were more vital than twenty years' lucubration. Further, a case appealed to the Supreme Court had already been heard by one of the six who had decided it on circuit. Yet Adams appointed none but members of his own party to these positions. It was only natural that Jefferson be provoked by this partisan move to dominate the courts.

In early 1802 Jefferson's lieutenants in Congress attempted to repeal the act. There followed a debate of epic proportions. Federalists maintained, of course, that the act was necessary, and that it could not be repealed. A federal judge, once appointed, could not be removed except by the process of impeachment, nor could his salary be diminished. His tenure—so long as he exercised "good behavior"—was expressly guaranteed by the Constitution. Any attempt to violate these conditions was to strike at the metacenter of our highly sensitive and delicately balanced federal system. "The independence of the judiciary," argued one Federalist, "is the felicity of our Constitution." Jefferson was to blame for attempting to "prostrate" the judiciary, and "the time may come, when he will be called upon to answer for it as his act." Republicans responded that the Constitution clearly gave Congress an unqualified right to decide on the power, numbers, and duties of inferior Federal courts. Congress could abolish district and circuit courts of its own creation. If not, hypothetically, countless judgeships might be created, sinecure positions which never could be cancelled. Once admit that this law could not be repealed, and this Government ceased to be a democracy.

After the Senate barely passed the act of repeal (Vice President Aaron Burr cast the decisive vote), and the lower house followed suit, Federalists decried the catastrophe. Daniel Webster, then a young teacher in Maine, reported to a friend that "the judiciary bill is knocked on the head." "The blow is mortal," echoed James A. Bayard, "and . . . we may bid a final adieu to the Constitution."

Actually, the repealing act was a comparatively conservative measure. Despite Federalist fears of a blood-bath, it simply overthrew, in the words of Henry Adams, "a mere outer line of defense." At one point in the debates Republicans touched upon a basic question: the treacherous battleground of judicial review. William Branch Giles warned, "The judges have determined that they are judges in the last resort upon the constitutionality of your laws . . . [I do not] propose to discuss this question, because . . . [I do] not think it pertinent to the question before us. . . .[I] only mention it to show . . . [the judges'] unlimited claims to power." John Randolph, Jr., went even further: "Are we not as deeply interested in the true exposition of the Constitution as the judges can be? . . . Is not Congress as capable of forming a correct opinion as they are?" Since Giles and Randolph were close political associates of Jefferson, co-leaders of the Republican party in the lower house, it is not unlikely that the President suggested this line of argument.

Jefferson's relations with the judiciary provide an excellent index of his alleged radicalism. To be sure, he attacked the courts. According to Albert Beveridge, this attack was "one of the few really great crises in American history." Jefferson, however, felt perfectly justified, since the judiciary had become a fortress of Federalist power. In other words, the assault was launched on political, not on theoretical grounds. Federalist judges, not judicial power, were the real enemy. Throughout his life, Jefferson never believed that the courts should be ultimate arbiters of all constitutional questions, for the result of this could only be judicial despotism. But as president, he never publicly proposed an act or amendment expressing this principle. Perhaps Jefferson remembered the negative response of most states to the Virginia and Kentucky Resolutions. Perhaps he did not wish to force the issue of judicial review during an ebb tide of political passions.

John Marshall, like most Federalists, deprecated the repealing act, but he also seemed to realize that Jefferson had not chosen to tamper with the essence of judicial power. Thus, when some Federalists demanded that the repeal be declared unconstitutional, Marshall counselled moderation. In the face of Republican power, it would not be wise to challenge them. The law should be abided.

Perhaps Marshall had a better case—a finer opportunity—in mind. This is quite possible, since William Marbury sought the help of the Supreme Court while congressional debate raged over the repealing act. Marshall's opinion in the Marbury case is so masterful that it was undoubtedly the result of careful forethought rather than sudden inspiration. Marbury was a Federalist, a "midnight" appointee of Adams as justice of the peace in the District of Columbia. His commission was approved by the Senate, signed by both Adams and Marshall (who was then secretary of state), but overlooked and undelivered in the rush of events at the close of Federalist rule. Jefferson and his secretary of state, James Madison, refused to give Marbury the already signed and sealed commission. What could Marshall do? If he recognized Marbury's motion for a mandamus, and issued the writ directing Madison to deliver the commission, it simply would be ignored. Instead, Marshall pronounced that the Supreme Court could not issue the writ and that the Supreme Court, in fact, had no jurisdiction in this type of case. Was this an expression of defeat by Marshall? In a very minor sense it was, for Marbury never received the commission. But in exchange, Marshall achieved for the Federalists a great precedent: judicial review of federal legislation. Part of the Judiciary Act of 1789 (Section 13, which gave the Supreme Court the power to issue writs of mandamus in certain types of cases), was declared unconstitutional. Whether Marshall could just as easily have construed that section constitutionally; whether his opinion was or was not partly *obiter dicta*; whether the decision in the Marbury *v.* Madison case was or was not a usurpation of legislative power, will always remain debatable. Twenty years after the decision, Jefferson wrote: "Marbury and Madison is continually cited by bench and bar, as if it were settled law, without any animadversion on its being merely an *obiter* dissertation of the Chief Justice. . . . The Chief Justice says, 'There must be an ultimate arbiter somewhere.' True, there must; but does that prove it is either party? The ultimate arbiter is the people of the Union." But Jefferson as president did nothing about the decision.

Instead, the Republicans concentrated their fire on Federalist judges who had frankly and nakedly propounded partisan doctrines from the bench. Two important impeachments took place—against district judge John Pickering and Supreme Court Justice Samuel Chase. The Pickering case was a poor one for the Administration to select. To be sure, Pickering had committed extraordinary breaches of conduct. In addition to his partiality to Federalists, he had appeared in court in an intoxicated condition, used profanity, and ignored the most elementary rules of law and due process. But Pickering was insane, and Federalists contended that he could not, therefore, be impeached. (The Judiciary Act of 1801 provided for the removal of insane judges; since that Act was repealed, there was no other way, save by the process of impeachment, to remove such persons. Yet some Republicans were squeamish about convicting a mentally-deranged individual.) Thus, a special form for the question on each article of impeachment was used in this case, omitting the words "high crimes and misdemeanors." It read: "Is John Pickering . . . *guilty*, as charged in the article?" John Quincy Adams, the young junior senator from Massachusetts, noted: "This form, by blending all the law and facts together under the shelter of general terms, put at ease a few of the weak brethren who scrupled on the law, and a few who doubted of the facts." By a strict party vote, Pickering was found guilty.

Samuel Chase was not insane, and in his trial the upper house returned to the older wording of the impeachment question. Every senator must decide whether Chase's acts were crimes. If his actions—execrable as they may have been—did not constitute "treason, bribery, or other high crimes and misdemeanors," then, in all honesty, the Senate could not vote to convict.

For almost a month all attention centered on the case of Samuel Chase. Visitors crowded into the Senate to see and hear the famous lawyer-orators, particularly John Randolph, Jr., and Luther Martin. Throughout the country their speeches were read and discussed, their merits argued, their conclusions debated. Most Republicans felt that Chase should not go unpunished, that his guilt was obvious. From the bench Chase, with venom in his voice, had accused Republicans of atheism, anarchy, and treason. Woe to any Jeffersonian who appeared before Chase; he was guaranteed an unfair trial. When the Judiciary Act of 1801 had been repealed, Chase spoke before a Baltimore grand jury of the "mobocracy" which was bringing ruin to America. Jefferson was inflamed. "Ought this seditious and official attack on the principles of our Constitution, and on the proceedings of a State, to go unpunished? . . . I ask these questions for your consideration," he wrote to a Congressional leader; "for myself it is better that I should not interfere."

Federalists were sure that John Marshall would be the next victim if Chase were found guilty. And, if that occurred, Jefferson's purpose of weakening the judiciary would be accomplished. But it is doubtful if Jefferson would have instigated or furthered the impeachment of Marshall, as he had suggested that of Chase. As much as he hated Marshall, personally and on principle, the Chief Justice had neither in word nor deed committed an impeachable offense.

Chase was declared innocent. Either because Jefferson had not pressed for party unity, as Randolph contended; or because the Federalist argument—that Chase's actions were not legal crimes or misdemeanors—was more skillfully presented, Chase escaped conviction by a narrow margin. Six Republicans broke ranks and joined with Federalists to vote "not guilty" on every article. "Impeachment," stated Jefferson, "is a farce which will not be tried again."

While the mind of Jefferson and the attention of America were concerned with judicial matters, the temporary peace in Europe was shattered in 1803. Foreign affairs soon assumed a precedence over every other issue; war or peace again became a common topic of conversation as the United States was forced into the perilous and difficult position of remaining neutral.

Napoleon planned to invade England. He concentrated an army at Boulogne to practice embarking and landing maneuvers; meanwhile, he assembled a fleet of flatboats. England fortified her coasts, stationed part of her navy in the channel, and signed alliances in the next few years with Russia, Austria, Sweden and Prussia. Whatever chance Napoleon had for successful invasion was shattered by Admiral Nelson's naval victory at Trafalgar. English supremacy on the high seas was thereafter uncontested; but Napoleon's supremacy on the Continent was equally impressive. His success at Ulm was followed by the celebrated victories at Austerlitz, Jena, and Friedland. In their respective spheres, therefore, the two powers seemed to be impregnable.

It was this state of affairs which indirectly caused American involvement, and which precluded any peaceful settlement. First, both England and France decided to employ economic weapons. The United States was then the leading neutral producer and carrier, the profit-making spectator in the Western world. But what could a spectator do when the players changed tactics and broke rules? Second, although British policy at times wavered, she would have preferred—indeed, many Englishmen would have welcomed—war to any recognition of American rights. Charles James Fox, some Whigs, and the Lord Treasurer may have realized the value of American trade and may have been willing to compromise or concede. But the Admiralty, Parliament, and public opinion, especially after Trafalgar, preferred to fight the hated Yankees.

The renewal of European war had a catalytic effect on American shipping. Not only did Yankee skippers carry exports of domestic goods; more important, they transported French West Indian products. Since the French merchant marine was small in numbers, virtually unprotected, and consequently no match for the British, Napoleon was gratified to have neutral shipping interests enter the West Indian markets.

At first the English allowed this trade to continue unmolested so long as Americans did not trade directly between the West Indies and Europe. Instead, a formality had to be observed, commonly called the "broken voyage." French West Indian cargoes were transported to a United States port, unloaded and reloaded, duties paid and often immediately refunded, and then shipped to Europe as American goods. In the *Essex* decision of 1805, however, a British court declared that French cargoes on American ships might be seized. Thereafter, English ships patrolled the Atlantic (indeed, blockaded key American ports) intercepting and boarding vessels suspected of engaging in this illegal trade. At worst, economically, the seizures and confiscations were a minor nuisance. The value of re-exports of West Indian products mounted from fourteen million dollars in 1803 to sixty million dollars in 1806. The commerce of the United States rose to unprecedented heights; nearly four thousand new seamen per year were employed on American merchant ships; and shipping increased at the rate of seventy thousand tons annually. Jefferson's protests to England were not based on potential economic ruin, but on the grounds of neutral rights guaranteed under international law. Most Federalists, during this period, continually demanded that effective steps, short of war, be taken by the President to compel Great Britain to cease its violations of American neutrality. And Jefferson's administration continually attempted, short of war, to induce Great Britain to stop its aggressions on American commerce. Not once, however, were the Federalists satisfied with Jefferson's unpleasant alternatives: either war, or some policy of economic coercion (that is, restrictions on trade), must be imposed against England to bring that country to terms. War, in view of Federalist pro-British associations, was out of the question. More important, it would probably bring about the complete destruction of American commerce. Economic coercion was equally contrary to Federalist interests. It would destroy the lucrative trade fostered by America's position as the leading neutral carrier; it would cause slow strangulation to the commercial classes. Yet, British aggressions continued unrelenting and disturbing, a constant irritant which all parties deprecated.

Besides England's blockades, her vague definition of contraband material, and her surly manner of boarding American vessels, quite the most insulting and provocative practice was her impressment of United States seamen. The British insisted that English citizenship was inalienable; once an Englishman, always an Englishman. American naturalization papers—real or fraudulent—were of no avail to the luckless sailors the British needed for their ships. Compared to conditions on American ships, the impressed sailor could look forward to filthier quarters, lower pay, more brutal treatment, and the possibility of being maimed or killed in naval engagements. No wonder impressment—aside from the insult to United States' sovereignty—was regarded as the prime offense of all British depredations.

In 1806, through pressure from Congress, Jefferson sent William Pinkney to join the American ambassador, James Monroe, in London. Their instructions were to secure from Great Britain the abandonment of the practice of impressment and resumption of the right of "broken voyages." No treaty could be signed without these two points specifically being guaranteed; if not, the United States would impose an act—recently passed but suspended pending the outcome of the diplomatic negotiations—prohibiting the importation of certain English goods. Jefferson hoped but never really expected that a treaty would be signed. He realized that England would not willingly grant all of our demands without some *quid pro quo*, and the United States had none to offer. Jefferson knew that diplomatic demands and protests would not budge the English; and war he rejected, as had his predecessors Washington and Adams, as absolute catastrophe for an unprepared America.

Monroe and Pinkney, however, violated the letter of their instructions and concluded a pact with the British. They did succeed in obtaining a strong diplomatic note promising to try to avoid impressment of bona fide Americans. But the formal treaty side-stepped the question of impressment. Thus, Jefferson's key ultimatum was abandoned. Further, the treaty stipulated that the United States would resist Napoleon's recently issued Berlin decree.

Had George Washington been president and the Federalists in control of Congress, this treaty, properly modified, might have been adopted. Jefferson, however, rejected it. "Would to God," thundered one Federalist in Congress, "that our President, wishing as sincerely as his friends profess for him, to accommodate the differences between the two countries, had . . . agreed to the arrangement made for him by his Ministers! . . . But, sir, in this lies the secret—a secret I will dare to pronounce. Your President never meant to have a treaty with Great Britain. If he had intended it, he would never have fettered the commissioners with *sine qua nons* which were insuperable. . . . Your President was taken by surprise when he found a British treaty laid at his door."

Some twentieth-century historians, mirroring the Federalist argument of that period, have severely criticized Jefferson's action. "He threw away an irreplaceable instrument," writes Professor A. L. Burt, "for stilling the growing strife between the two countries, and he also contributed to the increase of this strife." Nevertheless, Jefferson would not appease England on this matter of principle. He would yield no ground on the vital questions of national sovereignty and neutral rights. The policy Jefferson was eager to attempt—the only policy America could afford, the only policy that might force England to cease her violations, the penultimate policy, short of bribery or war—was economic coercion.

Between 1806 and 1808 England and France took further positive steps in their military-commercial war; but it was the United States that suffered. England proclaimed a blockade of Europe extending from Brest in France to the Elbe River in Germany. Napoleon launched his Continental System by issuing the Berlin decree. This order confiscated all British property in Europe, forbade all trade with Great Britain, and ordered the seizure of any vessel which touched at a British-owned port. England responded with an Order in Council to the effect that all neutral ships bound for Europe must enter and pay duties at an English port. Napoleon then countered with the Milan decree, which provided for the capture of any vessel which had complied with the British law. American shipping was now caught between two devils on the deep blue sea.

The fundamental causes for a declaration of war were present. On June 22, 1807, occurred an immediate provocation. A British man-of-war, H.M.S. *Leopard*, fired three broadsides at close range into the side of an American frigate—not a merchantman—the *Chesapeake*. The stricken vessel was then boarded by a British search party, and four alleged deserters were taken off. Two were Negro, two white, and only one was beyond doubt a British subject. Twenty-one of the *Chesapeake*'s crew were either killed or wounded. War fever swept the country as news of the attack radiated from Norfolk. Partisan differences were buried. One Federalist, speaking for many, wrote: "Without substantial reparation for the crying offense against our honor, rights and independence, we must go to war. . . . To be an American and not to feel upon the present occasion would be impossible." This was the Pearl Harbor of America's early national period, and Jefferson well understood the temper of his people. "Never, since the battle of Lexington," he wrote to Lafayette, "have I seen this country in such a state of exasperation as at present. And even that did not produce such unanimity."

After consultation with several Cabinet members, Jefferson issued a proclamation on July 2, 1807, in which he spoke of the attack as an "enormity . . . without provocation or justifiable cause . . . transcending all we have suffered, [it] brings the public sensibility to a serious crisis, and forbearance to a necessary pause." The proclamation announced that British warships would henceforth be barred from American waters. Congress was called into special session, but Jefferson carefully set the convening date in late October. By that time cool reason might prevail over hot-headed tempers.

Naturally, Jefferson demanded satisfaction. England was to disavow the act, grant reparations, recall Admiral Berkeley, and return the men taken from the *Chesapeake.* Even more, Jefferson again insisted that Great Britain discontinue the practice of impressment. Monroe was instructed by Secretary of State Madison that "as a security for the future, an entire abolition of impressments from vessels under the flag of the United States . . . is . . . to make an indispensable part of the satisfaction." Britain's answer could be anticipated. She was quite willing to apologize for the incident, but absolutely would not relinquish the principle of impressment. If this were cause for war, if America wanted to fight over the principle, then Britain was ready. As Britain well knew, America was not; and the *Chesapeake-Leopard* affair was not finally settled until after Jefferson left the presidency.

Jefferson's foreign policies have been roundly condemned, and defended, by contemporaries and by historians. Some, like Henry Adams, though fully understanding why Jefferson acted as he did, still maintain that his tactics amounted to appeasement, bringing nought but ignominious shame upon the nation. The United States, wrote Adams, "hesitated to fight when a foreign nation, after robbing their commerce, fired into their ships of war, and slaughtered or carried off their fellow-citizens. . . . Jefferson and his government had shown over and over again that no provocation would make them fight; and from the moment this attitude was understood, America became fair prey." The point Adams missed, however, is that Jefferson could but profit from a war, politically and personally, and a lesser man would have capitalized upon the passions of an aroused nationalism. Many of the disaffected, such as John Randolph, Jr., would have applauded a policy of force. And if the Essex Junto dissented, yet most Federalists, at least in 1807, would have admitted the complete justification of war. But the country, Jefferson felt, was simply not ready for war. Perhaps in ten years, he surmised, with continuing prosperity and the national debt paid, the United States would be *"hors d'insulte* from any nation." Perhaps then America could enter a conflict with the prospect of gain rather than loss. Perhaps then, said Jefferson as early as 1802, "we may say by what laws other nations shall treat us on the sea. And we shall say it."

Six months after the attack on the *Chesapeake* Congress passed the famous—to many, infamous—Embargo Act. Supplemented four times by additional legislation meant to strengthen its enforcement, the Embargo prohibited virtually all exports from the United States. Vessels engaged in fishing or coastal trade were permitted to continue their operations, but were required to post bonds guaranteeing that their cargoes were destined for a United States port. In general, then, this act was a measure of self-denial, meant to exert economic pressure on the belligerents so that they would cease their violations of neutral rights.

The concept was not new. Suspensions of commercial intercourse had been utilized since the revolutionary era three decades earlier; in 1794 Congress had passed a sixty-day embargo; and newspapers had discussed its possibilities all through Jefferson's presidency. The theory was old, but never really tested in full. All previous attempts at economic coercion had been limited either in time or in application. Jefferson realized this, and his embargo— for there is no question that Jefferson was its chief author, defender, and enforcer—was to be the first real trial of its merit as an economic weapon.

Later historians, criticizing the Embargo, have simply mirrored contemporary critics. One argument is that Jefferson was stupidly shortsighted; that he wanted peace but took steps which led to war. Richard Hildreth, for example, argued that "Jefferson did not expect nor intend to bring on war; for with war might come armies, navies, and public debt. . . . Yet that such a stickling for the extreme of [neutral] right[s], such an irritation [the Embargo] constantly kept up, must lead inevitably to war, the Federalists had foreseen, and had foretold from the beginning." Suffice it to say, in answer, that Jefferson regarded the Embargo as the only possible way to avoid war. If it was found wanting, Jefferson felt, "we must abandon it only for a state of war. The day is not distant, when that will be preferable to a longer continuance of the Embargo."

Albert Jay Nock, a shrewd critic of American history, has suggested that Jefferson might have solved the entire dilemma by the simple expedient of proclaiming "that every American ship that left its native waters did so at its own risk." In other words, by abandoning the sovereign rights of neutral nations, neither economic disaster nor war, but rather continuing peace and prosperity, would have resulted. Many anti-Jeffersonians had advised this course of action as the wisest of policies. Do not submit to Britain, one Federalist urged, but rather temporize on the points at issue, "as Britain was willing to do, and wait for a more propitious epoch, for the final arrangement of the dispute." In a sense, this is what happened after 1815. With Napoleon's defeat the contentions vanished, not to be resurrected for another century. Jefferson had considered and rejected such a negative scheme. For such a policy would be vile, abject submission. "We can never . . . let our vessels go out and be taken under these orders [in council]," he stated, "without making reprisal." Had Jefferson followed such advice, the possibility is that war might have come earlier than 1812. "There can be no question, in a mind truly American," Jefferson told the Tammany men of New York City, "whether it is best to send our citizens and property into certain captivity, and then wage war for their recovery, or to keep them at home. . . ."

The shrillest complaints against the Embargo concerned its effects on the American economy. The value of exports plummeted from 108 million dollars in 1807 to 22 million dollars in 1808. The Embargo hurt the commercial interests more than combined British and French spoliations had ever done. Agriculture also suffered; nevertheless, the South and West understood and defended Jefferson's program. In the North, however, where ships and sailors stood idle, bankruptcies and unemployment mounted. The threat of secession, latent ever since Jefferson won the election of 1800, was now voiced openly to a more receptive audience. Smuggling, mainly through Canada, became big business, and smugglers and law-breakers suffered no qualms of disloyalty. For, after all, whom was Jefferson coercing, England or New England? "Would to God," said one Federalist, "that the embargo had done as little evil to ourselves as it has done to foreign nations!" It seemed to many that the American economy must be ruined by the act before England or France was brought to heel.

In effect for only fifteen months, the Embargo was never given a fair trial. Despite Jefferson's rather desperate and even dictatorial gestures, it was constantly violated during that entire period. The Federalists began to enjoy a momentary recovery of political vitality. Even many Republicans had become discouraged and disillusioned and wished to see the Embargo either modified or abandoned. Just before Jefferson retired from the presidency, happily returning to the quiet of Monticello, the general Embargo was repealed. In its stead, an act was passed maintaining nonintercourse with England and France. Jefferson had been forced to retreat. The most dramatic act of his second administration proved an unpopular and costly failure.

But had it been a failure? Had he not, like Washington and Adams, gained time, "the most precious of all things to us"? Perhaps a more valid criticism is that Jefferson might more energetically have pursued measures of defense while the precious time was being gained. Had the Embargo not stimulated manufacturing? Naturally, this was not Jefferson's original intent. But he early saw this potential and eagerly capitalized upon it in his public addresses. Had not Jefferson maintained peace without sacrificing honor? In the cause of liberty, when tyrants were to be overthrown, Jefferson never flinched at the idea of blood or slaughter. But the cause of American republicanism, "kindly separated by nature and a wide ocean from the exterminating havoc of one quarter of the globe," could be advanced more readily by peaceful means. European wars and ways were contrary to American interests. "Happily," Jefferson once stated, "we deal in ink only; they in blood!"

"Your administration," John Adams told Jefferson, "will be quoted by Philosophers, as a model of profound wisdom; by Politicians, as weak, superficial, and short sighted." Adams was wrong on both points. Jefferson's administration reflected neither profound wisdom nor superficiality. Rather, it was compounded of three ingredients—liberalism, nationalism, and a healthy dose of common sense. Finally, Jefferson's success as a president may be weighed by his practical accomplishments. Very few have better understood or appreciated these accomplishments than William Wirt, who, in 1809, wrote the following address of the Virginia legislature. Its exaggerations are obvious and immaterial, for Wirt well understood why historians will always list Jefferson as one of America's greatest presidents:

"We have to thank you for the model of an administration conducted on the purest principles of republicanism;
For pomp and state laid aside;
Patronage discarded;
Internal taxes abolished;
A host of superfluous offices disbanded;

The monarchic maxim that a national debt is a national blessing, renounced, and more than thirty-three millions of our debt discharged; . . .

Without the guilt or calamities of conquest, a vast and fertile region added to our country, far more extensive than her original possessions, bringing along with it the Mississippi and the port of Orleans, the trade of the West to the Pacific ocean, and in the intrinsic value of the land itself, a source of permanent and almost inexhaustible revenue.

Peace with the civilized world, preserved through a season of uncommon difficulty and trial;

Good will cultivated with the unfortunate aborigines of our country, and civilization humanely extended among them;

The lesson taught the inhabitants of the coast of Barbary, that we have the means of chastising their piratical encroachments, and awing them into justice;

That theme, which, above all others, the historic genius will hang upon with rapture, the liberty of speech and the press preserved inviolate, without which genius and science are given to man in vain.

These are points in your Administration which the historian will not fail to seize, to expand, and to teach posterity to dwell upon with delight."

Andrew Jackson

by WILLIAM N. CHAMBERS

*T*he evil lay in schemes to make "rich men . . . richer by act of Congress," and deny the fundamental principle of "equal protection and equal benefits," Andrew Jackson proclaimed. He was defending in July, 1832, his veto of a bill to recharter the Bank of the United States for another twenty years. Privately, his confidante and later vice president recalled, he had exclaimed in the midst of a wasting illness, "The bank, Mr. Van Buren, is trying to kill me, *but I will kill it!*" The rhetoric, and Jackson's dogged conviction of his own rectitude as the voice of the popular will against sinister forces, suggest a key to his controversial presidency. Under scrutiny, they also point to ambiguities in the movement Jackson led.

Some presidents attain stature chiefly by their specific achievements; others, significantly by their symbolic representation of important national values. Among the first we find a Polk or a Truman; among the second a Jefferson, an Abraham Lincoln, or a Franklin D. Roosevelt—and Jackson. Some presidents, of course, are significant in both ways, but in the case of Old Hickory it is certainly less his accomplishments that make him memorable than what he stood for. The Bank issue and other acrid controversies of his two terms from 1829 to 1837 are dry dust. His basic moral and political perspective, and his political style, however, retain relevance a century and a quarter later. In short, Jackson was *the* complex, even contradictory, representative man of an era that was not only colorful and contradictory in itself, but formative of the nation as well. Not only his presidency, but substantially his whole career, symbolize deep forces in his America.

At the core of Jackson's importance for the American tradition are four great themes or issues: equalitarianism, democracy, and—as instruments—strong presidential leadership and political party action. Each was the product of earlier history; yet each also bore the imprint of Jackson's commitment and purpose. Finally, each contained the seeds of unresolved problems. Thus, Jackson has been subject to hero-worship and demonology not only in his own time, but at the hands of historians down to our own day.

Stresses toward broadened liberal democracy and equalitarianism were central elements in the Jacksonian perspective. A liberal tradition, in the sense of emphasis on the value of the individual, and a pervading equalitarian ethos as an aspect of the tradition, have been practically indigenous in American soil. In contrast with European nations with their feudal tradition, new America quickly achieved substantial democracy in the form of open competition of groups and parties, free elections, and representative government, together with substantial consensus on settling controversies by vote, not revolt. In addition, "this American, this new man," as Crèvecoeur called him, enjoyed relative freedom from fixed class and social distinctions, and relatively widely-diffused opportunity and welfare. This was the case well before Jackson's presidency. What Jackson as the leader of a many-faceted movement did, was to represent the impulses of equality and democracy at a critical juncture, and *extend* them in idea and action.

These impulses of equality and democracy were embroiled, in the context of the era, with conflicting views of the good life. To Jackson in certain moods, and to purist Jacksonians, one view represented welfare for the many; another, the interests of a few; but other forces in the Jacksonian complex saw the issue differently. The nation had begun as an agricultural domain of farmers and planters, with commerce and manufactures subordinate. As Jefferson, John Tyler, and other prophets of pristine democracy saw it, an agrarian base of small property-holding farmers in a rough equality of condition was the best of all soils for nurturing a simple, republican way of life.

The forces of trade, industry, and finance were not so easily contained, however. Factors from normal economic growth to the

ANDREW JACKSON

strenuous efforts of Hamilton and of Henry Clay in his "American System" to promote hothouse capitalist development through a national bank, protective tariffs, and "internal improvements," produced an economic expansion which was happily embraced by venturesome Americans with their eyes on economic gain. As one of Jackson's chief disciples put it, Americans were a "go-ahead people." In the 1830's opportunities to "go ahead" in making money seemed nearly everywhere.

Thus, the eighteenth-century dream of a simple, equalitarian freeholder's republic came into conflict with a new nineteenth-century vision of enterprise unlimited, in which "equality" would mean equality in chances for economic acquisition and advancement. This issue, the conflict of perspectives of Enterprise and perspectives of Arcadia, with all of the questions it posed for the meaning of equality in the American way of life, was the ordeal of the Jacksonian experience. Not only Jackson himself, but many of his disciples were torn by tensions between these two sets of values.

Old Hickory was always perceived by his followers as a "people's president." As one of them put it on the occasion of his first inauguration in 1829, a marshalling of popular fervor typical of his presidency, "It was a proud day for the *people*—General Jackson is *their own* president!" Repeatedly, Jackson drew on this reservoir of popular excitement to support a style of presidential leadership which was bold, dramatic, and aggressive. He performed in the office in a fashion hardly conceived by Washington and scarcely touched by Jefferson, to say nothing of such *rois-fainéants* among Jackson's immediate predecessors as the bedevilled Madison and the feckless Monroe. Jackson's presidential practice suggests the twentieth-century Roosevelts in manner, though not in content or policy. It was exhibited in his dramatic and often polemical messages to Congress and in his direct appeals to public opinion—in his frequent showdowns with the legislative branch, as well as in repeated instances of decisive executive action. Unquestionably, Jackson contributed powerfully to establishing the pattern of strong presidential leadership as a force for coherence in American government, fragmented as it is through the separation of powers and federalism.

He also played a catalytic role in party development, particularly as a folk hero and dramatic leader around whom party forces could combine. The decade previous to Jackson's advent was a period of party collapse. In the late 1820's, however, a new party began to grow around him as a "people's candidate." And during his presidency the work of party formation was carried forward through organization and patronage and through partisan issues his policies produced. Thus Jackson stands as the saint and symbol of the founding of the modern Democratic party—and also as the spur to the Whig opposition of 1834 and after. By 1840 the United States could at last claim a mass-based, institutionalized two-party system.

A nation, like a man, *is* in large degree what it *became* in its formative years. Thus Jackson and the American themes he symbolized at a crucial stage in national development possess immediacy today—not just on the ritual occasions of his party, but in our whole confrontation of public problems. He was not an intellectual in the sense Jefferson was; he left us no significant philosophy or reflections on fundamentals of politics. What Jackson did bequeath was an example of energy, and a perspective, a broad pattern of faiths, commitments, and loyalties.

Andrew Jackson's early career and political novitiate touch at many points intimations of the issues he met as president. They also present a curious but often-repeated irony of our politics— the metamorphosis of a man given primarily to private advancement into a national leader for popular values.

His origins, though scarcely of the lean-to or log-cabin variety that helped make Lincoln a figure in the democratic myth, were humble enough. His parents were Irish Presbyterian pioneers who had the ambition and resolution to leave their homes for the perilous trip to the New World in the 1760's, when fear held others back. They made their way to a rude settlement in the Waxhaw region on the South Carolina border. There Andrew Jackson was born on March 15, 1767, shortly after his father's death. In his first years he and his family lived with a more prosperous uncle. Young Andrew attended a local school and, briefly, a "classical school" in the area, though his formal education was never more than sporadic. He always had difficulty with the niceties of spelling, sentence structure, and punctuation, but his writing often exhibited a rough muscularity and vividness. His youth, however, was far more given to cock fighting, horse racing, gambling, and girls, than to concern with learning or career.

ANDREW JACKSON

His early character was an outline of the ruder parts of the man-to-be. His father's untimely death, his mother's death when Andrew was fourteen, and the wandering, venturesome life he led, may have helped form a disposition that was aggressive and often quarrelsome, as well as resourceful and self-reliant. At thirteen he became an orderly and messenger with revolutionary troops in heavy fighting against Lord Cornwallis' forces. Captured by the British, he refused in a fiery explosion of temper an officer's demand that he, Jackson, clean his captor's boots; for this personal declaration of independence Andrew suffered a sabre slash which left a permanent scar on his head. Before he was seventeen he received an inheritance of three hundred pounds from a grandfather, but he squandered it in gay living at Charleston, the Tidewater-planter capital, and was forced again to live by his wits. Fortunately, he had qualities for this kind of life—ebullience, a facile Celtic charm and sense of fun, and a handsome appearance marked by a tall, slender, erect body, and a long, mobile face set off by reddish-brown hair and intense blue eyes. In his late teens his impulsive drive began to mature into purpose and strength. He set out to read law at Salisbury, North Carolina, in 1784, moved steadily to his goal, and was admitted to the bar three years later.

The next year, 1788, Jackson secured an appointment as public prosecutor in the western range of North Carolina which was to become Tennessee, and at twenty-one travelled across the Allegheny mountains to the Nashville settlement. There he did what many immigrants did who were to fill the trans-Allegheny new West in the next several decades. He began to mark a trail toward the station of a frontier "gentleman," a trail toward property and position.

As public prosecutor, Jackson found entry to the ranks of frontier affluence. Many suits were between creditors and debtors; Jackson represented the creditor side, thereby winning important private clients. Establishing residence with the well-to-do Donelson family, he soon invested in slaves, mercantile trade, and land. In particular he acquired large uncleared tracts which he planned to hold as speculative ventures until prices rose as western settlement spread. By 1796 Jackson's status and connections were such that he became a delegate to the Tennessee constitutional convention, then the state's first representative in the Federal Congress, and in 1797 United States senator from Tennessee—a post he re-

85

signed after a few months of undistinguished service. Though he, along with most Tennesseeans, thought of himself as a Jeffersonian Republican, Jackson was antagonistic to canebrake, hill-country popular democratic tendencies in the state. He took the planter-merchant-gentleman's "beaver-hat" side against the "beaver-skinner" forces, led (somewhat cynically) by Governor "Nolichucky Jack" Sevier and his cohorts, who classed Jackson with the "nabobs." Jackson was, however, more interested in pursuing his personal and business fortunes than in politics.

Jackson's progress along the trail to success did not go unchecked. In 1795 he undertook a business trip to Philadelphia, planning to sell lands and buy on credit stock for a trading post he owned. A Philadelphia speculator, David Allison, gave Jackson a note for land claims he had purchased, and Jackson in turn used this note in payment for the supplies he bought. When Allison defaulted on the note, the Philadelphia wholesaler demanded cash; thus Jackson was forced to trade his store for land and then sell off the land in order to meet the debt. This reverse, and later similar "paper losses," gave Jackson a taste of the perils of credit and speculation. They did not lead him to alter his course, however, or become an agrarian radical, but only to liquidate his debts and labor in order to stabilize his finances. Jackson succeeded in this over the years, establishing himself as a cotton planter with twenty slaves, and drawing on his knowledge of horse racing for both pleasure and profit. His progress was marked by the development of his Hermitage tract near Nashville. He lived there at first in 1804 in a renovated blockhouse, then in a larger dwelling which he built in 1818, which in turn he had elegantly remodeled and refurnished several years later. When a speculative boom collapsed in the first great national financial panic in 1819, Tennessee politics echoed popular outcries for relief. Once again, the master of the Hermitage chose the creditor, conservative side.

Meanwhile, Jackson had become in 1798 a judge of the state Superior Court, a position he filled as a faithful, responsible public servant and as a refreshingly non-technical jurist, with a shrewd intuitive perception. "Do what is *right* between these parties," he often charged juries, "that is what the law always *means*." He resigned his judgeship in 1804 to concentrate on his business affairs. The title Hermitage was meant to signalize his retirement from public life.

Even in private life, however, Jackson seemed unable to avoid becoming a storm-center. His stay with the Donelson family led him to take the part of chivalrous protector to the beguiling Rachel Donelson Robards, who had left her unstable, violently-jealous husband. In August, 1791, Jackson married her and carried her off for a romantic honeymoon. Unfortunately, though both Andrew and Rachel were ignorant of the fact, her impending divorce from Robards was not yet legally complete; despite a second ceremony after the divorce was legally accomplished, they were subjected to charges of having lived in adultery. These charges were whispered against the devoted couple as late as Jackson's presidential candidacies of 1824 and 1828, and Jackson believed that they were in part responsible for his beloved Rachel's death a month and a half before his inauguration as president in 1829.

Gentle as Jackson was with Rachel, and as warm and hospitable as he was at the Hermitage, the fiery, combative side of his temperament was still subject to explosion. He became involved in numerous feuds and quarrels, including a formal duel in 1806 with Charles Dickinson. In this duel Jackson coolly stood and took first fire from Dickinson, a superior marksman, and then, despite a serious chest wound, killed his adversary. At a Nashville tavern in 1813, Jackson flailed a horsewhip at a younger man with whom he had been feuding, crying, "Now, defend yourself you damned rascal!" The upshot was a free-for-all, gun-blazing affray which ended with Jackson soaking two mattresses with his blood in the town square. His intended victims were Thomas Hart Benton (who later, as Senator from Missouri, became Jackson's staunch political and personal friend) and Benton's younger brother Jesse. Jackson's quarrels and his trigger-touchy frontier-gentleman's sense of honor won him a notoriety among Easterners as a wild man of the West. During the presidential campaign of 1828, opponents devised a "coffin handbill" consisting of an array of black casket silhouettes, each marking an alleged bloody death at candidate Jackson's hands, through personal quarrels or military discipline. Probably such exaggerations did him little or no harm, at least among his Western constituents. Feuds and violence were common on the frontier, and it was easy—particularly when Jackson came to be perceived as an agent of great popular purposes—to see folk virtues in his combativeness and courage.

There was, of course, another side to the mature Jackson. The critical New Englander, Daniel Webster, expressed a common, often-surprised reaction when he noted shortly before the election of 1824 that Jackson was "grave, mild and reserved," entirely "presidential" in his courtly manners. Yet even as president, Jackson's well-known bursts of temper were a commonplace. Sometimes, however, his tantrums were intentionally calculated to serve as a political weapon.

National fame came in middle life to Jackson, but it came in a sunburst that helped bring him to an eminence he had never envisioned. Popular adulation, and the sobriquets "Old Hickory" and the "Hero of New Orleans," were his, of course, because of his crowning victory in the War of 1812. This victory came, however, in special circumstances without which Jackson's image might never have acquired the lustre it did.

The war, always controversial, went badly. Pro-British or peace-minded Federalists opposed the conflict as pointless and wrong, and dubbed it "Mr. Madison's war." Most Republicans, however, and particularly men of the trans-Allegheny new West, saw it as a second battle for effective American independence from British arrogance and oppression. Yet defeats and frustration marked the American military cause, and in August, 1814, enemy troops marched unopposed into Washington.

The nation's nadir was, ironically, the threshold of the Tennessee border captain's good fortune. In the face of national disgrace and spreading defeatism, and particularly of humiliation for professional commanders, Jackson offered special ingredients for a popular military reputation. To begin with, he was a *citizen-soldier*, a plain civilian in general's uniform, and other plain citizens could take particular pride in his success. Succeed he did, first as major general of the Tennessee militia, and then in the Federal service. He led forays against Creek Indians in the wilderness south of Tennessee to the Gulf of Mexico, and in 1814 imposed a treaty which broke Creek power. In the process, furthermore, he had shared danger and hardship with his troops, and had shown daring and flinty resolution in mastering the obstacles of frequent debilitating illness and the unpredictabilities of ill-disciplined volunteers. Once he commanded in a fierce engagement despite wracking dysentery by having himself tied by his arms to two trees so he could remain standing. When word came late in 1814 that Lord Edward Pakenham had sailed with a veteran invasion army, many Americans feared that their old enemy would, surely this time, engulf the new nation. Again, auspiciously for Jackson, the point of attack was New Orleans, the strategic outlet for the produce of thousands of Mississippi valley farmers and traders. Thus Jackson's great patriotic opportunity came in an order to contain Lord Pakenham's thrust. He held back the attack swiftly and skillfully, mobilizing Tennessee and Kentucky hunter-sharp-shooters and other troops against superior forces in a series of engagements. The decisive triumph came on January 8, 1815.

There was a final irony even in the timing of the "glorious victory." Peace had been concluded at Ghent, Belgium, fifteen days before, but the news had not reached the United States. When it did, it did not dim the aura of Jackson's image as Old Hickory and the Hero of New Orleans. He had smashed the British thrust; he had given a much-needed lift to the threatened national pride. In any case, military triumph was palpably more dramatic than diplomatic negotiation.

The next several years of Jackson's life were, inevitably, anti-climactic. Military glory and a tendency to hero-worship, perhaps rooted in American individualism and perhaps fructified by needs in an equalitarian culture to find heroes as symbols of vicarious distinction and emotional identification, pointed toward Jackson's availability for high political office. It did not fall upon him immediately, however; and after a brief retirement at the Hermitage, Jackson went in 1818 to the then-Spanish province of Florida to subdue Seminole Indians who were raiding American territory. His peremptory policies and executions, including the hanging of one British adventurer and the shooting of another, made his stay there controversial and brought charges of "hangman" rule. When he retired again in 1821, following service as military governor after American acquisition of Florida, his reputation was some-what tarnished. To millions, however—and the fact remained por-tentous—the glory of New Orleans was still his distinguishing mark.

In the fifty-odd years from his birth to his return to Rachel and the Hermitage in 1821, Jackson had come a long way. His lean, salient face was now heavily lined, and his great shock of hair turning iron-grey. This, however, together with his tall, spare, still ramrod-erect frame, made him an even more command-ing figure than he had been. In the rude, mobile milieu of Ten-nessee, he had displayed the nerve, quick resourcefulness, and pan-amateurism which brought a man forward in varied careers. His was a strong, self-reliant personality—an inner-directed character, in David Riesman's term—which fitted well not only into the West, but into a prevalent Protestant ethic which valued striving, determination, purpose, and success. The flash of his eyes and his formal manner expressed this—as his abiding tenderness for Rachel and his urbanity among friends represented a calm-in-tempestuousness which was another side of his complex personality. Indeed, he often exhibited a self-possession or autonomy amazing to those who knew only his reputation for ferocity. He had developed a strong intuitive intelligence, which frequently enabled him to cut sharply through the thickets of complex questions, and which emerged in a natural talent for the evocative phrase. Preeminently, Jackson was a man who could "take hold." When he took hold, action generally followed.

The man was there; and the hero-image, which soon approached intimations of providential destiny—or what Max Weber called "charisma"—lay dormant in the minds of millions. There remained the involved series of events which gave him lasting fame as a major national spokesman.

In terms of political development and particularly in terms of party functioning, the events were a phoenix-like resurgence from chaos to something like democratic order.

The years from the end of Jefferson's administration in 1809 to 1825 saw the disintegration of his Republican party, its ultimate falling apart as an effective political engine. In a process common to dominant parties in the American system, the Republican combination came to embrace a wider and wider range of leaders, social groupings, aggregates of opinion, and sections. The desuetude of the Federalist party, particularly after 1816, further fed the Republican ranks. Furthermore, the near extinction of their traditional enemy sapped Republican cohesion and *élan;* there was no substantial rival to anathematize and oppose. These and other forces set the stage for an outburst under Madison of what, years before, he had called "the violence of faction" within the party. This factionalism was followed in Monroe's "Era of Good Feelings" by the denigration of the very idea of party. The Congressional caucus as a means of unifying the party on national candidates fell into disrepute, and patronage was distributed ineptly or on an eventually nonparty basis. In short, the cements of party cohesion loosened and gave way. Even Jackson pressed

Monroe in 1816 "to exterminate the *monster* called party spirit." At the time, presumably, Jackson was as ignorant of the impossibility of providing democratic choice in a complex society without parties as he was that he would become the beneficiary of party breakdown. The election of 1824 developed as a hurly-burly contest of four candidates, each supported by personal, interest-group, and sectional factions. The glory of New Orleans and the image that was presented of Jackson as an enemy of the "undemocratic" Congressional caucus gave him strong national appeal. He took the cue offered by his Tennessee friend Major John Henry Eaton: "Commit not your opinions." Despite some equivocal remarks about a "judicious" tariff and the dangers in a "moneyed aristocracy," his early support was amorphous rather than class-oriented, a relatively unstructured range of individual voters. He won a plurality of popular and electoral votes, but no candidate had a majority.

The election of John Quincy Adams in the House of Representatives began a long process of "re-establishing parties upon the basis of principle," as Benton put it grandiloquently. As a violation of the *demos krateo* principle, the selection of the "aristocrat" over the "people's choice" was widely perceived as a transgression of democratic practice. Then Adams seemed to out-Clay Clay in a design to promote commerce and manufactures by internal improvements, higher protective tariffs, and other measures. Finally, as if to symbolize the issue of political democracy for the Jackson men, Adams appointed Clay, whose support had been decisive in the election in the House of Representatives, as his secretary of state. The result was a strident, echoing, though unfounded cry of "corrupt bargain" between the dour New Englander and the Kentucky gamester. It was "the combination, unheard of till then," as the waspish John Randolph put it in a remark that got him into a duel with Clay, "of the puritan with the blackleg." In Congress; in the burgeoning, polemical popular press; in the towns, the county courthouses, and the canebrakes, an opposition brewed.

A delayed reaction from earlier events also contributed to the emerging Jackson charisma. The depression of 1819 had brought distress to at least a third of the population. Falling prices made it hard for farmers to hold property they had mortgaged—often to the Bank of the United States—while business and bank failures spawned latent animosity to banks, and particularly to the "monster" Bank, and drove unemployed Americans for the first time to soup kitchens and soup lines. As early as 1820 Adams and John C. Calhoun conversed gloomily about a general mass of disaffection to the Government, a vague but widespread discontent, ominously ready to seize upon any event and looking out anywhere for a leader.

Almost inevitably, Jackson became the beneficiary of the national winter of discontent and emerged as the sought-for leader. It was but a step from a vision of Old Hickory's recorded patriotic decisiveness at New Orleans to a perception of him as a symbol of political righteousness who could give government back to the people and put it right again.

The new cause, however, relied not only on the evolving image of Jackson-hero, but on skillful political action. The other side, sometimes seamy, lay in building a new political structure: an effective Jackson party. Adept political managers, emerging more and more in the guise of professional politicians, labored to mobilize an increasingly numerous mass electorate. Most notable among them was Martin Van Buren, trained in the hard, fast school of New York caucus organization and discipline. He had experience as William H. Crawford's chief manager in 1824. Seeking to join the old Crawford and Calhoun factions to Jackson, Van Buren wrote innumerable letters and travelled from state to state to assuage and convert local leaders. He labored to reconstruct the New York–Virginia alliance which had been the crossbeam of Jefferson's support; he effected a jerry-built information office in the cooperation of his Albany *Argus* and the bellwether Richmond *Enquirer;* and he put his New York joiners and carpenters to work on the new edifice. In Washington Calhoun, who had become vice president under Adams and was to continue in the post under Jackson, presided over the senatorial opposition, while his capital organ the *Telegraph* carried the word to the nation. At the local foundations, "efficient friends" from top state leaders to nameless thousands in the townships and wards sank the pillars of organization in meetings and rallies, town and county conventions and committees, and state conventions. They were flanked by local party presses taking their cues from organs of national influence. Across the country a variety of men, motives, and interests contributed to the process. The catalytic agent, however, was Jackson's name—Jackson the candidate for 1828.

The years 1825 to 1828 by no means saw completion of the

party edifice. In the 1830's and 1840's the framework was extended and surfaced. It was not until 1840 that American democracy possessed an effective two-party system. Among the Jackson men, Federal patronage provided new building materials; the name Democratic was adopted; a pattern of permanent state chairmen and state committees emerged; and printed ballots or "tickets" issued by local party units appeared. Such conceptions and procedures—largely copied by the Whigs after 1834 and the second Republicans in the 1850's—were institutionalized. The most significant innovation was the national convention as a replacement for the discredited Congressional nominating caucus. The idea was not entirely new, and the Democrats were not the first to apply it, but as the durable and dominant party they played a critical part in establishing it. A second term for Jackson was obvious in 1832, but he and other leaders urged a delegate convention to choose a vice-presidential candidate—the nomination went to Van Buren—and to plan the election campaign. Later conventions named both presidential and vice-presidential candidates and began the practice of shaping policy statements or platforms. In the 1840's the selection of delegates and voting in the conventions was regularized, and the Democratic convention of 1848 established the first national party committee. Thus, renovation of the political structure, begun in the 1820's under the aegis of Jackson's name, went forward on lasting foundations.

Such renovation and elaboration not only brought strength to the Democrats as a party, but to democracy as a political system. Two-party competition, particularly if there is significant differentiation between parties on issues, introduces an order and clarity of democratic choice which a politics of shifting, half-visible multi-factionalism cannot provide. A democratic party system can promote and sustain representative government by shaping attitudes and practices among government decision-makers, making them responsive to popular interests or sentiments. Though Hamilton, Jefferson, and others provided early blueprints, we owe our present party system largely to Jackson and the Jacksonians—and to the inevitable opposition they evoked.

Given the Jackson-image and Jacksonian political organization, the event of 1828 was practically foreordained. In a hurrah campaign characterized by broad mass appeals rather than explicit policy commitments, the Hero of New Orleans won 56 per cent of the popular vote. He carried majorities in every section except

Adams' New England, though even there he collected significant support.

The inaugural scene on March 4, 1829, was a veritable pageant of mass enthusiasm. Facing Jackson as he took the oath on the capitol portico was a crowd of more than twenty thousand. There were "the highest and most polished down to the most vulgar and gross," the old-Federalist Mr. Justice Story sniffed: "The reign of *King Mob* seemed triumphant." At the executive mansion the high-toned John Adams had first occupied, barrels of orange punch had to be placed in the yard to draw off the mob, lest it break through the floors. The ascendancy of equalitarian, *hoi polloi* democracy appeared to be at hand.

Analysis of the voting that made Jackson president only partially sustains such a conclusion. Voting in 1824, despite suffrage extension in the two preceding decades, had been only 26 per cent of the adult white males in states choosing electors by popular ballot. Higher percentages had been achieved in many states in earlier years, particularly in sharp party contests. The decline was probably due largely to the inanition of party under Monroe and the confusions of the multi-factional contest. Voting in 1828 rose to 56 per cent of white adult males—more than twice the turnout for important elections near the end of the party-formative decade of the 1790's, half as much again as participation at the turn of the century, and double the 1824 figure. Furthermore, six of twenty-four states, including populous New York, had named electors by legislature in 1824, whereas in 1828 only South Carolina and Delaware did so. Thus, political managers had a substantially larger potential presidential electorate to face. Nor was voting negligible considering that women, Indians, and nearly all Negroes were denied the ballot, and the fact that a mobile, mainly rural population works against participation. Nonetheless, turnout was hardly overwhelming in 1828; equally significantly, the proportion of those voting did not increase substantially in 1832 and 1836. It was not until 1840, with a competitive party system well established and Whigs aping Jacksonian *hoi polloi* appeals in a log-cabin, multi-hurrah campaign, that voting rose steeply, reaching 78 per cent.

The popular-democratic character of the response to Jackson lay, to an important degree, elsewhere. It was to be found first of all in quality more than mere quantity—in the emotional intensity of the feelings his following experienced. He probably evoked an enthusiasm more emotional than that accorded to any of his presidential predecessors, despite the deep affection countrymen felt for Washington and Jefferson. Furthermore, Jacksonian political practices marked a democratic development. To about 1800 party in America, whether under Hamilton and Adams or Jefferson, was to a considerable degree what Max Weber called the "party of notables." Such parties depend primarily on leaders of already-established position and prestige in their communities, and on patterns of deference to such leaders for a following. The Jackson or Democratic party, by contrast, originated as a party open to all comers in the spirit of the "plebiscitarian principle," or rule by popular majorities in elections. It was, thus, a full-scale national "party of politicians," in the sense of men who rise to or achieve standing through political endeavor. In addition, political participation other than voting also probably increased—in attending meetings, in reading the proliferating political press and pamphlets, and in "political talk."

Finally, the democratic character of the Jackson movement emerged in the perspective and policy it evolved in its years of national power.

In February, 1829, shortly before Jackson arrived in Washington to take office as president, Daniel Webster sketched some moody notes:

Nobody knows what he will do when he does come . . .
My opinion is
That when he comes he will bring a breeze with him.
Which way it will blow, I cannot tell . . .
My *fear* is stronger than my *hope*.

More concretely, Clay flatly predicted "dissolvents" for the Jackson party. Whatever the President proposed, "his friends [in Congress] must divide on certain leading measures of policy," such as the tariff, which might lose him support and thus deny him re-election.

Such comments by two men who became leading senatorial opponents of Jackson and all his works were apt. They reflected the pluralistic, heterogeneous, ambiguous nature of the popular response and of the political engine that had brought him to office. Yet they also underestimated the character and influence he brought with him.

Some foreshadowing of concrete policy, some indication of the way the breeze would blow, came in Jackson's first message to Congress. The Constitution, Jackson urged, should be amended to provide for popular election of the president and vice president, so that these critical choices could rest clearly on "the first principle of our system—*that the majority is to govern.*" Attacking the idea of property in public office, Jackson argued in an access of equalitarianism—and beneath the measured sentences, of party-building concern—that the duties of such offices were so plain and simple that any man of intelligence could perform them. On the economic side, Jackson noted the superior role of agriculture over commerce and manufactures while expressing a desire "to harmonize the[se] conflicting interests." He decried the public debt that Hamilton and his disciples had seen as a public blessing—to Enterprise, at least—and ran up a warning flag on the internal improvements issue. In view of the future, probably the most significant passage was a restrained but nonetheless reproving reference to the Bank of the United States.

In all of his succeeding annual messages but one, Jackson recurred to his proposal for electing the president and vice president by popular majority vote. Supporters in Congress also pressed the matter, but nothing was done, and the electoral college procedure remained.

Greater success attended Jackson's views concerning "rotation" in public office. A quasi-elite of officials had clung to their posts as a species of "property," growing frequently indolent and inefficient and sometimes corrupt, often out of step with the new policies elections turned on. Thus to Jackson and many others, removals seemed a salutary democratic reform. The *Telegraph* urged a thorough cleansing of "the Augean Stable," and Jackson back-country papers asserted that the people demanded from Hercules-Jackson "the *reform of all abuses.*" The cleansing went forward despite partisan criticism and outcries from the displaced and disappointed. Many later historians have scored Jackson for wrecking the Federal service by introducing a sweeping "spoils system"—or at least for carrying it from New York and Pennsylvania to the national government. In fact, his removals in the entire span of his presidency from 1829 to 1837 were less than 20 per cent of the offices, and appointments were not always strictly partisan or made in disregard of ability. Over-all, the shaking-up probably improved functioning in the Federal bureaucracy. While much of the impetus for renovation was democratic-reformist, another motivation was clearly partisan. This view was expressed by the senator from New York, William Learned Marcy, who declared blandly in 1831 that "the politicians of New York" would "boldly *preach* what they *practice*"–"to the victor belongs the spoils." Patronage was, thus, not only part of a popular reform but an arm of presidential power and a blood transfusion to the new "party of politicians," the developing Democratic organization.

An early exertion of presidential power in the economy marked a course Jackson was to follow thereafter. For years, as one of the twin pillars of the American System, internal improvements bills had made their way through Congress. Harbors, lighthouses, river channels, roads and turnpikes, canals–all were built, or improved. Frequently the interests served were local and special rather than general, and the means were Federal subscriptions in private corporations. Undoubtedly, many projects promoted a national market for mercantile and manufacturing Enterprise, in addition to the aid they gave particular enterprisers. To purist Jeffersonians, however, they seemed not only a questionable extension of Federal power under the Constitution, but dubious in policy. When Congress sent up a bill in May, 1830, authorizing a stock subscription in a company which was to build a road from Maysville to Lexington, entirely in Clay's Kentucky, Jackson vetoed it. He would support improvements he considered genuinely "national" or "general." But he would set his face against local projects financed by "unequal appropriations" at the expense–through higher prices occasioned by the tariff, the other pillar of the American System–of "the laboring and less prosperous classes of the community." Indeed, national projects, particularly for harbors and rivers, went forward at a rate exceeding that of the Adams administration. But the ringing Maysville veto put an effective stop to the system of improvements for "personal ambition and self-aggrandizement," or "partial instead of general advantages." The breeze was stiffening–and in a direction contrary to that of previous politics.

Further internal improvements vetoes in 1830, 1832, and 1833 reiterated the Maysville statement. The objections were partly constitutional and partly political—a slap at Clay, particularly in the Maysville issue, and a bow to Van Buren and New York interests opposed to Federally-sponsored projects, and to the South. In rhetoric and effect, however, they were broadly equalitarian and put the Administration in conflict with at least a portion of the nation's emergent Enterprise. Furthermore, the internal-improvements vetoes went far in establishing Jackson as an exponent of strong presidential power. Previous presidents, often assuming that they should reject only legislation they thought unconstitutional, had in forty years vetoed only ten bills all told. In eight years Jackson exercised the veto twelve times, and six of these vetoes blocked internal-improvement projects. Many of Jackson's followers had feared that the Maysville veto would hurt him politically; Clay and others raged against it and tried to blow up a popular storm. The preponderance of popular opinion supported Jackson's equalitarian action through presidential power, however.

As a partial counterweight to the American System, Jackson urged freer distribution of the public lands. This issue had been pressed repeatedly by the emerging Jackson leader in Congress, Senator Benton of frontier Missouri. The untold acres of Federally-owned lands in the new states, Benton urged, should be moved more quickly into cultivation by farmer-settlers by offering the public lands at reduced prices, and eventually as outright donations. By the end of 1832 Jackson had added his presidential voice to the chorus of support for such proposals, and he reiterated his views in 1833, 1835, and 1836. Every citizen who wanted it, he argued, should have "the opportunity of acquiring an independent freehold"; thus agriculture could advance as actual settlers took up lands at reduced prices in freehold-limited quantities. The old policy of selling off the lands primarily for revenue, first to meet the public debt and then to be siphoned to the states for internal improvements (under Clay's abortive Distribution Act), was another instance of "partial and interested legislation." Here again were equalitarian overtones, and a stress toward Arcadia. Major action was blocked by a complex of opposition in the 1830's. It was not until the Homestead Act of the Lincoln years that Jacksonian views on land policy came into operation as a system.

Elimination of the public debt, however, was accomplished. In Hamilton's economics, a national debt was another instrument for the catalytic promotion of Enterprise through its effect in providing business capital. As Jackson saw it, the debt was a prop to the restrictive land policy and to high tariffs—and through the latter, a continuing burden of "unnecessary taxation" on the general population. Extinguishing the debt, which was substantially accomplished by 1834, would weaken the high-tariff rationale and make it possible "to dispose of the lands for the common benefit." It was only after the retirement of the debt that Jackson spoke strongly for land distribution. Thus, at some cost to investors and manufacturing interests, "the people" and agriculture could be served.

The apogee of democratic and equalitarian perspectives came in what many Jacksonians, over-dramatizing the issue somewhat in a fashion common to politics, called the "Bank war." Here the breeze became a wind, and here also latent ambiguities in the emerging Jacksonian perspective were most clearly laid bare.

Proponents saw the Bank of the United States not only as a source of business capital through its bank-note credit issues. It had also become, in their view—a view with substance—a responsible agent for handling Government transactions and for maintaining a sound money policy through its role in keeping the Federal funds and discounting state bank notes received in Federal revenues. It was also, however, the giant corporation of the day, paying dividends to hundreds of stockholders and reaching out from Philadelphia through branches in two dozen cities. Furthermore, it was not only an economic but, inevitably, a political power. The Bank was a major financial "interest group" in itself, with connections with political leaders and editors; it was a central influence and representative among older-established commercial and manufacturing interests. As such, the "B.U.S." was a ready target of popular antipathy.

Despite forewarnings in his annual messages through 1831, Jackson did not initiate the original conflict. The first rally-call was a Senate attack on the Bank as a mechanism to "multiply nabobs and paupers," launched in 1831 by Thomas Hart Benton, who thus staked his leadership of the "radical" Democracy. The emergence of Jackson as commander of the anti-Bank forces came in the next year. Working closely with Nicholas Biddle, the Bank's conservative and adroit president since 1822, Clay, Webster, and other National Republicans, with a coterie of Bank Democrats, pushed through a bill for the early renewal of the Bank's charter, though it did not expire until 1836. The answer was Jackson's dramatic, polemical veto message. It was strewn with recurring equalitarian appeals: "monopoly"; a government charter as a "gratuity of many millions to the stockholders"; "odious because it does not measure out equal justice to the high and the low"; in his judgment, "*unnecessary* and *improper*, and therefore unconstitutional"; "advancement of the few at the expense of the many." "Distinctions in society," the President knew, "will always exist," and "every man is equally entitled to protection by law." But, "when the laws undertake to add to these natural and just advantages artificial distinctions, to grant titles, gratuities, and exclusive privileges, to make the rich richer and the potent more powerful, the humble members of society—the farmers, mechanics, and laborers—who have neither the time nor the means of securing like favors to themselves, have a right to complain of the injustice of their Government." Unfortunately, "many of our rich men have not been content with equal protection and equal benefits, but have besought us to make them richer by act of Congress." Bitterly attacked by Webster and Clay, the veto was nonetheless sustained—and not only by Congress, but in public opinion.

The immediate test came in the presidential election of 1832. Somewhat fatuously for so experienced a politician, Clay, the National Republican candidate, decided to make the B.U.S. the issue. Once again, popular response to Jackson's leadership was forthcoming, and he triumphed with 56 per cent of the popular vote.

Yet Jackson's support was equivocal in a fashion that underscored ambiguities in his own rhetoric. Its ranks embraced agrarians who saw Biddle's "monster" as the point in a capitalist phalanx marching ominously against Arcadia. Other thousands of citizens of many descriptions remembered the Bank's speculative credit expansions and contractions under pre-Biddle management in the boom and bust of 1819–21. To many the Bank issue was more a moral and emotional concern as a threat to a simple republican way of life, than an issue of economic interest. Another variety of opposition, however, lay with state banks, who saw the B.U.S. quite concretely as a competitor and an obstacle to speculation and venture through its power to discount state bank notes. Flanking the state bank interests were legions of new capitalists or proto-capitalists who, in confrontation with entrenched business, were excluded from the charmed circle of national Bank credit, and were dependent on easy state-bank credit. To them, the Bank was a bastion of old Enterprise against *their* new Enterprise—against their hopes of competitive gain. They had an active interest in circumscribing the Bank's power, or in destroying the Bank altogether.

For whom, then, did Jackson speak? Certainly he sought, at a crux in American development, to reinforce and extend equality; but how did he and his variegated following read the equalitarian theme? Some could identify with Jackson as an avenger of the cause of freeholding farmers and urban wage-earners. They would go about their tasks in a rustic version of "fair shares." Each would live by "the sweat of his face," as the aged purist republican Nathaniel Macon of North Carolina put it, in an approximate equality of social *condition* for "the humble members of society," with "artificial distinctions" through Government favor broken down. Others read Jackson as speaking for economic *opportunity*, equal business access, a leveling of strong-points of "monopoly" Enterprise in the interest of a liberalized capitalism in a socially-mobile population. In the Jacksonian symbolism and response, "the people" was a many-splendored entity. Near-doctrinaires like Benton, with a solid agrarian base in his far-west constituency, could cleave to strict Arcadian-equalitarian views. At other points, the base for political division was division in the business community itself, with the interests of the new men of Enterprise providing energy and direction for the Jacksonian forces. As a central leader in a complex movement, Jackson, himself a product of a mobile and mixed career, could not escape some degree of ambiguity.

The decisive blow against the Bank came in another exertion of executive authority. Convinced that the Bank's power must be broken both in the economy and in its impact, or potential impact, on politics, Jackson decided to remove the Federal funds from the B.U.S. and deposit them in selected state banks instead. When the Secretary of the Treasury refused to carry out the necessary steps, Jackson removed him; and when the replacement also balked, removed him too—until finally he got a secretary who agreed, Roger Brooke Taney. The order was issued in September, 1833. This time, the forceful action was defended in broad democratic terms. The B.U.S. was condemned as "an irresponsible power" which had deployed its funds "as a means of operating upon public opinion" in order to secure recharter. It was further stigmatized as "a vast electioneering engine."

In his veto of recharter and in his dramatic appeal to public opinion, Jackson had underscored his extension of the scope and weight of presidential leadership as an agent of popular purpose.

By removal of deposits, and two Cabinet secretaries in the process, he exerted strong presidential power within his official family. By making the Bank the differentiating issue in the election of 1832 in conjunction with Clay, Jackson had taken party leadership. In each instance he had supported his thrusts with a covering fire of democratic or equalitarian rhetoric, and had evoked intense popular response.

In its counterattack, the new Whig opposition balanced Jackson's charges of excessive private, *economic* power with charges of "executive despotism" in government. They even carried a Senate resolution censuring the President for removing the deposits. They thereby evoked against Jackson another traditional theme of American political culture—the fear of concentrated *political* power which Montesquieu had helped instill in the framers of the Constitution, and which Jefferson had shared.

The rising wind stirred more dramatic charges. The cultivated Nicholas Biddle, for example, called the veto message "a manifesto of anarchy, such as Marat or Robespierre might have issued to the mob of the Faubourg St. Antoine." The comment exemplifies not only some contemporaneous reaction, but also some later historical interpretations. Yet its portents of melodrama, like some of Jackson's own more purple "Bank war" polemics, can be misleading.

The "radicalism" of Jackson shared little with Marat, Robespierre, or other European revolutionaries. As de Tocqueville, after his visit in the Jackson era noted, Americans had in effect been *born* equal and had no need to make a revolution against prescriptive orders, estates, or a monarchial establishment in order to *become* equal. Thus American as compared with European political conflict has generally been contained within a moderate spectrum set by what Louis Hartz in our time has called a *liberal tradition*. Emphasizing free, atomistic individuals, this tradition has kept American politics from the extremes of Jacobin revolution or aristocratic reaction.

As individuals cohere into shifting groups, a continuing stress toward open pluralism has resulted. This stress has been balanced only by tendencies in crisis or under crowd-compelling leaders like Jackson toward majority-bent or dualistic alignments. The Jacksonian address was not in terms of a great war of *classes*, in a French-revolutionary sense, much less in the meaning Marx gave the concept. When Jackson used terms like the "productive classes," he was employing a loose, embracing concept, to mark off "useful" members of society from those who lived on bank credit and the like. The "productive classes" could include planters as well as freeholding farmers, tradesmen and professionals as well as mechanics.

Thus a cautious review of Jacksonian symbolism reveals a dialectic not of the Third Estate or bourgeoisie and proletariat, but a dialectic of "community," of general advantages as contrasted with partial and interested legislation, of a generalized will of the people through a variegated majority, and of hoped-for harmony of conflicting interests. Indeed, the notion of "community" good was almost a primary, yet still equivocal, meaning in the Jacksonian equalitarian theme.

The original attack on the Bank was followed by a new essay in economic policy. To many "Democrats *in principle*," as a contemporary called them in an intended sneer, the removal of the Federal funds and their deposit in state banks constituted only a half-way house. A hard-money system; a circulating currency of gold and silver; suppression of all bank notes except the largest, and these permitted only as a matter of convenience; banks operating only under close restrictions: such were the ultimate radical goals. These goals took on particular relevance in the mid-1830's. Increasing numbers of state banks, in part because of the new life they drew from the attack on the B.U.S. and the nourishment of Federal deposits, in part as a result of an economic boom resting largely on land speculation, greatly extended paper issues to provide land-purchase and venture credit. To neophytes in entrepreneurship, or "Democrats *by trade*," as a realization of their animating interest in expanding business opportunities, such developments were highly gratifying. On the other hand they were anathema to agrarians or urban-radical "Locofoco" elements.

As president, Jackson moved gradually to hard-money doctrines. In 1834 he expressed the hope that new gold coinage would provide a sound currency, and urged the states to reform their banking systems to prevent speculative expansion-and-contraction credit fluctuations. In succeeding years, rhetoric was stepped up and policy firmed. All notes below a value of twenty dollars should be suppressed—and later Jackson urged an even higher minimum. He worried about excessive issues by state banks as the "process by which specie is banished," drew parallels between the power of the national Bank and the burgeoning state banks as new corporate powers, and condemned their easy credit to land speculators. The equalitarian theme was increasingly put forward in references to the state banks as an interest distinct from that of the community, serving creditors and cautious capitalists but threatening ruin to debtors. Finally, Jackson was linking the state banks with avarice and fraud, and with the eager desire to amass wealth without labor, with the burden of losses falling upon the laboring classes of society who asked nothing but equal rights and equal laws. The "mischief"—read *evil?*—flowed from "the power which the moneyed interest derives from a paper currency."

The attack on the paper-speculation-venture system drew lines more sharply than the Bank issue had. As the democratic and equalitarian perspective was pointed toward hard money policy, it took on clearer agrarian and populist overtones. One cost was the loss of most of Jackson's support among the *arrivistes* of acquisition and proto-capitalists. Once again, however, the new campaign had its ambiguities. In the laboring classes of society, Jackson himself listed not only the farmer of the old-republican, freeholders' Arcadia, but also the planter, who of course might possess substantial capital and hundreds of slaves, and the mechanic and the laborer. In the parlance and practice of the time, such terms included working employers as well as apprentices and employees —who often looked to becoming masters—and, by extension, self-employed grocers, small merchants, tailors, and the like. Even the rhetoric and appeal of hard-money radicalism was not in terms of strict "class," much less of "yeomen" and wage-workers only. Furthermore, their states' rights doctrine, though hardly extreme, ironically denied the Jacksonians the course of comprehensive, effective attack through Federal power on the state banks, even if all of them had wanted to go this route. In vain, more-determined hard-money men proposed a prohibitive Federal tax on state bank note issues as a means of drying up the streams of paper credit. Even this would hardly have held back the flood-force of Enterprise—and probably no Government action could have done so. However emotionally gratifying Jackson's moral perspective was to agrarian sentiments, however hopeful or effective many of his measures were, much of the total result of his Bank policy and its intended hard-money sequel lay elsewhere. The effort to serve equality in Arcadia brought parallel or counter-balancing gains for new Enterprise, for equality in liberalizing an expanding capitalism. Thus ambiguity in appeal and in effect remained—particularly in unanticipated consequences.

Another irony of Jackson's presidency came in a flutter of

ANDREW JACKSON

financial panic and, later, depression. Low points in 1819 and in
the late 1820's were followed by onrushing expansion in the 1830's,
capped by the bank-credit land boom. These economic currents,
of course, provided the foundations for the heady spirit of venture
and gain which made so many of the old-Jeffersonian aspects of
the Jacksonian address to economic issues an ordeal. In 1834 the
"Bank war," and the response of Biddle and the Bank men in sharp
credit contractions and bearish talk, precipitated a brief panic. In
1837 the boom collapsed, partly of its own imbalance in piling
speculation on speculation, but partly also because of Jacksonian
policies against speculation. The distress of 1819–21 was repeated
in darker tones. Political consequences also followed in the defeat
of Van Buren for re-election as president in 1840.

Despite obstacles, opposition, panic, and depression, the hard-
money forces pressed what purposeful action they could. In June,
1834, the indefatigable Benton, supported by James K. Polk in the
House, carried bills to increase the gold coinage; Jackson declared
that they deserved "golden medals" for their work. This action
won Benton the sobriquet "Old Bullion," and the small yellow
coins his legislation spread through the nation were often called
"Benton mint drops." In July, 1836, after attempts to win further
legislation for the purpose had failed, and despite opposition from
most of his Cabinet, Old Hickory, in collaboration with Old Bullion, prepared a Treasury order to prohibit the receipt of paper
in payment for public lands, and to require gold or silver. In the
face of capitalist development and speculative boom riding toward
bust, the Coinage Acts proved too little, and the Specie Order too
late. The twilight of Van Buren's term accomplished the divorce
of Government and banks in an Independent Treasury Act. It established Federal subtreasuries to replace the state banks as depos-
itories for the Federal funds, further requiring that only gold and
silver be accepted in *all* Federal revenues after 1843. The Act was
repealed following the Whig triumph of 1840, however, and
when it was restored under Polk four years later the hard-money
receipts stipulation was left out.

In the 1830's Jackson and his cohorts were generally triumphant in rhetoric and politics. As a dramatic, charismatic leader and
president he did much to shape the outlook and character of the
age. In succeeding decades the capitalist development and spirit
of Enterprise which also cut channels across the 1830's, sometimes
in crosscurrent to Jacksonian directions, sometimes in a parallel
stream, surged to new high-water marks. The dream of Arcadia—

in the age of Jackson already part myth, part nostalgia—became in the age of Carnegie the pathos of a lost cause. Long after Jackson died at the Hermitage in 1845, however, already in the process of being canonized as a popular saint, his essence lived on. It survived in the broad perspective he symbolized and bequeathed to the American tradition.

Although most of the drama on the Jacksonian stage evolved from the tension of moral perspectives addressed to economic impulses, other issues appeared on the scene to mark Jackson's presidency and measure his stature.

One was an almost explosive conflict over the tariff, states' rights, and the Union. In the second half of the 1820's, Southern planter-slaveholders, as well as other agricultural groupings, had chafed at increased protective tariff rates, which reached a new high in 1828. In that year and the next, South Carolina and three other planter states set the stage for the ensuing drama by protesting this "Tariff of Abominations" through their legislatures. The first act was played in the famous debate in 1830 between Robert Y. Hayne of South Carolina and Daniel Webster of New Hampshire, with Hayne arguing the doctrine of nullification, or the right of a state to void Federal statutes in its domain, while Webster eloquently defended the Union and Federal authority. A second act was played the same year at a Jefferson birthday dinner. There Jackson, having sat through a series of nullification toasts, proposed one of his own which was repeated and echoed in fateful decades to come: "Our Union: It must be preserved." The third act came in 1832, when a convention in South Carolina formally nullified the tariffs of 1828 and 1832. Promptly Jackson declared his intention to enforce Federal law, issuing a proclamation in which he condemned nullification as a disruptive absurdity, insisted on the supremacy of an indivisible Union, and characterized any move threatening disunion by violence as treason. He favored reductions in protective tariff duties, however, and labored to find a compromise. On the Union he stood firm and called on Congress in 1833 for a "force bill" to enable him to subdue South Carolina nullification, if necessary. The denouement of the immediate conflict came in a compromise devised chiefly by Clay, which kept the tariff issue off the stage for a decade.

This drama of Jackson's day was an intimation of bloody melodrama to come. The North-South conflict exploded in the 1840's and 1850's in the annexation of Texas and in the disruptive issue of slavery or nonslavery in the vast reaches to the California coast which were added to the American domain by war with Mexico under Polk. It led finally to civil war.

The nullification issue and conflicts over economic policy brought some of the party "dissolvents" Clay had predicted. The great antagonist in each act of the tariff-nullification controversy, even when he remained offstage and let others speak for him, was Calhoun. Calhoun had other causes for antipathy: rivalry as a presidential hopeful with Van Buren, whose star rose under Jackson; tiffs over the chastity of a tavern-keeper's daughter who married Jackson's friend, Major Eaton; and Calhoun's own image of Jackson's "executive despotism" in the President's forceful opposition to nullification. In 1831 Calhoun led his clique or faction out of the Democratic ranks, and in 1832 resigned as vice president to become an opposition senator. Along with most of the great Southern planter-slaveholders he turned to the new Whig coalition of 1834, though he himself left the Whigs a few years later and became at least a quasi-Democrat again. Meanwhile, the economic policy Jackson set, particularly in the national Bank, state-bank, and hard-money issues, brought intraparty factional divisions between "radicals" like Benton, Van Buren in his later years, or Blair, in contrast to "conservatives" like Marcy of the "spoils," and Lewis Cass of Michigan, who was the party's presidential nominee in 1848. Still others deserted to the Whigs on economic or sectional issues, including John Tyler of the "Tippecanoe-and-Tyler-too" campaign of 1840.

Like the Jeffersonians before them, the Democrats experienced the strains that beset a dominant party. The centrifugal forces of intraparty pluralism in interest and opinion, however, were countered for two decades by centripetal forces: Jackson's leadership and aura, the popular and electoral appeal of "radical" perspectives, organization and the provender of patronage, the discovery of formulas of agreement, and party identification and *élan*. Not until the 1850's, when new factional intensities based on fundamental sectional cleavage precluded agreement or compromise, did the Democrats suffer disruption. Even then, separation occurred only on the eve of civil war itself and helped precipitate the resort to arms.

National self-discovery is never-ending, and reflective reconsideration of the themes of Jackson's presidency may help promote the quest. We can never in an age of organization recapture the simple, atomistic democracy he spoke for; his nineteenth-century policy prescriptions provide no specifics for the health of the twentieth-century body politic. Yet his larger perspective is relevant today—in part because it contained the seeds of still unresolved problems.

The equalitarian urge gives rise to a tangle of complex questions. Under Jackson, it was bent against economic and social privilege; life's good things were to go not only to "the few, the rich, and the well-born," as a Federalist ideologist put it, but to the "many" or "majority." Today the "many" no longer own the property from which they derive their living. Concentration in great corporations employing vast thousands sets an economic and bureaucratic climate for gradations of status and power. Supplemented by insensitivity to personal distinction, this atmosphere generates a compensatory scramble for materially-based status and recognition. How, then, can the equalitarian impulse be sustained as a living force? Unless we are indeed doomed to invidious rule by a "power elite"—in the dubious hypothesis of C. Wright Mills—the hope of equality may lie in further diffusion of economic well-being and social acceptance, and in a calmer climate which reduces the anxieties of status-seeking through greater assurance in individual identities and roles. Over-all, lacking a Jacksonian base of self-sufficient freeholders, equality today may depend on a pattern in which nineteenth-century economic individualism is circumscribed, and concentrated economic power is met by countervailing powers of Government, union organization, regulation for public purposes of both business and unions, and of group associations of many kinds. Equality and well-being may also be promoted by a more purposeful balance of expenditure in the public sector of the economy, from schools to housing and parks, as compared with the private sector. Such possibilities hardly revive the pristine, individualistic equalitarianism of Jackson, but any attempt at such revival can only be a form of nostalgia. They may, however, constitute contemporary applications of his basic theme.

The still-unconquered frontier of minimum equalitarianism, of course, is in overt discrimination and unspoken prejudice against racial and religious minorities—a problem that requires not only good will but energy (public and private) and time for solution.

Yet, other questions remain. A latent danger in being born

ANDREW JACKSON

equal, which de Tocqueville noted in Jackson's era, lurks in the
potentiality of negation of the exceptional by the mediocre, of
conformist leveling of individual personality. To our own day,
such stresses have prompted ambivalent denigrations of intellect,
judgment, and meaningful leaders-in-action, while we exalt organ-
ization-age "smooth dealers" or special heroes. Such figures, particularly as they may be shaped by Madison Avenue image-mon-
gering, can deceive us. The charisma of Old Hickory pointed the
way to hurrahs for meaningless Old Tippecanoe in a cynically-
contrived bandwagon campaign in 1840 and to future triumphs for
hero-images from Grant to Eisenhower. It is easy to see as "great
men" figures whose aura is commanding but whose creativity
and boldness in leadership is at least debatable. The problem,
which Jackson only touched in a more inner-directed age, lies in
reshaping the equalitarian perspective to accept personal individuality, encourage variety, cherish the exceptional, and extend
intellect and critical judgment. In this connection, Jackson's personality and address have something to offer for our day in his
very individuality, ahead-of-the-crowd leadership and dogged
commitment.

Such questions, together with much of Jackson's political style,
also raise problems for democratic functioning. To an important
degree, his appeal evoked mass emotive identifications with Jackson-hero and with ambiguous rhetoric. Thus, the satisfactions he
provided were composed as much or more of cathexis and symbolism as of fulfillment of concrete interests. This is often the way
in politics—we may find warm gratification in seeing *our* men, and
thus *our* perspectives or *our* hopes, ascendent in public symbolism.
So reformers could enjoy happy identification with Franklin
Roosevelt, innumerable middle-class Americans with the likeable
image of "Ike" Eisenhower, and intellectuals with Adlai Stevenson, because each seemed to speak in *their* way—whatever they
meant to others. A crucial distinction remains for democracy,
however. It is the extent to which appeal-and-response involves
not only personality images, but also some measure of popular
choice on concrete issues—some chance to judge candidates on
the grounds of policies they espouse. As Jackson became a spokesman for significant policies, he, with his party, helped to extend
such choice. Successor hero-candidates have not always undertaken such commitments. When elections are left to revolve
around candidate-orientation to the detriment of issue-orientation,

the meaning of electoral choices is smudged, the effect of elections on public decisions is attenuated.

Strong presidential leadership, by shaping policy and clarifying alternatives, may further democratic values. A president who seeks to harness the wonderful three-horse shay of the separated executive, legislative, and judicial branches, who grasps the whip of party leadership, may make much of the potential scope and weight of presidential power as an agent of purposes of the "many," even of a "majority." He may use it, as Jackson largely did, in a negative fashion to restrain impulses he and the preponderant opinion oppose. He may make it, as Franklin Roosevelt did, a majority-based force for positive Government intervention through policy innovation. If he does so, he is bound to provoke counterappeals to the deeply-ingrained American fear of concentrations of political power, such as the Whig cry of "executive despotism." In fact, strong presidents from Jackson and Lincoln to the two Roosevelts have not subverted our liberties. Furthermore, an age of complex problems, massive economic organization, and nuclear threat seems particularly to require energetic presidential leadership as a force for coherence. Yet, how much dependence do we want to place on one man, or more properly on one office? and how may we hold him responsible? There is no ready answer; presumably proximate solutions will evolve, as they did in Jackson's era, as different men take the presidential reins. One answer, however, which can be argued as an extension of the Jacksonian sense-of-purpose in our less-individualistic, organized contemporary context, may lie in efforts to strengthen tendencies toward coherence at other points of power. These would include parties, Congress, Federal-state-municipal relationships, and administration.

Such considerations inevitably raise continuing problems of party structure and action, again taking us back to Jacksonian origins. At the outset, the Jackson party was a democratic instrument, not only in terms of interparty democratic competition, but of intraparty democracy in its structure. Internally it was broadly representative of its popular power-base. Yet it was also a party of organization, and a "party of politicians"—who became more and more like Disraeli's contemporaneous fictional characters, Tadpole and Taper, who swam in the muddy waters of opinion and lined up votes. As the professionalization of politicians spread, the party was increasingly vulnerable to domination by the cadre who managed it and who saw the chance to make their own purposes the party purposes. *Hoi polloi* symbolism derived from Jackson's ascendency, gradually emptied of all but residual meaning, became a cover for manipulation. Thus, both Democrats and Whigs tended to what Ostrogorski called "democratic formalism," in which party organs, particularly conventions, often spoke in the name of "the people," without significant interaction between that "people" and party managers. Thus by the 1850's the party of Jackson had spawned prototypes of the classical boss and machine depending on patronage, other spoils, corruption, and coercion. The old-style boss and his graft-greased behemoth are practically extinct, but problems rooted in organization and professionalization remain. By its very nature, the party structure Jackson and his followers bequeathed to us entails a continuing tension between tendencies to oligarchy and self-serving manipulation on the one hand and impulses to intraparty democracy on the other. The result depends on popular attitudes and participation, as well as on the conduct of professional politicians. The issue marks another point at which unresolved problems of the Jacksonian perspective intersect our own times.

Finally, as the broadest link between the public on one side and public decisions on the other, parties offer potentialities of mobilizing support for coherent policy. Furthermore, the intraparty democracy of electoral competition and continuing criticism may provide some check over presidential power. Thus the radical Jackson, like the conservative Burke before him, could see party action as "a situation of power and energy," though Jackson left the notion of party as a checkrein mostly to his Whig opposition. Today, however, we may wonder if our parties will develop the requisite power and energy. Despite organization superior to that of Jackson's day, American parties are still relatively loose-jointed, federal, and heterogeneous—ill-equipped to channel the pluralistic swirl of groups and opinions into coherent action. This is the structure many party figures believe the parties ought to maintain, to be sure, though some tendencies toward articulation and nationalization are discernible. The complex tensions of the twentieth century, meanwhile, make the job simply bigger than it was in Jackson's easier era. Finally, the 1950's, somewhat like the span of the Monroe years, have shown signs of decline in party standing with the electorate. This decline is evidenced in negative attitudes toward parties and in more independent or "floating" voters, or ticket-splitters and "switchers." Whether our parties will enjoy a new resurgence as instruments of democracy, as they did under Jackson, is an open question.

"A second-class intellect," Mr. Justice Holmes remarked, *"but a first-class temperament."* Though he was speaking of Franklin Roosevelt, the comment might well have been made of Jackson, who offered little in the way of philosophy but much in energy, perspective, and example. The themes of democracy and equalitarianism he symbolized remain with us—as presidential leadership and party action continue to be our best public hopes for implementing them.

James Polk

by NORMAN A. GRAEBNER

"*Who is James K. Polk?*" *demanded the Whigs contemptu-*
ously of their Democratic opponents during the presidential canvass of 1844. In feigning astonishment at the Democratic
choice, these men were exploiting a dilemma which long characterized Polk's political career. Except among his close associates
he was unloved and unappreciated in his own day; throughout
the nineteenth century Americans all but ignored him. Perhaps
the reason is clear. Men are remembered for their unique qualities,
and Polk had none. In oratory he lacked the elegance of Daniel
Webster; in intellect, the preciseness of John C. Calhoun. In reputation he was no match for the Whig party's gallant hero, Henry
Clay. Not even in personality or appearance was he conspicuous.
He was below average in height, with thin face and piercing grey
eyes. He wore his hair long and brushed back behind his ears. He
was an uncompromising Presbyterian—a man honest and incorruptible, thoughtful and meditative, slow and measured in speech,
methodical and industrious. Polk's personal attributes were
worthy, even admirable, but they hardly conveyed distinction.

Yet Polk's gradual eclipse during the decades that followed his
presidency resulted as much from historic as from personal factors. His identification with the Texas and Mexican War issues
made him appear to post-Civil War historians as the chief pro-
ponent of slavery expansion. These writers consigned him, along
with Calhoun, to that large and seemingly contemptible category

of southern leaders whose aggressiveness allegedly plunged the nation into civil war. But the publication of his diary in 1910 quickened an interest Polk at a time when historians no longer accepted the abolitionist interpretation of the forties uncritically and were willing to judge the Tennessean by the evidence of his written record. Since that time few scholars have doubted that Polk was the most significant figure in the presidency between Andrew Jackson and Abraham Lincoln.

Polk was forty-nine years old when he entered the presidential office in March, 1845—the youngest incumbent of the White House up to that time. If he was not marked for greatness, his success was neither inconsequential nor accidental. His political experience was deep and long, giving him a knowledge of party behavior as thorough as that of any of his contemporaries. He achieved his first political prominence in Congress when, as a Representative from Tennessee, he joined the vanguard in the attack on the Maysville Road bill and the Bank of the United States early in Jackson's presidency. His devotion to the Jacksonian cause led him eventually into the camp of Martin Van Buren and two successful terms as speaker of the House of Representatives. His leadership in the House brought him a wide acquaintance and revealed his remarkable capacity for detail. Polk followed his Congressional career with a term as governor of Tennessee. A vigorous campaigner, a thorough Jacksonian, a man of parts in national Democratic circles, Polk had become by 1842 a man mentioned widely for the vice-presidency. This did not presage his nomination and election to the White House two years later, but it indicated that his "availability" was clear.

Polk's nomination was largely accidental. Former President Van Buren had been the titular head and front-running candidate of the Democratic party before the Baltimore convention of 1844. But the New Yorker faced the determined opposition of two groups. Southern Democrats attempted to put Calhoun in contention for the nomination by exploiting the powerful Texas issue in the South. But another Democratic clique, led by Lewis Cass of Michigan, Robert J. Walker of Mississippi, James Buchanan of Pennsylvania, and William L. Marcy of New York, quickly nationalized the Texas issue with appeals to "manifest destiny," and forced the question on the party as a national concern. Van Buren's anti-slavery leanings caused him to balk at immediate annexation. This hesitancy permitted his Southern and national opponents to join forces against him, prevent his nomination with the two-thirds rule, and eventually secure the nomination of a compromise candidate—Polk of Tennessee. For the moment Polk's Jacksonianism satisfied the Van Burenites just as his stand on Texas appealed to Southerners. Under Polk, however, it was the national Democratic faction that reached new heights of power and influence, both in Congress and in the Cabinet. During his four years in office this group comprised the core of Democratic power.

Polk had more than experience and an ambitious party bloc behind him. He had an unsuspected feel for leadership. He accepted the dictum of Alexander Hamilton that the American system provides no substitute for energy in the executive. Not long after he entered the presidency, one Washington editor said of him: "Few men are capable of the labors which he encounters; and few in his place would devote themselves with the same assiduity to the public service. He works from 10 to 12 hours in every 24. He holds two Cabinets a week. He sees visitors two hours every day when the Cabinet is not employed. . . . He is also in frequent communion with his secretaries."

So persistently did Polk remain at his official tasks that during his term he was outside the capital only six weeks. He spent one day at Mount Vernon early in his administration. In the summer of 1846 he vacationed briefly at Old Point Comfort. In May and June, 1847, he visited the University of North Carolina from which he graduated in 1819. Later that summer he toured New England for two weeks; and, lastly, in August, 1848, he rested for ten days at Bedford Springs, Pennsylvania. Shortly before he left office, Polk explained this devotion to duty: "No President who performs his duty faithfully and conscientiously can have any leisure. If he intrusts the details and smaller matters to subordinates constant errors will occur. I prefer to supervise the whole operations of the Government myself rather than intrust the public business to subordinates, and this makes my duties very great."

Polk was guide and master of his administration. Ten weeks before his inauguration he wrote to Cave Johnson of Tennessee, later to become his postmaster general, ". . . I intend to be myself President of the United States." Polk demanded absolute cooperation from members of his Cabinet, and required assurances that they would retire at the moment they became aspirants for the presidency. For Polk this appeared essential, for his announcement, at the time of his nomination, that he would not seek re-election raised the issue of the succession even before he entered the White House. In Cabinet sessions Polk encouraged free discussion. He listened attentively, but seldom abandoned his convictions. Gideon Welles, never an admirer of the President, reported early in Polk's administration that several Cabinet members "have been at particular pains to tell me that the President has his own way . . . does as he had a mind to." Later the reluctant Welles admitted that Polk "had courage and determination and shrank from no labor or responsibility." Judge John Catron wrote to Andrew Jackson in the spring of 1845: "Our friend is very prudent, and *eminently* firm, regardless of consequences. He came here to be—THE PRESIDENT—which at this date is as undisputed as that you was The GENL at N. Orleans." Jackson discovered how little he could influence Polk when the new President, ignoring the General's admonition, removed Francis P. Blair and the *Globe,* and established the Washington *Union* under Thomas Ritchie as the official organ of the Administration.

George Bancroft, the eminent historian and Polk's first secretary of the navy, has left the most impressive testimony of Polk's administrative capacity. Fifty years after the events of the 1840's, he recalled that Polk, on his inauguration day, informed him that he had four key objectives as President: tariff reduction, reestablishment of the Independent Treasury, the settlement of the Oregon boundary, and the acquisition of California. That Polk achieved these goals led Bancroft to the conclusion that he was "one of the very foremost of our public men and one of the very best and most honest and most successful Presidents the country ever had." Polk's administration succeeded, Bancroft added, "because he insisted on being its centre, and in overruling and guiding all his secretaries to act so as to produce unity and harmony."

Polk's rigid control of his administrative machinery accounts only partially for his success. Every aspect of his program required the eventual approval of Congress. That he achieved Congressional majorities on his pet measures has been written off by some historians as a simple expression of public opinion. Had he tried to dominate Congress, say his critics, his lack of color would have proved fatal. Only as a mirror of Jacksonianism was he equal to the task. But public opinion is never clearly defined or easily converted into policy. Polk's Democratic party was no longer united in 1845 on any philosophy. Throughout the expanding industrial and commercial centers of the North were powerful Democratic voices which sounded less and less Jacksonian as they demanded that the Federal government underwrite the economy with a variety of special dispensations. In both houses of Congress were determined Whig minorities that maintained a persistent attack on Polk's leadership. Against his enemies the President commanded the allegiance of only a segment of the party which had elected him.

Van Buren's followers were sullen. Since the Texas issue had carried Polk into the White House, they predicted logically that the friends of annexation would dominate the new administration. When Polk's Cabinet appointments favored "Texas" men, the Van Burenites concluded that the President had sold out to their enemies.

Actually, Polk, knowing the magnitude of their power as well as their discontent, made repeated efforts to pacify the Van Buren clique with a Cabinet post. He proffered the Treasury to Silas Wright, who declined because of his election to the New York governorship. Van Buren, in return, recommended another New Yorker, Benjamin F. Butler, for the State Department, and either Azariah C. Flagg or Churchill C. Cambreleng for the Treasury. Instead, the President incurred the wrath of the Van Burenites by placing Buchanan in the State Department, and, in deference to the South and Vice President George M. Dallas, he tendered the Treasury Department to Walker. For New York he now reserved the War Department. He offered this post to Butler, who refused to accept anything but the Treasury. Polk then decided on Marcy, also of New York but Van Buren's chief rival in New York politics. At the eleventh hour Butler reversed his decision, but his acceptance arrived in Washington too late.

Neither was Calhoun's powerful Southern faction represented in the Cabinet. Party spokesmen had prophesied that if the South Carolinian were not retained as secretary of state he would bolt the party, and that to dismiss him while the Texas negotiation was pending would be an irreparable insult. Calhoun professed delight at his return to private life in March, but the astute Webster observed that the Southern leader stood "at the head of the aggrieved." The Calhounites, in voicing their animosity toward the Administration, erroneously accused the President of bowing to the Van Buren group. Calhoun had but one explanation—"that I stood in the way of the restoration of the old Jackson Regime." Whatever the motive behind the Cabinet appointments, Polk, as president, faced resentment in two of the three important factions of his party. It was doubtful in March, 1845, if the Democratic organization was sufficiently united to carry any measure against a resolute Whig minority. Thomas Corwin, the partisan Ohio Whig, saw the Administration's dilemma clearly. "The truth is," he wrote, "Polk is not far from the category of Tyler. He is like Tyler an accident. He knows this. His friends know & feel it, and if his friends were United they would compel him to many a wild & wicked freak. But his friends are not united."

Polk was unawed by this opposition. When Congress met in December, 1845, he not only confronted it with a carefully-prepared program but he also made it clear that he was determined to carry this program into law. From the moment that Congress assembled, he exerted continuous pressure on key Democrats in both Houses through personal interviews or through members of the Cabinet. To Polk every administration proposal was a party measure to be forced through Congress as a matter of party responsibility.

Such determination merely reflected the President's deep conviction. Early in his career Polk had imbibed the philosophy of Thomas Jefferson. He entered political life an enemy of Clay's American System, and never ceased to condemn the protective tariff, the national Bank and credit system, internal improvements, and the distribution of Federal surpluses among the states. "I would keep no surplus revenue there to scramble for, either for internal improvements, or for any thing else," he once remarked. "I would bring the Government back to what it was intended to be, a plain economical Government." Even as President he never compromised with these beliefs.

Southern Democrats had led a continuous, if unsuccessful, assault on the high Whig Tariff of 1842. Polk renewed the attack in his message to Congress in December, 1845. He admitted that Congress had the power to levy taxes and could institute a tariff for that purpose. "But care should be taken," he added, "that all the great interests of the country, including manufactures, agriculture, commerce, navigation, and the mechanic arts, should . . . derive equal advantages from the incidental protection which a just system of revenue duties may afford." Taxes, he said, should be imposed on all classes according to their ability to pay. The existing tariff was wrong because it imposed "heavy and unjust burdens on the farmer, the planter, the commercial man, and those of all other pursuits except the capitalist who has made his investments in manufactures." Secretary of the Treasury Walker prepared the new tariff bill, mildly protective but proposing a general reduction of rates. In addition, the Walker bill introduced a simplified form by separating all dutiable goods into groups and providing *ad valorem* rates for each classification.

Opponents of tariff revision declared repeatedly throughout the ensuing debate that they comprised a majority in Congress, but Polk and Walker, aided by George Dwight, a little-known Massachusetts Whig, maintained a steady pressure on Congress. Dwight occupied a large parlor in one of the capital's leading hotels and there dispensed generous, if discriminate, hospitality as an agent of British manufacturing and mercantile interests. When the President in March learned that the Committee on Ways and Means was prepared to introduce specific duties on iron, he called in its chairman, James I. McKay of North Carolina, and extracted from him a promise to report the bill in its original form. Late in April word reached the White House that the Whigs in the Senate had managed to postpone action on the tariff bill. Polk reminded Dixon H. Lewis, chairman of the Senate Finance Committee, of the recommendations of the annual message. "I told him," the President recorded in his diary, "that I considered them as administration measures and that I intended to urge them upon Congress as such, and that I considered the public good, as well as my own power and the glory of my administration, depended in a great degree upon my success in carrying them through Congress." So occupied was Polk with Congressional affairs that seldom did he miss having evening callers when Congress was in session.

July was the critical month for the tariff. Shortly before the House vote was taken on July 3 the President reminded Daniel Dickinson of New York that the vote would be close and that the fate of the measure lay with the Democratic delegation from his state. Dickinson left immediately for the Capitol while Polk dispatched other members of Congress to exert similar pressure on doubtful votes. That afternoon Dickinson was able to report the successful passage of the bill in the House. The Senate decision remained doubtful. Scores of lobbyists had invaded Washington to defeat the measure. "The absence of a single democratic Senator will probably enable them to effect their object," observed the President. "I considered the passage of the bill before the Senate the most important domestic measure of my administration, and therefore I take so great an interest in it."

So tightly were the lines drawn on the tariff that everyone in Washington knew the Senate decision hinged on every vote. Polk learned that James Semple of Illinois was about to leave Washington on business. After a long conversation Polk secured Semple's agreement to remain. As the Senate vote neared all attention was focused on two men, William H. Haywood of North Carolina and Spencer Jarnagin of Tennessee. Haywood, a Democrat, balked at voting for tariff reduction. Polk warned him that he would be the only Southern Democrat voting against the measure and that he "would strike a severe blow upon my administration, inflict grave injury on the country, and . . . would ruin himself." Haywood resigned his seat rather than vote against his conscience or his party.

Now the fate of the new tariff was in the hands of Jarnagin, a Whig under instructions from the Tennessee legislature to vote for tariff reduction. Polk dispatched Hopkins Turney, a Tennessee Democrat, to encourage Jarnagin to obey his instructions. Webster, leader of the protariff forces in the Senate, brought the full weight of his prestige to bear on Jarnagin, but at the White House the Tennessean promised Polk that he would vote for the Walker bill and thereafter refused to discuss the matter with the Whigs. During the fateful session, Jarnagin stalked from the Senate chamber and permitted Vice President Dallas to cast the deciding vote for engrossment. Then the Tennessee Whig returned to vote for the final passage. Executive leadership was decisive throughout.

Polk achieved his second legislative ambition a few days later when his Independent Treasury bill passed Congress by a narrow party vote. His recommendation for the graduated reduction of Federal land prices, a measure favored earlier by both Jackson and Van Buren, failed through the combined votes of Whigs and Northern Democrats. But Joshua Giddings, the Ohio Whig and bitter opponent of the Administration, complained of the presence of members of the Administration on the House floor during the final vote on the bill. "Discussion had ceased," he recalled,

> they did not therefore attend to listen to our debates; yet we saw the Secretary of State, the Secretary of War, the Secretary of the Treasury, the Secretary of the Navy, the Postmaster General, the editor of the Executive organ, and the President's private secretary, busily engaged with individual members of the dominant party, with every indication of exerting their influence to induce gentlemen to vote for that Executive measure. . . . It was a shameless prostitution of the Executive character, which may well cause a blush upon the cheek of every American who feels an interest in the honor of his country, or in the purity of our institutions. . . .

Demands throughout the North and Northwest for river and harbor improvement at Federal expense had been accumulating for several years when Congress began to debate the River and Harbor bill of 1846. This was neither an Administration nor a party measure, and the debate on internal improvements, unlike the debate on the tariff and the Independent Treasury, revealed a sectional rather than a party cleavage. The South, representing the Jacksonian tradition, stood firm against the measure whereas Northern Whigs and Democrats tended to support it. Polk remained noncommittal, reminding callers at the White House that when he was in Congress he had voted against all such measures. To the astonishment of many Democrats, Polk greeted the passage of the River and Harbor bill early in August with a resounding veto. There was bitterness in the Northern reaction, for only Southern Democrats had voted in a bloc against the measure. Here was evidence, charged Polk's critics in the North, that the President was playing a Southern game.

Undaunted by such sectionalism, Polk was prepared to veto every internal improvement bill that reached his desk. Perhaps his most uncompromising lecture to Congress on that issue came in December, 1847, when he declared that the power of Congress to improve inland waterways must be conceded completely or must be denied altogether. "If it be admitted," he said, "how broad and how susceptible of enormous abuses is the power thus vested in the

General Government! There is not an inlet of the ocean or the lakes, not a river, creek or streamlet within the States, which is not brought for this purpose within the power and jurisdiction of the General Government."

Polk's tenacious control of domestic policies through White House interference and executive veto increasingly embittered his opponents. Some accused him of wielding so much authority over Congress that he was undermining the American democratic system itself. The pent-up resentment of one Whig finally exploded on the floor of Congress early in 1848:

> What great measure, whether of a financial or of any other character, has not been originated by the President or one of the heads of department who may have been selected to do his pleasure? I detest and abhor this one-man power. I am utterly opposed to a consolidated government. What honeyed language do we not hear on this subject from gentlemen on the other side? How eloquently they can declaim against the threatening dangers of a consolidated government, yet what else is our government at this hour? All power, the whole Government, is now virtually in the hands of the President, and he wields and exercises that power just as he pleases. Let a man have the boldness to differ from his views, and let him have the temerity to avow that difference on this floor, and he is denounced in the [Washington] Union before the next twenty-four hours. Forthwith he must walk the plank. He has but one alternative, either to stand on the platform with the Executive, or be pushed into the sea. . . . The President is elected by the people, and measures are willed by the President; *ergo*, whatever measures he wishes are the measures of the people, and his will is the will of the people. That is the will of the people. That is the argument. But I go for a truly popular government; by which I mean a government in which all great measures of public policy originate with the people themselves.

Polk's Jacksonianism became more militant as his administration progressed. During the summer of 1848, while Congress was in session, he kept a veto message in readiness. "Should another veto become necessary," he confided to his diary, "I desire to make it a strong paper, so that if I should be over-ruled, as I may be, by a united Whig vote and a part of the Democratic members, making a vote of two thirds, I may leave my full views on record to be judged of by my own countrymen & by posterity." His last night in office, March 3, 1849, Polk carried that message to the Capitol to be prepared if any river and harbor bill pending before the Senate should pass. But Congress never forced the President to read it.

To Polk internal improvements were the key to the entire American System of Henry Clay. Every aspect of that program had been overthrown—the Bank, the protective tariff, the distribution of the proceeds of Western lands, and internal improvements. But if the last principle were revived, he feared, all other aspects of the system would be revived also. Against this danger there was no defense except that of the Presidential veto. To make this clear, in his message of December, 1848, he lectured the Whigs on the nature of the American constitutional system: "Any attempt to coerce the President to yield his sanction to measures which he cannot approve would be a violation of the spirit of the Constitution . . . and if successful would break down the independence of the Executive department and make the President, clothed by the Constitution with the power to defend their rights, the mere instrument of a majority of Congress. . . . If it be said that the Representatives in the popular branch of Congress are chosen directly by the people, it is answered, the people elect the President. . . . The President represents in the Executive department the whole people of the United States as each representative of the legislative department represents portions of them." This message reveals how completely Polk's concept of the presidential office was Jacksonian.

Polk's distinction as president rests even more on diplomacy than on the management of his domestic program. Of the two expansionist issues (Texas and Oregon) raised by the campaign of 1844, Texas offered no challenge to his leadership. It had been an independent republic for almost a decade when Congress, through the Joint Resolution of early March, 1845, invited the region to join the United States. The Texas convention, called the following summer, accepted the invitation of Congress. In December, 1845, Texas became a state in the Union. Yet annexation had one troublesome result. In the spring of 1845 Mexico carried out its threat to break diplomatic relations with the United States if this nation ever voted to annex the former Mexican province.

Oregon was the more serious challenge, but the difficulties it presented the President were largely self-imposed. The traditional American diplomatic offer of the forty-ninth parallel had been eminently reasonable, but under the stimulation of manifest destiny doctrines Western Democrats demanded all of Oregon to the Alaska boundary and forced their platform on the Democratic party in 1844. If this stand had some appeal politically, it was impossible diplomatically. There was no apparent way in which the nation could gain the line fifty-four forty without more or less fighting. Yet Polk in his inaugural reaffirmed the party's conviction that the American title to Oregon was "clear and unquestionable." He was in no mood to challenge the Western Democrats by abandoning the campaign platform. Nor did he run much risk of antagonizing his expansionist friends in his subsequent negotiations with Great Britain during the summer of 1845. Actually only two minor issues still separated the two nations, those of Vancouver Island and the navigation of the Columbia. Privately both Polk and the British government had arrived at the necessity of reaching an agreement at the forty-ninth parallel, but Polk was still too encumbered politically to pursue details. He assured his secretary of state that his party commitments would not tolerate another offer of compromise. "I told him," Polk recorded, "that if that proposition had been accepted by the British Minister my course would have met with great opposition, and in my opinion would have gone far to overthrow the administration; that, had it been accepted, as we came in on Texas the probability was we would have gone out on Oregon."

Polk, still clinging to the Baltimore platform, raised the fifty-four forty issue again in his message to Congress in December, 1845. He warned the nation that the British rejection of his July offer, which he assured the Democrats had been made only in deference to his predecessors, was evidence enough that "no compromise which the United States ought to accept, can be effected." Upon Polk's recommendation that it was time to terminate the convention of joint occupancy in Oregon (renewed by England and the United States in 1827 in lieu of a diplomatic settlement), Congress proceeded to debate a resolution to extend the necessary twelve-month notice to England. Immediately the President found himself trapped by the enormous discrepancy between his political commitments to his party and the diplomatic realities in the Oregon situation. Since any Congressional action would convey to the Executive a mandate for a prompt and final settlement of the Oregon dispute, it made considerable difference to members of Congress how the President would use his authority.

William Allen of Ohio, chairman of the Foreign Relations Committee in the Senate, rushed to the defense of the notice, assuring Congress that the President would settle for nothing less than the whole of Oregon. Southern Democrats, led by Calhoun, challenged the Western bloc and argued that the President's message actually cleared the way for a settlement at the forty-ninth parallel. Nothing, declared Walter T. Colquitt of Georgia, could be "clear and unquestionable" that had been in dispute for thirty years. Haywood of North Carolina reasoned that Polk had accepted the necessity of compromise once and would do so again. But the Democrats were divided, and as late as April, 1846, John C. Rives wrote to Silas Wright, the Democrat governor of New York: "The 54° 40 & the 49° men both allege that the President is with them, *certain;* & I suspect that both are about half right. They both say they can prove it if necessary."

Polk's Whig opponents recognized his self-inflicted dilemma and plotted to embarrass him. "The Democratic leaders," observed William C. Rives, "have gotten themselves into a narrow defile, between warring sections of their own party, with a solid phalanx of the public arrayed against them—a position from which no art can rescue them, retreat and advance being alike impossible or fatal." What gave the Whigs such broad latitude for political maneuvering was the general conviction that the Executive would avoid war at all costs. They noted that neither the President nor the extremists in Congress were making any provision for the defense of the country.

Whig strategy demanded that the Administration be held responsible for an Oregon settlement, so that the President could not escape his commitment to fifty-four forty without first divesting himself of his political advantage. Polk, at the moment of settlement, must be made to face the full fury of the super-patriots in Democratic ranks. "The question of peace or war is with the Administration," observed Thurlow Weed's Albany *Evening Journal,* a powerful Whig publication, early in January, 1846. "If England is disposed to settle the question upon fair terms, the President can close the matter at once. He 'opened the ball' in his

Inaugural. His organ and party have been making political capital out of it quite long enough. They have had what there is of glory in the alarm—let them now take the responsibility of their own issue." By appearing to take an uncompromising stand against England, the Whigs hoped to force the Administration to carry the complete burden of diplomatic responsibility between war and peace. In one case it would face the country; in the other, the extremists within its own party. In either case the President would suffer the consequences of taking the nation to the brink of war. As Weed wrote in February, "The Administration must settle the question or stand guilty of blundering as well as of crime, in the eyes of the world."

In Congress the Whigs attacked and ridiculed the President for causing confusion in Congress. They observed that week after week he neglected to throw any light on the question of his future action. Senator Jacob W. Miller of New Jersey observed that the President's stand seemed "like the mercury in the barometer, to go up and down according as gentlemen placed their fingers on the bulb. When touched by the warm hands of the Senators from Indiana, from Illinois, and from Ohio, it immediately went up to 54° 40'; but when the cool and distinguished Senator from North Carolina put his finger upon it, it fell as quickly to 49°." Alexander Barrow of Louisiana declared with considerable truth, "There never was, before, a period when some one in the Senate was not authorized to speak for the Executive, made regularly acquainted with his views, and ready to put right those who misconstrue his plans or language." Whigs insisted on knowing how the President planned to dispose of the Oregon question. "I want light," shouted George Evans of Maine, "I want further assurance how the notice is to be used if we pass it."

These Whig jibes sent a constant stream of Democrats to the White House to seek the President's views. Polk refused to commit himself. When early in January, 1846, James A. Black of South Carolina sought the President's opinions, Polk recorded: "I told him that my opinions were contained in my message, that they had been well considered, and that I had not changed them; that I had recommended the Notice and thought it ought to be given." Such an answer was hardly satisfactory when Congress could not agree on the meaning of the message, but it served Polk's purpose and was repeated. When Turney sought to ascertain the Administration's intentions to better govern his own conduct in Congress, Polk discreetly referred him to the message. Still the compromise views of Calhoun could not be ignored. Polk assured him privately that he would submit any fair British proposal to Congress for its previous advice before rejecting it.

It was Haywood who stimulated the extremists into action early in March when he professed in Congress to speak the views of the Administration. The exasperated Edward Hannegan of Indiana prophesied that if this were true, the President "would sink so deep that the Trumpet of the Angel of Resurrection would not reach him!" The Indianan stormed into the Executive office and demanded a clear-cut decision. "I answered him that I would answer no man what I would do in the future," the President hedged, "that for what I might do I would be responsible to God and my country and if I should hereafter do anything which should be disapproved by himself and others, it would be time enough to condemn me." Similarly he informed the inquisitive Cass that his views on Oregon were contained in his message. Allen argued logically with Polk that he required the authority to speak for the Administration if he were to regain his position as the Senate's spokesman on foreign affairs. He presented to Polk a prepared statement for his endorsement, but the President would not be trapped. "I told him I could give no authority to him or any one else to say anything in the Senate," replied the President, "that I had given no such authority to Mr. Haywood and I would give none such to him; that I did not wish to be involved in the matter & that what he said he must say on his own responsibility." Polk refused to believe that he was responsible for the confusion in Congress, and attributed the party divisions rather to personal ambitions. "The truth is," he wrote in April, "that in all this Oregon discussion in the Senate, too many Democratic Senators have been more concerned about the Presidential election in '48, than they have been about settling Oregon either at 49° or 54° 40'."

Gradually Polk's duplicity antagonized all factions of his party. At the White House Calhoun reminded the President repeatedly of his promise to avoid war, but he could wrest no assurance from Polk that the Administration would accept a compromise settlement. In April the Senator wrote to his son, "The Oregon negotiation has been wretchedly managed. The differences ought to have been adjusted long since; as it is, it is so entangled, that much uncertainty still hangs over it." So completely did Polk avoid a showdown with the extremists that Calhoun believed to the end that the final settlement was achieved against the influence of the Executive.

During the spring the Van Burenites in Congress joined Calhoun in demanding a compromise arrangement. But this faction, too, found the Administration unfathomable. Thomas Hart Benton of Missouri, who gradually took the lead in denouncing the Western Democrats, complained that he was assailed daily in the *Union* for attempting to carry out what the President had asked the night before. To John A. Dix of New York, an important member of the faction, Polk's persistent effort to create the illusion that compromise was being achieved against his will while he secretly favored it was nothing short of treachery. "The whole matter of the Oregon question," he wrote in June, "has been scandalously mismanaged from the President down. . . ."

Polk was saved further embarrassment by the rapid shift in public and Congressional sentiment. By late spring it was quite obvious that the extremists had been isolated by Congressional argument, newspaper editorials, and the wearing out of public emotion. Even for the calculating Weed the time had come to join the general movement toward compromise. Whigs and Democrats alike could rejoice at the passage of the resolution for notice, for a peaceful settlement was now assured. England seized the diplomatic initiative and proposed an acceptable boundary along the forty-ninth parallel. Polk, through the device of seeking the prior approval of Congress, managed not only to rid himself of a political dilemma but also to escape the condemnation of all but the most extreme. Allen resigned his post as chairman of the Senate Committee on Foreign Relations; a few Western Democrats professed humiliation at what they termed a loss of national honor. But the Oregon settlement was so satisfactory that even the extremists were soon willing to permit the fifty-four forty issue to rest. Little of the nation's approbation was reserved for the President. Polk, refusing to face a divided party, had permitted the question to drift. Exerting no leadership himself, he was unable to associate his Administration with the final triumph in the minds of his contemporaries. That victory belonged to Calhoun and other Congressional leaders.

Even while Oregon negotiations were pending Polk involved himself in the question of California. The key to this significant diplomatic maneuver was the American declaration of war against Mexico in May, 1846. Behind that decision lay months of semi-obscure negotiation with Mexico over a series of unsettled issues— the claims of American citizens against the Mexican government for property stolen or destroyed in Mexico, the Texas-Mexican boundary, and the future of such California harbors as San Francisco, Monterey, and San Diego. Polk had attempted to reopen diplomatic relations with Mexico through the John Slidell mission of November, 1845, instructing Slidell to secure a satisfactory boundary line which would include the Rio Grande and as much of the coveted California coast as possible. In exchange, the United States would assume all American claims against the Mexican government and pay additional millions, the precise amount depending on the extent of ocean frontage which Mexico might concede to the United States.

Slidell was not recognized by the government in Mexico City, and Polk, to strengthen his diplomatic arm, dispatched General Zachary Taylor with an American force to the region of the Rio Grande. To Mexico this had all the appearance of aggression, and with a few scattered shots in that distant wilderness the uneasy peace vanished. With the notice of hostilities, the Cabinet agreed unanimously on war. On May 13 Congress accepted the President's request for a formal declaration.

Polk did not want war. In his diplomacy with Mexico he had hoped to secure California by purchase. His eagerness had provoked a clash of arms, but having become involved in war, he was determined to prolong the conflict until he could drive Mexico into a cession of California. To admit such war aims publicly, the President feared, would be fatal. The principle of indemnity, clearly recognized under the law of nations, was acceptable only to those Americans who placed responsibility for the war on Mexico. What disturbed Polk was the refusal of the Whigs to do so. His own action in sending Taylor to the Rio Grande left sufficient doubt in the minds of his opposition that it elicited an unending review of the war's causes. Politicians who attacked the war could hardly approve the annexation of California as the fruit of that struggle. Polk did not want to be accused of conducting a war of conquest. To the American public and members of Congress, therefore, he remained silent on the subject of California. Benton knew the Administration well and saw its predicament clearly when he wrote:

It is impossible to conceive of an administration less warlike, or more intriguing, than that of Mr. Polk. They were men of peace, with objects to be accomplished by means of war; so that war was a necessity and an indispensability to their purposes. They wanted a small war, just large enough to require a treaty of peace, and not large enough to make military reputations, dangerous for the presidency. Never were men at the head of government less imbued with military spirit, or more addicted to intrigue. How to manage the war was a puzzle. Defeat would be ruin: to conquer vicariously, would be dangerous.

In his conduct of the Mexican War, Polk faced a challenge of major proportions. To achieve California he had to keep the nation involved until Mexico was ready to negotiate. Yet how could he prevail upon Congress to furnish the sinews of war without revealing his purpose in continuing the struggle? Polk admitted simply that his aim was a just peace. In his war message he declared it his desire "not only to terminate hostilities speedily, but to bring all matters in dispute between this Government and Mexico to an early and amicable adjustment." Official policy, noted the Washington *Union*, was that of seeking peace through war. In a circular to American ministers and consuls the Administration declared its military objectives in Mexico as the conquest of an "honorable and permanent peace." Fearing that no administration in Mexico that ceded California could remain in power unless it received, at the moment of the treaty, sufficient funds to support an army, Polk requested two million dollars from Congress to overcome the chief obstacle to peace. This, he said, was "the adjustment of a boundary between the two republics." In his message to Congress in December, 1846, he again declared his purpose in demanding additional troops to be that of obtaining "an honorable peace and thereby secure *ample indemnity* for the expenses of the war, as well as to our much injured citizens. . . ." Yet he carefully avoided any precise definition of that indemnification.

What embarrassed Polk was his need of pursuing the war against an ephemeral enemy that continued to lose all the battles but refused to ask for terms of peace. If the purpose of the war was peace, at what stage in the progression of American victories would a peace be conquered? In complete disgust, Giddings attacked the President's message of December, 1846: "The people of the nation are demanding of the Executive a statement of the objects of the war. What are the ulterior designs of the government in its prosecution?" The Ohioan recounted the successes of American arms in Mexico, professedly achieved in the name of defense, and continued: "What estimation must the author of this message have placed upon the intelligence of this body, and of the nation, when he penned these statements? Such absurdities defy argument." Despite the logic of such attacks, the Whigs ultimately voted additional troops and equipment under the conviction that if they gave the President enough rope he would eventually hang himself.

But the challenge to the President's equanimity ran deeper. The Whig party never forgot, nor permitted the nation to forget, that Winfield Scott and Zachary Taylor, the two leading generals in the war, were Whigs. Polk observed Taylor's unique capacity to attract favorable attention to himself from all segments of the American public. The President believed him unfitted for military command. In September, 1846, he complained that Taylor "simply obeys orders and gives no information to aid the administration in directing his movement." But the beleaguered President continued, "After the late battles, which were well fought, the public opinion seems to point to him as entitled to the command." Although he trusted Scott even less, Polk offered him command of the Vera Cruz expedition late in 1846. Eventually the President attempted to resolve the question of partisanship in the military command by obtaining the appointment of Benton as a lieutenant general to serve as supreme commander over the American forces in Mexico. The Senate defeated the President's proposal. Without the power to replace them, Polk followed the actions of the two Whig generals with mounting fear and agitation. "I am held responsible for the conduct of the War," he complained, "and yet Congress refused to give me a commander in whom I have confidence, & I am compelled to employ the officers whom the law provided, however unfit they may be."

Some Democrats joined the Whigs in opposing the wartime Administration. Many of the Van Burenites rejected Polk's rationalization for the war, yet they supported the President as a party obligation. Calhoun deserted the Administration completely and openly used his prestige in Congress to undermine and embarrass it. He charged the President with bungling American diplomacy with Mexico, for if Texas annexation alone were the cause of the war, the burden would fall on the South Carolinian as the author of the treaty of annexation. Calhoun accused the Administration of stupidity in involving the country in a war which would furnish popular Whig presidential candidates for a decade. Calhoun and his friends joined the Whig minority to defeat one wartime measure after another. In one succinct paragraph of February, 1847, Polk summarized the many political pressures beating against his wartime leadership:

> It is now in the third month of the Session and none of my war measures have yet been acted upon. There is no harmony in the Democratic party. . . . In truth faction rules the hour, while principle & patriotism is forgotten. While the Democratic party are thus distracted and divided and are playing this foolish and suicidal game, the Federal party are united and never fail to unite with the minority of the Democratic party, or any faction of it who may break off from the body of their party, and thus postpone and defeat all my measures. I am in the unenviable position of being held responsible for the conduct of the Mexican War, when I have no support either from Congress or from the two officers highest in command in the field. How long this state of things will continue I cannot foresee.

Slavery added another dimension to the political confusion of Congress. David Wilmot, a little-known Pennsylvania Democrat, anchored the question of slavery expansion to the Mexican War with his Proviso of August, 1846, which declared that slavery should not exist in any territory acquired from Mexico as the result of the war. Polk was dismayed at the ensuing debate over slavery, for he insisted that it had no connection with the war. He reminded members of Congress that the institution could exist in neither New Mexico or California. "The state of things in Congress is lamentable," he noted early in 1847. "Instead of coming up to the mark as patriots and sustaining the administration and the country in conducting a foreign war, they are engaged in discussing the abstract question of slavery. . . ." Abolitionists attacked the war savagely because they regarded it as the conspiracy of slaveholders to expand the area of slavery at Mexico's expense.

Whig conservatives, fearful of the impact of the slavery issue on the Union, accepted as their wartime program Senator John Berrien's proposed amendment of February, 1847, which declared that "the war with Mexico ought not to be prosecuted by this Government with any view to the dismemberment of the republic, or to the acquisition by conquest of any portion of her territory."

Polk's resourcefulness was equal to the occasion. While politicians and editors attacked the Mexican War and demanded its immediate cessation, the President in April, 1847, dispatched Nicholas P. Trist, chief clerk in the State Department, to join Scott's headquarters in Mexico and attempt to establish direct negotiations with the Mexican government. Trist's instructions were specific, for the President knew precisely what he wanted. He had made that clear in his earlier instructions to Slidell and in his Cabinet deliberations following the outbreak of war. He would settle for no less than the acquisition of San Diego bay and the entire California coast to the north of it. Trist was told to run the boundary down the Colorado "to a point directly opposite the division line between Upper and Lower California; thence due west, along said line, which runs north of the parallel of 32° and south of San Miguel, to the Pacific Ocean. . . ." This line, Polk believed, would bring San Diego bay into the United States. Trist was committed to absolute secrecy, but the news of his mission leaked to the press, and by June the *New York Herald's* Washington correspondent had secured a copy of the Administration's boundary proposals. Thereafter it was futile for the President to deny his war aims.

Through Trist, Polk eventually escaped his wartime dilemmas and achieved his territorial objectives in the Southwest. But even this diplomatic achievement was gained without his approval, for he had recalled Trist from Mexico as early as October, 1847. During a brief armistice with the Mexicans in August, Trist had agreed to forward to Washington a Mexican proposal that would have conceded all California ports except San Francisco to Mexico. Polk explained his decision to recall Trist in one diary notation: "Mr. Trist is recalled because his remaining any longer with the army could not, probably, accomplish the objects of his mission, and because his remaining longer might, & probably would, impress the Mexican Government with the belief that the United States were so anxious for peace that they would ultimate[ly] conclude one upon the Mexican terms. Mexico must now first sue for peace, & when she does we will hear her proposition."

Unknown to the President, Mexico complied with these conditions when it asked Trist to remain in Mexico and conclude a peace treaty. Having been assured by the Mexicans in advance that they would concede a boundary along the thirty-second parallel, Trist agreed to ignore his instructions. During January, 1848, he negotiated the treaty of Guadalupe Hidalgo which conveyed California and New Mexico, including the port of San Diego, to the United States. Polk knew that Trist was involved in treaty negotiations but took no measure to terminate his efforts until late in January when the decision could have no effect on events in Mexico. Polk accepted the treaty, but he rejected Trist, for his agent had become a close friend of Scott and, after January, the President could only interpret Trist's actions as an effort to embarrass him and his administration.

Peace had become a prime requisite. Despite the succession of American victories in Mexico, it required over eighteen months to terminate the war. "It was not brief, cheap, and bloodless," observed Benton. "It had become long, costly, and sanguinary." Polk demanded that the Senate examine only the treaty, not the circumstances surrounding the negotiation. This assured its ratification. The treaty became the law of the land, but Polk refused even to compensate its author for his expenses in Mexico. Benton recalled regretfully, "Certainly those who served the government well in the war with Mexico fared badly with the administration. . . . Trist, who made the treaty which secured the objects of the war, and released the administration from its dangers, was recalled and dismissed."

Polk's achievements in diplomacy were among the most remarkable in American history. If his own role was often confused, his fundamental demands on other nations were so precise and limited that he could achieve them despite the enormous domestic pressures under which he labored. In his message of December, 1847, he declared that the bay of San Francisco and other harbors on the California coast "would afford shelter for our navy, for our numerous whale ships, and other merchant vessels employed in the Pacific ocean, [and] would in a short period become the marts of an extensive and profitable commerce with China, and other countries of the East." Polk was concerned primarily with frontage on the Pacific, and even after the ratification of the treaty with Mexico he defined his diplomatic gains in no other terms.

Polk's career raises fundamental questions concerning political success and its conditions. That singleness of purpose which made possible his presidential triumphs also exposed his Administration to endless criticism. He pressed toward his goals, unmindful of consequences. So narrow and all-consuming were his policies that he was probably never fully conscious of the bitter sectional controversy which they created. He never perceived the relationship between the acquisition of California and the rise of freesoilism in the nation. In this Polk was sincere, for he was convinced that terrain and climate would bar slavery from the Southwest. But for millions of Americans the relationship between slavery and territorial expansion was distressing indeed. It was not the President's actions alone that laid the foundations of civil strife; it was primarily his refusal to recognize their impact on the American consciousness.

Unfortunately Polk's deviousness almost matched the dexterity which he revealed in the management of his office. Vice President Dallas once observed that Polk suffered from the same defects of character that applied to Charles I. To the President he applied the words of Macaulay's History of England: "He was, in truth, impelled by an incurable propensity to dark and crooked ways. It may seem strange that his conscience, which, on occasions of little moment, was sufficiently sensitive, should never have reproached him with this great vice. But there is reason to believe that he was perfidious, not only from constitution and from habit, but also on principle. He seems to have learned from the theologians whom he most esteemed . . . that, *in every promise which he made, there was an implied reservation that such promise might be broken in case of necessity, and that of the necessity he was the sole judge.*" Dallas was especially disturbed at Polk's habit of announcing one purpose publicly and pursuing another privately. To him it was an administration of "frauds and falsehoods . . . brought home by undeniable evidence." Cunning, the Vice President added, so completely dominated Polk's actions that even his "most devoted friends could not refrain from complaining to each other, with bitter grief and shame, of his crooked politics. His defeats, they said, gave them less pain than his intrigues."

For Polk a successful presidency, measured by his own standards, required both a vast expenditure of energy and a high degree of expediency, for he had few genuine political assets. He lacked the magnetism and popularity to build a large personal following. The public almost ignored him. When he visited Chapel Hill in May, 1847, for example, no one came to see him off. "You would be surprised to see how little attention the President or his family receives here," wrote one Washingtonian, "—if it were not for the office-hunters, he would hardly receive any." Polk's journey to New England produced little enthusiasm, and whatever cheers he received were meant for the President, not the man.

Nor was Polk successful in building political support through the Federal patronage. Perhaps the distribution of offices won some key votes in Congress, but the President's insistence on making appointments himself sent a wave of discontent through Democratic ranks. Politicians who had campaigned enthusiastically for the party felt dismayed and abused at the denial of public offices. Some Democratic leaders took offense at almost all of Polk's diplomatic appointments since they appeared to serve no party purpose. The *New York Tribune* concluded that Polk's patronage policy was "deplorably odious to a vast majority of the leading Democrats of the country." Calhoun asserted in November, 1846, that the President through his patronage decisions had "distracted and divided and disheartened and alienated the party to an extent unknown heretofore."

Federal patronage brought no greater satisfaction to the President than it did to the disaffected members of his party. Polk saw clearly that it was a source of presidential weakness. He had been in office scarcely four months when he wrote to Governor Silas Wright of New York, "I sincerely wish I had no office to bestow." On his first anniversary in the White House he noted in his diary that the absence of patronage "would add much to the happiness and comfort" of his office. By January, 1847, he felt the pressures of the system so keenly that he predicted defeat for any president who sought re-election if he were forced to wield the Federal patronage. Polk wrote of the trials of the system: "In every appointment which the President makes he disappoints half a dozen or more applicants and their friends, who . . . will prefer any other candidate in the next election, while the person appointed attributes the appointment to his own superior merit and does not even feel obliged by it." Polk recognized one basic principle in the distribution of patronage—that the withholding of office might garner support, but that offices once bestowed are no guarantee of future loyalty.

Polk's insistence on wielding the selective power brought to his office a monotonous stream of office-seekers who nearly drove him to distraction. His lamentation so dominates his diary that historians have noted little besides this aspect of his patronage experience. He admitted that he had utter contempt for the hordes who took his time to set forth their merits and claims. "It is a great and useless consumption of my time, and yet I do not see how I am to avoid it without being rude or insulting, which it is not in my nature to be," he noted with complete resignation. On March 4, 1846, he recorded that all was not pleasant at the White House: "I am ready to exclaim, will the pressure for office never cease! It is one year to-day since I entered on the duties of my office, and still the pressure for office has not abated." During the Mexican War the President wrote that the begging for rewards was "not only disgusting, but is almost beyond endurance." Even after the war ended, he declared that it required "great patience & self command to repress the loathing I feel towards a hungry crowd of unworthy office-hunters who often crowd my office."

Occasionally members of Congress sought to protect themselves from their constituents by submitting applications to the President and then instructing him privately to ignore their candidates as unworthy of public office. One day David R. Atchison of Missouri voted against his own applicant in the Senate and quickly proposed another name to Polk. When the irate President demanded of him why he had opposed his first nominee, the Senator replied simply that "we are obliged to recommend our constituents when they apply to us." Polk recorded in his diary that he was tired of the trickery and treachery practiced on him by some members of Congress. He threatened to prepare a treatise on the evils of the Federal patronage as a warning to his successors. "If God grants me length of days and health," he wrote in January, 1847, "I will, after the expiration of my term, give a history of the selfish and corrupt considerations which influence the course of public men, as a legacy to posterity. I shall never be profited by it, but those who come after me may be."

Polk, never physically strong, declined markedly under the burdens of office. Long before his term expired, his friends detected his shortened step, his air of languor and exhaustion.

Charles J. Ingersoll, the noted Democratic politician, warned Mrs. Polk that her husband was wearing himself out—that unless he had some recreation he would die in office. He suggested that she order her carriage and demand that the President accompany her on an occasional drive. "I did so," she replied, "and the carriage waited and waited, until it was too late. It would have been obliged to wait all day, for somebody was always in the office, and Mr. Polk would not, or could not, come. I seldom succeeded in getting him to drive with me." So completely did his official cares dominate his being that Polk found no relaxation in entertainment or anecdote.

For Polk the price of leadership came high. He had never sought the presidency; throughout his last year in the White House he looked forward to his retirement to private life. "I have now passed through two-thirds of my Presidential term," he observed in November, 1847, "& most heartily wish that the remaining third was over. . . ." On March 3, 1848, he noted in his diary, "This day closes my third year in the Presidential office. They have been years of incessant labour, anxiety, & responsibility." On the day that he left the White House he recorded, "I feel exceedingly relieved that I am now free from all public cares." But with leisure did not come the recuperation of body and serenity of mind he required. The labors and anxieties of the past had been too exhausting. His health continued to fail, and he died on June 15, 1849, three months after leaving office.

Abraham Lincoln

by RICHARD N. CURRENT

Abraham Lincoln, sixteenth President, is both a historical figure and a hero of folklore. It is not always easy to distinguish the two, the man and the myth. Either way, he is the most famous of all the presidents. He has surpassed George Washington as first in the hearts of his countrymen, according to various opinion polls. More than Washington or any other, except perhaps for very recent heads of the government, he is known at least by reputation to people outside the United States. His name has a kind of magic appeal in countries as far away, both geographically and culturally, as India and Japan. In India he often is compared with the native folk hero Mahatma Gandhi. In Japan he is a source of inspiration to Emperor Hirohito, who keeps a Lincoln bust in his Tokyo laboratory-study.

The fame of Lincoln is nourished by a swelling stream of books, pamphlets, newspaper and magazine articles, and radio, television, and stage productions. The books alone total more than five thousand, or an average of about one a week since the day he died.

Much of this material is tendentious, and much of it also is trash. So potent is the Lincoln legend that politicians, peddlers, and others with followers to win or commodities to sell are at great pains to show that Lincoln really was one of them—a prohibitionist, Communist, spiritualist, or what not. Some writing, not necessarily self-interested, is praiseworthy as literature but

misleading as history. The plays by the Englishman John Drinkwater and the American Robert E. Sherwood have provided
many thousands, both in America and abroad, with their conceptions of Lincoln. Drinkwater could not help losing himself in hero
worship. Sherwood emphasized themes that had dramatic but no
historical value: he dwelt upon the sad romance which was supposed to have involved young Abe with the backwoods beauty
Ann Rutledge; and he pictured the rising Lincoln as a rather aim-
less and ambitionless person, who would have got nowhere without the prodding of his rather shrewish wife.

Even in footnoted biographies and history books it is sometimes hard to tell fiction from fact. Despite the vast quantity of
materials published—or, in some cases, *because* of it—there are gaps
in our knowledge of Lincoln, and there are areas of dispute about
him. Sincere and informed scholars continue to debate certain
issues of his career. Did he (to mention but one of the oft-debated
questions about him) deliberately start the Civil War by maneuvering the Confederates into firing the first shot at Fort Sumter?
A considerable part of the writing about Lincoln is controversial,
and controversy begets more controversy. There is, morever,
something intriguing in the uncertain and unknown. Herein lies
part of the explanation for the continuing interest in Lincoln.

There are other and more compelling reasons for his hold upon
the minds and hearts of people everywhere. The "self-made man"
is generally admired, and Lincoln was a self-made man. Brought
up in the wilderness of frontier Kentucky and Indiana, the child
of semiliterate parents, he had few opportunities for schooling or
for intellectual stimulation of any sort. Yet, as a youth, he acquired somehow a deep desire to learn, and learn he did, mainly
by his own efforts. After moving to Illinois, he succeeded in his
chosen profession, the law, before rising to the very top in politics.
In short, he exemplified and gave reality to the great American
dream of the nineteenth century, the dream that anyone by honest effort could rise from poverty to comfort, from obscurity to
fame. Among the nineteenth-century presidents, however, he was
not the only one who made the long ascent from log cabin to
White House. James A. Garfield, too, was born in a log cabin,
and so was Millard Fillmore.

The timing and circumstances of Lincoln's death partly account for his lasting grip on the popular imagination. Struck down
at the very moment of triumph, he seemed a martyr to the causes

for which the war had been fought. As it happened, he was shot on Good Friday, the anniversary of the Crucifixion. Perhaps this was more than mere coincidence, or so it appeared to many ministers of the gospel, who on the next Easter and on later Sundays preached upon the similarities between Abraham Lincoln and Jesus Christ. Thus he was deified in a way that the other assassinated presidents, Garfield and William McKinley, were not.

Lincoln had personal qualities that give him a unique appeal. His very appearance—his towering, awkward figure and his rough-hewn face—made him as hard to forget as he was easy to caricature. His expression, now vacant and sad, now beaming as he joined the laughter at one of his own stories, left and still leaves the feeling that he could sympathize with a wide range of human emotions, though sometimes he was moody, wrapped up in feelings he did not share with anyone. Uncommon he was, and yet he seemed a common man, one with whom other common men could identify themselves. Above all, he was unaffected and "natural," humble and humane. Not that he felt or acted inferior to the men around him, but neither did he lord it over anyone. Power and place never went to his head.

The events of 1861–65 would have made memorable anyone who happened to be president at the time. In proportion to the size of the country, the Civil War was much the hugest of all wars that Americans have participated in. It left much the deepest impression upon its own and later generations. This war was won, the Union was preserved, and the slaves were put upon the way to freedom while Lincoln was president. He would be remembered if he had been no more than the quaint and at times pathetic figure he often has been pictured—a man who for the most part merely presided, at a distance, over the stirring and fateful events of those four years.

Lincoln did not merely preside. His best and most solid claim to greatness is to be found in his positive achievements as president. Only in recent years has historical scholarship made it possible to do full justice to Lincoln the actual leader. Though mysteries about him remain, it has become clear enough that he was the dominant and decisive American figure of his day. In sum, he used rare political skill not only to gain and hold office but also to unite the North and thus reunite the nation. A statesman as well as a politician, he led the way cautiously but surely toward the emancipation of the slaves as well as the preservation of the

Union. As commander in chief of the Army and the Navy, he took responsibility for making and seeing to the execution of the strategic plans that at last brought victory. And he gave point and meaning to all the bloodshed by symbolizing and putting into deathless words the ideals which, alone, were worth fighting for.

In political skill, as in many other respects, Lincoln grew remarkably, especially during the last four years of his life. He had been slow to attain national prominence, much slower than, for instance, his Illinois friend and rival Stephen A. Douglas. Before becoming president, Lincoln had had comparatively little experience in winning and holding office. He had served several terms in the Illinois legislature and one in the national Congress. That was all. His backwardness in politics was due to no lack of aspiration for prestige and place. As his long-time law partner William H. Herndon said of him: "His ambition was a little engine that knew no rest."

While in the House of Representatives, as the "lone Whig" from Illinois (1847–49), he gave much attention to politics and little attention to anything else. Most of his congressional speechmaking consisted of campaign oratory. Throughout his first year in Congress, he had his eye on the presidential election of 1848. Not yet did he aspire to the presidency, but he hoped to unmake one president, a Democrat, and to make another, a Whig. He set out to discredit President James K. Polk, whom he accused of unnecessarily and unconstitutionally bringing on the War with Mexico. Meanwhile he labored to elevate as Polk's successor the popular general Zachary Taylor, whom he praised for winning victories in that same unnecessary and unconstitutional war. To some extent, Lincoln succeeded with his political tactics: Taylor was duly elected. Yet these tactics failed to strengthen Lincoln or his party among his own Illinois constituents, most of whom were enthusiastic about the war that he decried. He himself was not a candidate for a second term in Congress, but if he had been he could not have obtained it. What was for him much worse, he was unable to get the Government job (as commissioner of the general land office) which he sought as a well-earned reward for his services in the recent presidential campaign.

Frustrated and despondent, he withdrew almost entirely from active politics and remained for five years in a kind of exile. At last he saw a new challenge and a new opportunity when the Kansas-Nebraska bill was passed in 1854. This Act, the work of Douglas, reopened to slavery an area that Congress earlier had defined as free soil. Embodying Douglas' "popular sovereignty" principle, the law provided that the settlers of Kansas and Nebraska territories should decide for themselves whether to permit the owning of slaves. The measure provoked violent opposition, though there was little probability that slavery would take root in Kansas or Nebraska, and in fact few slaves ever were carried into either territory. The "anti-Nebraska" movement led to the founding of the modern Republican party.

Joining the new party, Lincoln made himself one of its leaders in Illinois, and he continually attacked Douglas' idea of letting the people choose. No doubt he was sincere in taking the stand he did, but he also advanced himself in politics thereby. Eastern Republicans, among them Horace Greeley of the powerful *New York Tribune*, began to talk of adopting Douglas and his program after he quarreled with slavery expansionists in the Democratic party. Whether he became a Republican or remained a Democrat, Douglas threatened to win the following of many other Whigs throughout the West. He stood in the way of Lincoln's advancement. Boldly challenging him, Lincoln made Illinois politics pretty much a running duel between the two, a contest that reached a climax in the senatorial campaign of 1858. All along, Lincoln denounced Douglas as a pro-slavery conspirator, and "popular sovereignty" as a device to prepare the way for fixing slavery upon the territories—indeed, upon the entire nation. Lincoln insisted that Congress must take positive action to prevent slavery from spreading and put it on the way to ultimate extinction. Eventually he won the duel with Douglas. Though Lincoln lost the Senate race, he gained a reputation that made it possible for him to reach the White House.

As the Republican presidential candidate in 1860, Lincoln personally laid down the basic strategy for his own campaign. He had learned a great deal about the art of politics since 1848, when he took up a cause which, though successful in the nation at large, proved unpopular at home. Now, in 1860, he was determined to avoid issues that might be troublesome in this locality or that. His idea was to concentrate upon the one principle that had become fairly safe throughout the North—the principle of free soil. Though he made no stump speeches (it was not yet the accepted thing for a presidential candidate to speak in his own behalf) he gave advice to those who did. He counseled them to say nothing about the tariff, political rights for foreigners, prohibition, or any other subject that might offend prospective Republican voters anywhere. This strategy of avoidance no doubt helped to hold dissident Republicans together. With the Democrats divided, Lincoln managed to garner a comfortable majority of the electoral votes.

Of the popular votes, however, he got only a plurality and not a majority—only about two in five of the total cast. The Republicans were in the minority until Southern Democrats seceded with their states. Even after that, the Democratic party remained strong in the North, strong enough to recover many congressional seats in the mid-term elections of 1862. Throughout the war, this party was beset by factional strife, especially as between the War Democrats and the advocates of a compromise peace. But Lincoln's party, too, had its internal disagreements. Among Republicans were former Whigs and former Democrats, high-tariff and low-tariff men, native Americans and recent immigrants, abolitionists and people more or less indifferent to slavery. Among Republicans were also rival leaders with personal or local differences. And at the time of Lincoln's first election there existed no true Republican organization on a national scale: there was but a congeries of Republican parties organized state by state.

As President and party leader, Lincoln faced the task of holding the support of Republicans and gaining the cooperation of Democrats. He needed, furthermore, to consolidate his party, strengthen its internal ties, and make it a truly national (or at least all-Northern) organization. During his slightly more than four years in office he succeeded, admirably if imperfectly, in accomplishing all these objects.

What were the secrets of his success as a politician? It often has been supposed that his strength lay chiefly in a kind of mystical communion with the masses. Perhaps he did keep intuitively in touch with them. This would be hard to prove—or disprove.

Certainly he watched the trends of opinion as closely as he could at a time when no technique of "scientific sampling" had yet been devised. Certainly, too, he undertook now and then to influence the views of the public. Lacking such means of mass communication as radio and television, he could speak only to a crowd assembled immediately before him, and while President he actually did this rather seldom. To reach a larger public, he could resort to the newspapers, and occasionally he did so. He talked with Washington correspondents, wrote letters to editors like Greeley, and even composed a few editorials of his own, to be published anonymously in one of the Washington papers. His various proclamations were featured in the news. Still, he developed no system of publicity, no institution comparable to the later White House press conference or press secretary.

On the whole, President Lincoln depended much less upon direct appeals to the voters than did other strong Presidents before and after him, such as Andrew Jackson, Woodrow Wilson, and Franklin D. Roosevelt. He was less inclined than they to take an open stand on one side or the other of a clear-cut, controversial choice of policy. In politics he dealt more effectively with people as individuals than as masses. With a knack for personal relationships, he could smooth over differences that would have frustrated anyone else, and he could hold the allegiance of men who disagreed with him and with one another. His humor was an important part of his technique for getting along. Sometimes he told funny stories to ease a tense occasion, and sometimes he told them to distract visitors from complaints they had come to make. He used his winsome arts most frequently upon Cabinet colleagues, congressmen, governors, and other men who themselves had political influence. Essentially he was (as David Donald has aptly said) a "politician's politician."

In unifying and strengthening the Republican party, Lincoln made very effective use of his powers of patronage. To his Cabinet he appointed, among others, his former rivals for the presidential nomination, and, all in all, he gave a place to every important faction of the Republican party and to every part of the Union, including even the border slave-states. He tried, in vain, to include also an outstanding Unionist as a representative from the South. In the number-one Cabinet position, as secretary of state, he put William H. Seward, the foremost of the "Conservatives" who opposed making war upon the private property of the Confederacy. He named to the number-two position, as secretary of the treasury, a champion of the "Radicals" who demanded abolition as a war aim—Salmon P. Chase. Cleverly he managed (till 1864) to keep Seward and Chase in his official family, despite a factional conspiracy to oust Seward and despite efforts by both men to resign. And then, after Lincoln finally had accepted the resignation of Chase, he made him Chief Justice of the Supreme Court (delaying the actual appointment till after the election of 1864, so as to be sure of Chase's wholehearted support during the campaign). By keeping the various factional leaders in the Government, Lincoln managed to tie the party together at the top, and to hold the strings pretty much in his own hands.

He interested himself also in the disposal of lesser jobs. The clamor for these, from spoilsmen eager for a place on the Federal payroll, sorely tried the patience of the President, a patient man if ever there was one. Yet, day after day, to the very last day of his life, he carefully considered the claims to Government jobs—a postmastership here, a marshal's office there—and in disposing of the jobs he always took political consequences as well as personal qualifications into account.

The election of 1864 provided a test of his political skill. To be sure, he was aided by good news that came from the front not long before election day, especially the news of Sherman's capture of Atlanta. But he left nothing to chance as, once more, he masterminded his own electoral campaign. He desired, and got, the nomination of Andrew Johnson as his running mate. He did this so that, with a Southern Democrat on the ticket with him, he could run as a "Union" candidate, the candidate of a kind of Northern and Southern, Republican and Democratic coalition (the Republicans accordingly called themselves the "Union" party for the time being). He accepted the resignation of an unpopular Cabinet member, Postmaster General Montgomery Blair, in time to rally Blair's critics to the party standard. Once the campaign was well under way, Lincoln removed a number of uncooperative jobholders, gave electioneering advice to party workers in various states, designated certain key speakers and laid out their itineraries, and made arrangements for as many soldiers as possible to cast ballots. The boys in blue being mostly Republicans, the soldier vote helped Lincoln considerably and may indeed have made the difference between victory and defeat.

Northern governors this time looked to Lincoln for aid in their own campaigns. Previously, in 1860, *he* had depended heavily on *them*. This reversal suggests the extent to which, in four years, he had made the party a unified, Washington-centered organization, and himself the master of it.

Still another indication of his success in politics is the fact that, so long as he lived, the Radical and Conservative factions most of the time worked together fairly well within the Republican fold. He remained on friendly terms with men of both groups, though some of the Radicals had bitter things to say about him. The party remained much more closely knit than it was to be after he was dead and Johnson, a comparatively inept politician, had become president.

If Lincoln had been merely a shrewd politician, he would have given little cause to be remembered. A great president must not only get power (by legitimate means, of course): he must also use that power effectively for worthwhile public ends. Lincoln did both. Through his skill as a politician he was able to achieve as a statesman. In the record of his presidency (as in that of other notable presidencies) politics and statecraft cannot always be neatly disentangled.

Statesmanship is the art of the possible. The statesman realizes that he seldom if ever has an option as between the wholly good and the entirely bad. Instead, he most of the time must choose between evils of varying degree. And he sometimes must sacrifice one object in order to achieve another that he values more. So it was with Lincoln.

To him, as indeed to most Northerners, slavery had come to seem, by 1860, a terrible wrong. He said once, during the war, that he could not remember a time when he did not so think and feel. At least as early as 1837, while he was a member of the Illinois legislature, he put his thoughts on record. With a colleague, he presented a set of resolutions declaring that slavery was "founded upon both injustice and bad policy." Yet, in those same resolutions, he opposed its immediate destruction, saying that "the promulgation of abolition doctrines tends rather to increase than to abate its evils." Then and afterwards he seemed to feel, as did some other Northern leaders, like Daniel Webster, that abolitionist agitation only had the effect of riveting the chains of the slave more firmly upon him, by frightening Southerners and provoking them to defend and strengthen their "peculiar institution."

But Lincoln also had other reasons for hesitancy. Even if immediate abolition had been attainable, he doubted whether it would be a good thing, as he made clear on more than one occasion during the 1850's. He had no desire to smash, at a single blow, the way of life that Southerners had developed from a time when very few Americans, North or South, had looked upon slaveholding as a sin. And he wondered what would become of the Negroes once they had been freed; he could guess the grievous handicaps that white prejudice and the slavery background would impose upon them. To sum up: As of 1860 Lincoln thought of slavery as "an evil not to be extended," and to be tolerated and protected only to the extent that its actual presence made toleration and protection necessary. He hoped that, if the institution was prevented from spreading to new areas, it would eventually die out in the states where it already existed.

After the Civil War had begun, a growing number of Northerners demanded that abolition be made a war aim. Lincoln still held back. He overruled two of his generals, John C. Frémont and David Hunter, when in their respective military districts they proclaimed freedom for the slaves of disloyal masters. He declined to enforce the confiscation acts which Congress passed in 1861 and 1862, empowering him to seize enemy property, including slaves. For his hesitancy, he was condemned by anti-slavery zealots in the North.

But he had been elected on a party platform that pledged no interference with slavery in the states. He had taken an oath to abide by the Constitution, and in the Constitution he could find no clear authority for emancipating slaves. Even if he had such power, he knew that its exercise would outrage people in the border slave states—Maryland, Delaware, Missouri, and above all Kentucky. A rash and premature step might cause one or more of them to leave the Union and join the Confederacy. Then the war might be lost, and if it were, Lincoln would be powerless either to save the Union or to free the slaves.

As between these two objectives—reunion and emancipation—Lincoln boldly stated his preference in a letter to Greeley (August 22, 1862). "My paramount object in this struggle," Lincoln wrote, "*is* to save the Union, and is *not* either to save or destroy slavery. If I could save the Union without freeing *any* slave I would do it, and if I could save it by freeing *all* the slaves I would do it; and if I could do it by freeing some and leaving others alone I would also do that." He added: "I have here stated my purpose according to my view of *official* duty; and I intend no modification of my oft-expressed *personal* wish that all men everywhere could be free."

He believed that this "personal wish" would in time be realized, whether or not he undertook a deliberate and official anti-slavery program. He was confident that, no matter what he did, slavery could not survive the war very long. As he told congressmen from the border states in 1862, the institution would be worn away "by mere friction and abrasion—by the mere incidents of war."

In telling the congressmen that, Lincoln was trying to persuade them to accept an emancipation plan he had devised. He still dreaded the social and economic problems that might arise from the sudden freeing of millions of slaves, but he hoped by this particular plan to avoid most of those problems. According to his proposal, emancipation was to be gradual and it was to be carried out by the slave states rather than the Federal government. The Government would provide financial aid, however, so that the slaveowners could be compensated. The Government also would help the Negroes, once they were freed, to resettle in Africa, the West Indies, or other places outside the United States.

Only after he had encountered resistance to this plan did Lincoln decide to issue his Emancipation Proclamation (in its preliminary form on September 22, 1862, and in its final form on January 1, 1863). The proclamation declared free only those slaves in areas still in rebellion. It did not apply to slaves in the loyal slave states or in those parts of the South already recovered by the Union armies. As contemporary critics both at home and abroad observed, Lincoln proclaimed freedom only in places where, at the moment, he had virtually no ability to make it real. These critics failed to take his constitutional scruples into account. He based the proclamation on his presidential war powers, which would have authorized him to act, in this case, only against those who were at war with the Government. Despite its limitations, the decree was important as a symbol. It produced a general impression that abolition as well as reunion was thenceforth a Northern war aim. And the proclamation actually led to freedom for some 200,000 slaves who made their way from rebeldom into the Union lines.

The rest of the more than 3,500,000 slaves would have remained in bondage if nothing else had been done for them. But something else was done: The Thirteenth Amendment was adopted, abolishing slavery throughout the land. Lincoln was largely responsible for this. The Amendment had been held up in the House of Representatives until, in January 1865, he used his resources of patronage and persuasion upon reluctant Democrats, so as to obtain the needed two-thirds majority for its passage. After the Amendment was sent out for ratification, he rejoiced as it was approved by Illinois and then by other states. He did not live to see its final adoption, before the end of 1865.

There is a certain irony in Lincoln's reputation as the Great Emancipator, since he was so slow to take effective steps for freeing the slaves. There is even greater irony in the fact that he deserves his reputation. He deserves it because of his very slowness, his unwillingness to move until the time was ripe, until Northern opinion and the fortunes of war had advanced to a point where he could act without jeopardizing everything, including emancipation itself.

On the slavery question, Lincoln was not a doctrinaire, nor was he one on the question of reconstruction. His peace planning was flexible: it changed with changing circumstances. At the very beginning of the war, his peace terms as well as his war aims could be expressed in but a single word—*reunion*. If the process of reunion were quick and easy, he seemed to think, the rebels might be encouraged to lay down their arms. When they continued to resist, his terms became somewhat more difficult, though never so harsh as some of his fellow partisans desired.

In his annual message of December, 1863, he proposed a reconstruction plan for the states which by then had been substantially reconquered—Louisiana, Arkansas, and Tennessee. According to the plan, any of these states could apply for readmission to the Union when 10 per cent of the voters had taken an oath of future loyalty and adopted a constitution repudiating secession and abolishing slavery. Practically all of the former rebels could expect pardons, Lincoln promised. These terms undoubtedly had two general purposes. One was to hasten the end of the war by encouraging Southerners still in rebellion to give up the fight: many of them would have comparatively little to lose by doing so. The other purpose was to hasten reunion once the war was over.

The generous pardon policy induced a number of individual Confederate soldiers to surrender, but the "10 per cent plan" did not weaken the determination of the Confederate government and people to resist. Nor did the plan meet with universal approval in the North. The Radical Republicans condemned it and offered as a substitute the Wade-Davis bill of 1864. This bill would have made reconstruction much more difficult by requiring a majority, not merely 10 per cent, of a state's voters to approve the new

constitution, and by compelling them to take an oath of past instead of future loyalty. Lincoln, while pocket-vetoing the bill,
announced that he would gladly accept any states which might
choose to re-enter the Union according to its terms.

Later, as the war was drawing to a close, some Republicans
began to insist upon more extreme measures than those provided
in the Wade-Davis bill. These Republicans demanded that political
rights be taken from leading Confederates and given to the freed
slaves.

It is hard to say exactly to what point Lincoln's planning for
the post-war South had developed by the end of the war. He still
believed, as he had believed all along, that the main object should
be to restore the "seceded states, so-called," to their "proper practical relations" with the Union. He still maintained that some of
the states, like Louisiana and Tennessee, should be admitted on
the basis of his 10 per cent plan. In the case of other states, like
Virginia and North Carolina, he seemed willing to recognize the
existing rebel governments, at least as a temporary expedient. He
intended to leave the problem of race relations to the Southern
states; he hoped they would discover some way by which whites
and Negroes "could gradually live themselves out of their old relations to each other, and both come out better prepared for the
new." He advocated that the states provide education for the
freedmen. He also suggested that the states give the vote to some
of the colored people—"as, for instance, the very intelligent, and
especially those who fought gallantly in our ranks." But he offered
no uniform, detailed plan to be enforced upon the South.

His approach to reconstruction was guided by the spirit of his
second inaugural: "with malice toward none, with charity for
all." Whether, if he had lived, he could have carried on in such
a spirit—that is another question.

War aims and peace plans occupied a great deal of President
Lincoln's attention because they were subjects of raging controversy as well as fundamental importance. Important matters of
economic policy also came before him, but these required less of
his time and energy, because on them he had fewer differences
with his fellow Republicans in Congress and the country. "The
legitimate object of government," he thought, "is to do for a community of people whatever they need to have done, but cannot
do at all, or cannot do so well for themselves, in their separate
and individual capacities." In his younger days, as a Whig, he had

heartily approved Henry Clay's program of encouraging business and developing resources by means of a national bank, a protective tariff, and Federal expenditures for improving transportation. As president, he favored a similar program, which the Republicans had inherited from the Whigs. During the war, Congress passed, and he signed, bills establishing a national banking system, raising the tariff, and providing aid for the construction of a "transcontinental" railroad.

Generally he left the details of finance to his secretary of the treasury, and the details of foreign affairs to his secretary of state. Never did he abdicate responsibility; sometimes he overruled his department heads. Early in his administration he had to show who was boss. Before the firing on Fort Sumter, Seward urged an aggressive policy toward France and Spain, even at the risk of foreign war. Seward believed that an international crisis would distract Americans from their domestic quarrel, rouse them to a patriotic fever, and thus reunite the North and the South. Later, at the time of the "Trent affair," he came close to provoking England to a fight. On both occasions, Lincoln rather gently checked his secretary of state. Indeed, from the outset he made it plain to Seward and all others in his Cabinet that *he*, not any of them, was the chief executive.

According to the Constitution, the president not only has duties as the civilian head of government: he also is the military head, the commander in chief of the Army and the Navy. President Lincoln was no more inclined to evade his military responsibilities than he was his civilian ones. Besides making decisions on patronage and policy, he continually faced problems having to do with the conduct of the war.

In the beginning he was ill-prepared for dealing with them. He possessed no military experience except for his brief service in the Black Hawk War (1831-32), during which he saw no "live, fighting Indians" but had "a good many bloody struggles with the mosquitoes," as he afterwards joked. As president, he again and again confessed his ignorance of the art of warfare. Eager to learn, he gathered books on tactics and strategy and studied them night after night. He also went to army officers and listened to their advice. Before long he discovered that the experts did not always agree among themselves, did not always trust their own views, and did not always make sense. So, despite his inexperience, he often had to judge for himself about military as well as civilian matters.

His first big decision, as commander in chief, had to do with Fort Sumter, in Charleston Harbor. At the time of his inauguration, United States troops still held this fort, but they could not hold it long, for they were running short of essential supplies. The Confederates claimed the fort and threatened it with their harbor batteries. Lincoln was in a dilemma. If he permitted Sumter's evacuation, he would be going back on his oath to execute the laws, and he would yield a psychological advantage to the Confederates. But if he undertook to strengthen the garrison, he would risk a war. His general in chief and top military adviser, the veteran Winfield Scott, urged him to withdraw the troops. Lincoln decided, instead, to send a relief expedition, after first notifying the Confederates. Without waiting for the expedition to arrive, they opened fire on the fort (April 12, 1861). Thus they became the aggressors, so far as the North was concerned. Though losing Sumter, Lincoln won the psychological advantage of rallying his people to defend themselves against attack.

His second important decision was to proclaim a blockade of the Southern ports, and he did so just one week after the first shell had exploded over Sumter. This was his own idea—not the suggestion of any of his generals. "Judicious indeed," G. F. R. Henderson has said, "was the policy which, at the very outset of the war, brought the tremendous pressure of the sea-power to bear against the South; and, had her statesmen possessed the knowledge of what that pressure meant, they must have realized that Abraham Lincoln was no ordinary foe." Month after month, as the Navy grew, the blockade became increasingly tight, and it contributed beyond measure to the final winning of the war.

In his next crucial decision, Lincoln adopted the idea of advancing his armies on several fronts at once. Again he disagreed with General Scott. The general proposed what has been called the "Anaconda" plan. This was a comparatively passive and bloodless strategy of avoiding battle with the Confederate forces in Virginia, moving down the Mississippi valley and getting control of the river, and then simply holding the South in what might be viewed as a gigantic squeeze. Unimpressed by Scott's proposal, Lincoln could not help feeling that the war would have to be actively fought if it ever was to be won. So (in July, 1861) he ordered a direct advance on the Virginia front, an advance which resulted in defeat and rout at Bull Run. For the next several days he pondered the lessons to be learned from this defeat. "I state my general idea of this war to be," he later wrote to one of his generals, "that we have the *greater* numbers, and the enemy has the *greater* facility of concentrating forces upon points of collision; that we must fail, unless we can find some way of making *our* advantage an overmatch for *his;* and that this can only be done by menacing him with superior forces at *different* points, at the *same* time."

Lincoln had the right basic idea; he now needed a general in chief who would see that it was carried out. He accepted the resignation of Scott (November, 1861) and put George B. McClellan in his place. But McClellan, after training and equipping a fine, large army, refused to do anything with it until Lincoln finally ordered him to advance. When McClellan did start out he chose a roundabout route that Lincoln disapproved. So Lincoln demoted him to the command of the Army of the Potomac alone, compelled him to alter his plans, and, after the Seven Days Battle outside of Richmond, ordered him to abandon his campaign. Then Lincoln tried a succession of army commanders in Virginia—John Pope, McClellan again, Ambrose E. Burnside, Joseph Hooker, and George Gordon Meade—but was disappointed with each of them in turn. Meanwhile, for a few months, he got along as best he could without a general in chief. He had only a nominal general in chief even after he appointed Henry W. Halleck to the post, for Halleck was willing to give advice but shrank from responsibility.

For nearly two years President Lincoln, General Halleck, and War Secretary Edwin M. Stanton acted as a kind of war council. Lincoln transmitted official orders to his field generals through Halleck. He also sent personal suggestions directly to the generals. Some of these suggestions were excellent, as for example the hint that he once telegraphed to General Hooker: "I think *Lee's* army, and not Richmond, is your true objective point." But Lincoln would have done better to provide for the transmission of all orders and suggestions in a regular and unconfusing way. For the most effective prosecution of the war, he still had two vital decisions to make. He still had to select a supreme commander whom he could trust, and he had to devise a system for unifying and maximizing the entire war effort.

At length he looked to the West for a general to take charge of all the armies. He had admired the Vicksburg campaign of Ulysses S. Grant. Nine days after the Vicksburg surrender (in July, 1863) he sent Grant a "grateful acknowledgment for the almost inestimable service" he had done the country. As he did so, he incidentally showed one of his own best qualities as a war leader—his willingness to learn, his readiness to admit his errors. He said he had expected Grant to bypass Vicksburg and go on down the Mississippi, instead of crossing the river and turning back to approach Vicksburg from the rear. "I feared it was a mistake," Lincoln wrote in his letter of congratulation. "I now wish to make the personal acknowledgment that you were right, and I was wrong." In March, 1864, he promoted Grant to lieutenant general, the highest rank at that time, and put him in command of the Union armies as a whole. Lincoln had found a man who—with such able subordinates as William T. Sherman, Philip Sheridan, and George H. Thomas—could complete the work that remained to be done in giving reality to Lincoln's strategic concept.

Preferring to have his headquarters in the field, Grant accompanied and directed the Army of the Potomac instead of staying in Washington. This made it difficult for him to coordinate the day-to-day movements of all the armies. After a Confederate raid on the capital (July, 1864) Lincoln took steps to assure the fullest coordination. He put the finishing touches on an over-all command system that had been gradually developing. The key members were Grant, Halleck, Stanton, and Lincoln. Grant, the general in chief, directed all the armies, as before. Halleck, the chief of staff, continued to advise the President and to serve as a liaison with the military men. Stanton, the secretary of war, took charge of raising soldiers and procuring supplies. Lincoln, the commander in chief, supervised and integrated the work of the other three.

And he did something else of importance to the successful waging of the war. Thousands of inventors brought forth new kinds of arms and ammunition which presumably might help to win it. Some of these inventions were useless, or worse than that, being unreliable and dangerous to the user, but others had real promise. The promising ones needed to be sorted out, tested, further developed, and perhaps adopted. There was, during the Civil War, no Government agency for seeing that all this was done—no agency comparable to the Office of Scientific Research and Development which took the responsibility during the Second World War. So Lincoln acted as a kind of one-man OSRD. He welcomed inventors and promoters, who sought him out with sketches, models, and samples. If interested, he arranged for demonstrations and tests, sometimes firing an experimental gun himself. To the Army and Navy ordnance officials he recommended the adoption of weapons he approved. Thus he contributed much to wartime progress in military technology, to the development and introduction of explosive bullets, incendiary shells, mortars, repeating rifles, and even machine guns.

Lincoln has been severely condemned—and extravagantly praised—for his conduct of the Civil War. On the one hand, he has been accused of amateurish meddling with the business of professional soldiers. On the other, he has been hailed as a military genius. Certainly he demonstrated a remarkable capacity for growth in military knowledge and leadership, becoming much more effective as a commander in chief the last year than the first. His lack of training and experience in military matters may have been more an advantage than a handicap. Unhampered by outdated concepts of warfare, he could all the better apply his practical insight and common sense to the changing requirements of victorious strategy.

Professionals like McClellan thought that Lincoln, a mere "politician," should have left war-making entirely to them. They protested against any "political" interference with strategy. Yet, in a democracy at war, it would be neither feasible nor desirable to eliminate "politics" (in the broad sense of policy-making by civilian leaders politically responsible to the people). In the Civil War Lincoln was doing what politicians have done in war time before and since. Congress "interfered" in the conduct of the Revolutionary War and gave instructions to General Washington. President Madison along with his Cabinet ran the War of 1812; and President Polk, the war with Mexico. Franklin D. Roosevelt, in cooperation with Winston Churchill, seldom hesitating to overrule the highest brass, shaped and directed strategy in the Second World War. These civilian leaders acted essentially as Lincoln did, but, considering the peculiar difficulty of his task, he stands out above them all.

"Our popular government has often been called an experiment," Lincoln said in 1861. "Two points in it, our people have already settled—the successful *establishing*, and the successful *administering* of it. One still remains—its successful *maintenance* against a formidable attempt to overthrow it."

This was the central issue of the Civil War, in Lincoln's view. From time to time he was to rephrase the issue, elaborate upon it, put it in words of increasing eloquence. He also had to deal with the problem as a practical matter, in his day-to-day use of his presidential powers. This meant facing one dilemma after another, and often a dilemma of excruciating sharpness. For he was undertaking to maintain a popular government, that is, a democracy, and so he hesitated to use other than democratic means. Yet these sometimes seemed hardly adequate to the emergencies that he continually faced.

After the war had begun he called Congress to meet in a special session—but not for nearly three months. During that time he took, on his own, a number of rather drastic steps, such as enlarging the Army and suspending the writ of habeas corpus (so that persons of doubtful loyalty could be arrested without formal charges and held without a trial). Had he done otherwise, the war might have been lost at the very outset. The state of Maryland presented a special danger, for that state contained numerous Confederate sympathizers and outright secessionists. In Baltimore a mob attacked a regiment of Massachusetts troops bound for the defense of Washington. Some Maryland legislators planned to hold a secession convention in the state. Only by prompt and drastic action could Lincoln be sure of protecting the routes between Washington and the North and holding the capital itself. He acted promptly and drastically, authorizing many arrests.

He was accused of acting illegally and, indeed, tyrannically. When Congress met, he sought (and obtained) justification for what he had done. He reminded Congress that he had taken an oath to see that the laws were faithfully executed. Suppose it were true that he himself had violated a law—with respect to the writ of habeas corpus. "The whole of the laws which were required to be faithfully executed, were being resisted, and failing of execution, in nearly one-third of the states," he said. Then he asked: "Must they be allowed to finally fail of execution, even had it been perfectly clear, that by the use of the means necessary to their execution, some single law, made in such extreme tenderness of the citizen's liberty, that practically, it relieves more of the guilty, than of the innocent, should, to a very limited extent, be violated? To state the question more directly, are all the laws, *but one*, to go unexecuted, and the government itself go to pieces, lest that one be violated?"

On later occasions Lincoln also authorized his generals to make arbitrary arrests, but he was careful to go no farther than the needs of the emergency made absolutely essential. He thought that, as the war progressed, the opinions and actions of the people would become less confused and more regular, so that the necessity for arbitrary measures would gradually decrease. "Still," he said, "I must continue to do as much as may seem to be required by the public safety."

Of all the military arrests, the most spectacular was that of Clement L. Vallandigham, an Ohio Democrat who, in and out of Congress, opposed the war and insisted that the draft was unconstitutional. The seizure of such an important politician proved embarrassing to Lincoln. He dared not let Vallandigham go scot free. "Must I shoot a simple-minded soldier boy who deserts," he asked, "while I must not touch a hair of a wily agitator who induces him to desert?" On the other hand, he did not wish to make a martyr of Vallandigham by holding him as a prisoner. Lincoln disposed of this dilemma by banishing the "wily agitator" within the Confederate lines.

In several instances Lincoln allowed his generals to close down hostile newspapers, but not for long. He stated his policy in these instructions to an army officer: "You will only arrest individuals and suppress assemblies or newspapers when they may be working palpable injury to the military in your charge, and in no other case will you interfere with the expression of opinion in any form or allow it to be interfered with violently by others. In this you have a discretion to exercise with great caution, calmness, and forbearance."

Lincoln was repeatedly called a dictator by his political opponents and the opposition press. He was in fact no dictator, and he had not the slightest inclination to be one. He found no easy way to dispose of questions regarding free speech in wartime—questions that still defy the best minds and wills of democratic leadership. But he proceeded cautiously and, on the whole, quite sanely. Indeed, considering the dangers and provocations of his time, he stands out as an exemplar of liberal statesmanship. He acted like a democrat.

And he spoke like one. Perhaps his greatest and most lasting contributions to the democratic cause are to be found in things he said as much as in things he did. He was a self-taught master of the literary art. Sensitive to words, he could use them to convey ideas with the utmost precision, or to stir the spirit with subtle and moving overtones. As a young man, he wanted to be a poet. Though he failed to write more than passable verse, he succeeded in writing some of the most poetic prose in the English language. The best of his prose embodies in enduring form the ideals and aspirations of the American people—and of all peoples with hopes of governing themselves.

Again and again Lincoln declared that his main object, as President, was to save the Union. He was a spokesman for the nation's interest, for nationalism. But he stood for more than that. To him, the Union was valuable in itself, but it was even more valuable in what it meant, to his own country and to the rest of the world. He repeatedly pointed out that the Civil War involved a principle of universal concern. "And this issue embraces more than the fate of these United States," he once put it. "It presents to the whole family of man, the question, whether a constitutional republic, or a democracy—a government of the people, by the same people—can, or cannot, maintain its territorial integrity, against its own domestic foes." He added: "It forces us to ask: 'Is there, in all republics, this inherent, and fatal weakness?' 'Must a government, of necessity, be too *strong* for the liberties of its own people, or too *weak* to maintain its own existence?'"

Surely this is the fundamental difficulty confronting all democratic governments—the difficulty of reconciling liberty and authority, the rights of the individual and the welfare of the group. No political theoretician or philosopher, Lincoln did not write treatises on methods of dealing with this difficulty. But he accurately viewed it as the essential issue of the war and thus helped to give the war the broad significance it deserved. His own commitment to democracy he stated in more and more effective language, culminating in those final words of the Gettysburg Address: "that from these honored dead we take increased devotion to that cause for which they gave the last full measure of devotion —that we here highly resolve that these dead shall not have died in vain—that this nation, under God, shall have a new birth of freedom—and that government of the people, by the people, for the people, shall not perish from the earth."

Lincoln came to see a deep spiritual as well as political significance in the war. He adopted no simple and self-righteous view that God was on his side, and the devil on the other. Not that he supposed the rebel cause was just and would win, but neither did he believe wickedness was a monopoly of the South. More and more, as the war dragged on and the casualty lists lengthened, he thought he saw the will of God at work. God, being all-powerful, could have prevented the war or could have ended it promptly with a victory for either side. Yet the struggle continued. Lincoln concluded that there must be some divine and unseen purpose in the protraction of the bloodshed. The purpose must be not only to preserve the Union but also to remove the sin of slavery and at the same time to punish the people, North as well as South, for their common guilt. Lincoln said in the second inaugural: "If we shall suppose that American slavery is one of those offences which, in the providence of God, must needs come, but which, having continued through His appointed time, He now wills to remove, and that He gives to both North and South, this terrible war, as the woe due to those by whom the offence came, shall we discern therein any departure from those divine attributes which the believers in a Living God always ascribe to Him?"

Lincoln lives because he could perceive the universal in the things about him, the eternal in the passing events of his time.

Grover Cleveland

by VINCENT P. DE SANTIS

Surveying the American scene after the Civil War, Walt Whit-
man hailed "with pride and joy" this country's technical
achievements, the "beating up of the wilderness into fertile
farms . . . her railroads, ships, [and] machinery." Yet he lamented
that with all this:

> unprecedented materialistic advancement—society, in these
> States, is canker'd, crude, superstitious, and rotten. Political,
> or law-made society is, and private or voluntary society, is
> also. . . . Never was there, perhaps, more hollowness at heart
> than at present. . . . Genuine belief seems to have left us. . . .
> We live in an atmosphere of hypocrisy throughout. . . . The
> official services of America, national, state, and municipal,
> in all their branches and departments, except the judiciary,
> are saturated in corruption, bribery, falsehood, mal-adminis-
> tration; and the judiciary is tainted.

Other thoughtful Americans agreed with Whitman's harsh indict-
ment of politics and politicians of the post–Civil War generation.
"No period so thoroughly ordinary has been known in American
politics since Christopher Columbus first disturbed the balance of
power in American society," wrote Henry Adams, the mordant
commentator of the Gilded Age. "One might search the whole list
of Congress, Judiciary, and Executive during the twenty-five

years 1870-1895 and find little but damaged reputations. The period was poor in purpose and barren in results."

The impulse to spring to the aid of the underdog has brought forth champions of the cultural, literary, and technological achievements of the Gilded Age but none to defend its political record. "Even among the most powerful men of that generation," said Adams, speaking of the politicians, there were "none who had a good word to say for it." Most historians have felt that at no other period in American history was the moral and intellectual tone of political life so uniformly low or were political conflicts so concerned with patronage rather than with principles. James Bryce in his classic, *The American Commonwealth*, found that "tenets and policies, points of political doctrine and points of political practice have all but vanished. . . . All has been lost, except office or the hope of it." The two major parties in this period, concluded Bryce, "were like two bottles. Each bore a label denoting the kind of liquor it contained, but each was empty."

Likewise, American historians have censured the politics of these years for being barren, dreary, and monotonous. They have condemned the parties for evading issues, for dodging the responsibility of enacting major legislation, for not reflecting the moods and purposes of the American people, for deteriorating into a group of spoilsmen, for ignoring the needs of the farmer, the laborer, and the consumer in the industrial age, and for best serving the ends of business as they were themselves best served by business collaboration. It is no wonder then that historians have pictured the twentieth century of Woodrow Wilson and of the two Roosevelts as a time when America struggled out of the darkness into the light.

It has become a historical convention to represent Grover Cleveland's presidency as the most distinguished one of the Gilded Age. "He alone of the Presidents of this generation had some suspicion of the significance and direction of the economic changes that were transforming the country and made some effort to grapple with the problems created by change," writes Professor Henry Steele Commager. "He alone of the titular leaders of either party had sufficient courage to defy the privilege groups and the pressure groups that were using the government for selfish purposes and to risk his political career in defense of what he thought was honest and right." Professor Allan Nevins, who has made the most exhaustive study of Cleveland, associates four achievements with his name. He restored honesty and impartiality to government;

he planted deep in the American mind the idea that the evils of the protective tariff system ought to be abolished; he saved the nation from the abandonment of the gold standard at a time when abandonment might have produced economic chaos; and he taught the American people that in their handling of foreign affairs, conscience should always be the one dominant force.

Yet, Cleveland's greatness as a president commonly rests, not so much upon his accomplishments or brilliance, as upon his character. According to Professor Richard Hofstadter, Cleveland stood out "if only for honesty and independence, as the sole reasonable facsimile of a major president between Lincoln and Theodore Roosevelt." Many historians have praised Cleveland for his courage, firmness, uprightness, self-direction, and common sense. "It is as a strong man, a man of character, that Cleveland will live in history," writes Professor Nevins. "It was his personality, not his mind, that made so deep an impress upon his time." In fact, says Nevins, Cleveland's greatest service to the country was to leave to subsequent generations an example of "courage that never yields an inch in the cause of truth, and that never surrenders an iota of principle to expediency." Thus the image of a fearless and heroic figure hewing the line developed about Cleveland, and in general, historians have maintained this portrait.

Actually Cleveland was stolid, unimaginative, stubborn, and indifferent to his popularity. Yet he appealed to Americans, because he seemed to be a plain man of the people and because he persistently appeared to do what he believed to be right. William Allen White has described Cleveland's appeal in the following manner:

> He was plain-spoken. If he thought a proposition was a steal he said so, and he used the short word. A robber, a thief, a sneak, a liar, and a cheat wore no perfunctory titles in the bright lexicon of Cleveland's veto messages. Naturally the people were pleased. . . . What the people desired just then with a furious passion was a vigorous, uncompromising man . . . who would save the State from its statesmen. The times crying out for an obstructionist to stem corruption found young Grover Cleveland.

In spite of his solid personal qualities Cleveland's presidency was largely a negative one. While it might be possible to praise his good intentions it is impossible to credit him with any major achievements. "He was too conservative to be a great constructive statesman," writes Professor Nevins. More to the point is the fact that Cleveland seemed to be unaware of, or unable to comprehend the fundamental economic and social problems of his day. He simply did not understand the sweeping changes that had come to America with the rise of industrial capitalism. Because of his intense opposition to what he called "paternalism," Cleveland was unsympathetic to the needs and protests of the nation's farmers and workers during the greatest depression that the country had yet seen. Still, if the total achievements of Cleveland's administration were more negative than positive, says Professor Commager, "it may yet be maintained that the ability to say 'no' and mean 'no' was in itself no mean achievement." To have bequeathed the country "such an example of iron fortitude," writes Professor Nevins, "is better than to have swayed parliaments or to have won battles or to have annexed provinces."

Cleveland's winning of the presidency in 1884 disrupted twenty-four years of unbroken Republican rule in this high office. He became the first elected Democratic president since James Buchanan, and while this event was looked upon by old-time Republican leaders as a major catastrophe, Democrats hailed it with gun salutes, fireworks, and hymns of joy. The Republicans referred to Cleveland as "His Accidency," and there was much truth in the phrase. His climb to power was rapid and favored by fortune. Until 1881 his only political experience had been as a young Democratic ward worker, as assistant district attorney, and as sheriff of Erie County in the state of New York. Then, in four years, he rose from the mayor's office in Buffalo to the executive mansion in Washington.

Cleveland, the son of a Presbyterian clergyman, was born in the small town of Caldwell, New Jersey. A few years later his family moved to Fayetteville in western New York, and there, and in nearby Clinton, the future president spent his boyhood. Cleveland's father died when the boy was sixteen leaving the mother with nine children on her hands. After a few years of earning his own living, Cleveland went to stay with his uncle in Buffalo, and this relative, being rich and influential, was able to put him into one of the best law offices in this rapidly growing city.

For the next twenty-six years, 1855–82, Cleveland remained in Buffalo and seldom went anywhere else for business or pleasure.

Perhaps the most significant aspect of Cleveland's years in Buffalo was the inadequate preparation for public life and the parochial outlook which they furnished him. Since he rarely traveled beyond the limits of the city, this provincialism imposed a limitation upon his understanding of the economic and political problems in other parts of the country. To him such pressing questions as unemployment, long hours of work, and low pay, seemed remote and unimportant. Like many other citizens of Buffalo, Cleveland felt that other communities should and could take care of themselves just as his own city did. Being kind and sympathetic, Cleveland did help the needy, but his name never appeared on the published lists of contributors to causes, such as the Buffalo Hospital or the Chicago Fire sufferers. Cleveland never served on the board of trustees of a charitable institution or supported the idea that charitable activity was one of the functions of government.

On the other hand, in these same years, Cleveland developed some of the qualities that he displayed in the presidency. It was by dogged industry and reliability rather than by any outstanding talents that he became one of the most prominent lawyers in Buffalo. If his apprehension was slow it was sure, and he exhibited a near genius for application and a resolute purpose to master every question that came before him. He had phenomenal physical energy and a striking ability to disregard comfort. "His power of concentration was only limited by physical demands," one of Cleveland's fellow attorneys noted, "and he worked for twenty-four hours at a stretch without feeling the need for rest—indeed, I think he was insensible to his physical requirements. When his task was ended, his physical reaction was like that of a suddenly released spring." At times he would spend the noon hour studying, when his law partners were at lunch, and when pressed would stay at his desk until two or three in the morning. But his deliberation and industry were no more remarkable than his honesty, a trait so dominant, according to one of the most distinguished members of the Buffalo bar, that "everybody felt it."

By 1880 Cleveland, with a lucrative, business-connected law practice, appeared to be a permanent fixture in the life of Buffalo. Then a series of chance events pushed him into the political limelight. A group of Buffalo citizens had become aroused over the corruption and inefficiency that characterized the city government for many years regardless of the party in power. When the Republican leaders failed to heed this danger signal and nominated dubious characters for mayor and other city offices, a large number of their own party suggested to the Democrats the plan of choosing a respectable candidate. The reformers and practical politicians were seeking a watchdog of the public funds. What better choice than this lawyer of candor and conservatism, Grover Cleveland? Showing no outward ambition for party leadership, Cleveland reluctantly agreed to run. His platform called for honesty and economy, and in view of the Republican revolt, his election was never in doubt. Proceeding to carry out his promises once in office, Cleveland began to win recognition in New York state as an able city administrater and for his blunt vetoes of questionable measures proposed by the city council rather than by a positive program of his own.

As a result, Cleveland now developed the ambition to become governor. To obtain this goal he resorted to a political technique that was to characterize the rest of his career in public life. Cleveland's carefully cultivated public image was that of a reluctant candidate who sought office without seeming to be a self-seeking candidate; who quietly accepted machine support, yet maintained an air of independence. While this formula was as old as politics itself, few public men have had such remarkable success with it as Cleveland. That success resulted not so much from his particular abilities as from his extraordinary luck. For example, Cleveland's nomination and election as governor of New York in 1882 were accidental. With few Democratic leaders of outstanding qualities in the state, with the party leadership unable to unite on a candidate, and with the public in a mood to vote against machine politicians, Cleveland's reputation for independence and uprightness gained for him the nomination on an early ballot. He went on to win the election largely because of a split in Republican ranks.

As governor, Cleveland offended Democrats and Republicans alike. He scorned Tammany Hall, flouted the labor faction of his party, and vetoed a bill to compel elevated railroads to keep their passenger fares at five cents. He had few friends and no inner group of advisers. He usually played a lone hand. Brutally forthright and lacking in congeniality, Cleveland was also quite stubborn and uncompromising. It should also be noted that he showed little understanding of the broader and more positive role that government could play. He held the prevalent view of his day that government ought not to interfere in the economic and social life of the people except to maintain law and order and to protect property rights. Known as a veto governor, Cleveland contented himself with pointing out the technical weaknesses of the bills he returned unsigned, but rarely urged or inspired remedial action. With such a reputation Cleveland endeared himself to the conservatives and businessmen in both parties. After he had vetoed the bill to maintain elevated railway fares, Andrew White exclaimed that Cleveland had overcome his "sympathies for the working people," and praised him for having "not the slightest germ of demagogism." Jay Gould, who controlled the elevated railroad in New York City, sent Cleveland a telegraphic message of congratulation in 1885: "I feel . . . that the vast business interests of the country will be entirely safe in your hands."

Grover Cleveland's election to the presidency in 1884 represented more of a change in spirit than it did in policies. The Democratic party was largely in the hands of Eastern conservatives who did not differ basically from their Republican counterparts. This Eastern conservative faction had gained control of the Democratic party machinery in 1868 and used it to suppress agrarian and labor discontent, as well as to fight corruption and inefficiency. These Democrats believed that governmental interference with the natural laws of economics was both futile and wicked. Government regulation and government aid should be kept to a minimum. Since taxation was a drag on the economy, it too must be severely limited. Yet they also opposed the protective tariff on similar grounds: that it interfered with the economic natural law, was government paternalism, and was a subsidy to privileged interests. Most protariff manufacturers were Republicans; most antitariff bankers, merchants, and railroad operators were conservative Democrats. While the latter could have friendly relations with their fellow Republicans, they became outcasts with the party hierarchy if they made concessions to farmers or workers. In fact, conservative Democrats did not shrink from electoral defeats if only party control remained firmly in their own hands.

While Cleveland had the reputation of a reformer, it was not expected that he would enter office with a bold progressive program or that he would display vigorous leadership. Rather it was anticipated that he would bring greater honesty and sincerity to the presidency. His campaign speeches had emphasized the need for a new moral attitude. To Cleveland the need for corrective action took precedence over that of constructive action. A great many Americans agreed with him.

The Republican party seemed to be losing whatever moral fiber it once possessed. All the political crimes in the catalogue—nepotism, corruption, inefficiency, misrule, bitter partisanship—appeared to flourish in the Republican party. According to one of its members, Senator James Wilson Grimes of Iowa, it was "the most corrupt and debauched political party that had ever existed." One of the principal needs of the country at the time of Cleveland's election was a thorough elimination of the baser elements of political life. Because of his reputation as a reformer many Americans looked to Cleveland to clean the Augean stables.

The key to Cleveland's presidency was his dislike of paternalism in government. He opposed the idea of the Government's giving aid to anybody in distress, and his political philosophy in this respect is best illustrated in his veto of the Texas Seed bill early in 1887. Certain Texas counties had suffered from a drought and were in pressing need for seed grain. In response to the pleas of a number of sufferers Congress passed a bill appropriating ten thousand dollars to allow the Commissioner of Agriculture to distribute seed. The amount was trivial, but the measure sharply challenged Cleveland's belief. He returned the bill unsigned, with a strong protest, for he felt it was wrong "to indulge a benevolent and charitable sentiment through the appropriation of public funds" for this purpose. "I can find no warrant for such an appropriation in the Constitution, and I do not believe that the power and duty of the General Government ought to be expended to the relief of individual suffering which is in no manner properly related to the public service or benefit." Then he added significantly: "A prevalent tendency to disregard the limited mission of this [the Government's] power and duty should, I think, be steadfastly resisted, to the end that the lesson should constantly be enforced that though the people support the Government the Government should not support the people."

In other phrases of this memorable veto which have been quoted again and again in behalf of the same philosophy, Cleveland reminded Americans that, "Federal aid in such cases encourages the expectation of paternal care on the part of the Government and weakens the sturdiness of our national character. . . .

The friendliness and charity of our countrymen can always be relied upon to relieve their fellow-citizens in misfortune." In his second inaugural address in 1893, Cleveland returned to this theme when he dwelt at length on the "unwholesome progeny of paternalism," and when, in the midst of acute distress for a large number of Americans, he complacently added, "while the people should patriotically and cheerfully support their Government its functions do not include the support of the people."

The thrifty liberalism of Cleveland appealed to the conservative businessmen, but it provided little consolation to the masses of the people. Cleveland fought the idea of the social service state. He believed that government should seldom intervene except for a negative end. He would do nothing to assist the farmer in his economic plight, but he would stand against inflation. He would not help to maintain the worker's wages in a depression, but he would use the army to break a strike. Cleveland's political and economic beliefs were the prevalent ones of his day, the point of view known as Social Darwinism that linked evolution with mechanical progress and the survival of the fittest with the economic theories of laissez faire. Actually Cleveland was an extreme conservative, and the people's quest for social justice advanced no further under Cleveland's administration than it had under his Republican predecessors and successors in the post–Civil War generation. In his political and economic thinking Cleveland so closely resembled the Republican presidents of the Gilded Age, that when Woodrow Wilson, a progressive Democrat, entered the White House in 1913, he believed he was the first Democrat to do so since James Buchanan in 1857. "This country has never had a Democratic administration since the Civil War," Wilson told a group of senators visiting him. "You may think Cleveland's administration was Democratic. It was not. Cleveland was a conservative Republican."

In Cleveland's opinion Americans were entitled to economy, purity, and justice in their Government and nothing more. There was to be a fair field for all and favors for none. Cleveland's conception of his role as president was that of a righteous watchdog whose business it was to look after other politicians and to prevent them from giving favors and taking graft. Thus he opposed tariff favors to business, pension favors to veterans, and land favors to railroads. Cleveland's two terms of obstruction mark his place in history as an almost purely negative president, who believed it was his duty to prevent bad things from occurring, but not to make good things happen.

When Cleveland took office he knew nothing about being president and nearly nothing about the great national issues. Yet, he intended, he said, to have around him the best minds, which would shun "extravagance and waste." In his first inaugural address he declared that "The people demand reform in the administration of the government, and the application of business principles to public affairs." He had a Cabinet of able conservative businessmen to help fulfill this demand. All of them had been successful in politics, law, or business, and they favored lower tariff rates and opposed extensive Government regulation and subsidies. But nowhere in the Cabinet was there a representative of the farmers, who made up the largest segment of the population, or of labor, or of various minority groups. And as Cleveland began the actual work of being president it was quite clear that he meant to keep the words of his inaugural. Practically ignoring the matter of legislation, Cleveland spent all his time at his first Cabinet meeting and most of his time at the next six meetings discussing departmental reforms.

Cleveland had no inner group of counselors who had accompanied his progression from Buffalo to Albany to Washington. Daniel Lamont had been his private secretary as governor and came to Washington to serve the President in the same capacity until Cleveland made him secretary of war in the second administration. Lamont was indispensable as a political adviser, although the President also relied heavily upon the counsel of Daniel Manning and William C. Whitney who headed the Treasury and Navy Departments respectively. Manning represented the influence and point of view of Samuel J. Tilden and the Democratic party in New York state. His appointment also pleased the friends of sound money, for he was a strong conservative on economic matters. Whitney was an added counselor from the New York organization. He was fully attached to Cleveland, who held him in great respect, and the ties between them became even stronger during the years in Washington.

There was little staff assistance in the White House executive office in Cleveland's day to help the President with major policy matters. There was no brain trust to supply the President with ideas and to provide him with a friendly opposition. Neither was there a group of administrative assistants to put his ideas into form and to do important tasks. "As the executive office is now organized," Cleveland observed, "it can deal, with a fair amount of efficiency, with the routine affairs of Government; but if the President has any great policy in mind or on hand, he has no one to help him work it out." To remedy this situation, Cleveland considered naming William L. Wilson, who had served both in the Cabinet and the House of Representatives, as assistant to the president at a salary of ten thousand dollars a year. When he could find no appropriation, Cleveland gave up the idea, saying, "I have even half a notion to offer him the place anyhow and pay him out of my own pocket."

Another major difficulty for Cleveland, particularly in handling public opinion, was his inability to get along with the press. Urged to invite friendly editors and publishers to dinner, he refused on the ground that he should not make himself "familiar with them" simply because they were personally agreeable. Neither was he much more cordial to reporters and correspondents. Cleveland looked upon this liability of temperament as an asset when he declared himself "thankful that the efforts to create an unconscious but effective censorship of the press never had any encouragement from me at any point in my public career."

In his relations with Congress, Cleveland made little effort to bring the political branches of the Government into an effective unit as did some of his distinguished successors. In fact, in his first years of office, he was one of the least inclined of all presidents to quarrel with Congress over a matter of power. Cleveland had great reverence for the doctrine of separated powers, and his favorite political theme was the "Independence of the Executive." This view, however, caused him a great deal of trouble, and in the end he had to give it up. But his reluctance to interfere with Congress was the despair of his friends. William L. Wilson, quite disappointed by the outcome of the Wilson-Gorman Tariff of 1894, confided to his diary how he felt about Cleveland's relationship with members of Congress. He regarded Cleveland as woefully "lacking in the tact of making ordinary men and especially representative public men feel a personal friendship and personal loyalty to him by little social and conventional attentions. Always courteous, frequently kindly, always frank and business-like he yet did not seem to think of the power he had, and possibly the duty he was under, to tie men to him by personal ties, rather than by political or business relations." Wilson believed that Cleveland could have kept many members of Congress personally friendly "by a casual invitation to lunch, or a formal invitation to dinner, a stroll together or a carriage drive." In the opinion of Woodrow Wilson, Cleveland "thought it no part of his proper function to press his preference in any other way [than by recommendation in a message] upon the acceptance of Congress. . . . But he deemed his duty done when he had thus used the only initiative given him by the Constitution and expressly declined to use any other means of pressing his views on his party. He meant to be aloof and to be President with a certain separateness as the Constitution seemed to suggest."

An excellent example of Cleveland's unwillingness to influence Congress was his handling of the monetary question shortly after he took office in 1885. In his first annual message to Congress, Cleveland said, "I recommend the suspension of the compulsory coinage of silver dollars, directed by the law passed in February, 1878." This being a major issue on which he had taken a position before his inauguration the country expected that he would use the full power of his administration to bring about the repeal of the Bland-Allison Act. But instead he publicly stated his intention of doing nothing. On January 4, 1886, he told the press:

> I believe the most important benefit that I can confer on the country by my presidency is to insist upon the entire independence of the executive and legislative branches of the government, and compel the members of the legislative branch to see that they have responsibilities of their own. . . . I believe that this is an executive office, and I deem it important that this country should be reminded of it. I have certain executive duties to perform; when that is done my responsibility ends.

When he was asked whether Congress would act favorably on his recommendations on silver, he replied he did not know. As far as he was concerned the matter was out of his hands. He did not want to prod Congress any further. This meant that the Democratic party had no leader in the legislative struggle over silver, and one Congressman complained:

If only Mr. Cleveland had been content to say nothing, he had the game in his own hands. The opposition to his policy was melting away like snow in a thaw. He need not have done anything, if only he had said nothing. We should presently have had a united party, confident and happy, with the President as our natural and proper leader. It makes me sad—for what he so needlessly said is a direct invitation to confusion and discord.

One of the first problems that Cleveland faced was that of patronage. He had to please the Mugwumps, who had done much to secure his election, and who opposed any wholesale removals from office. Yet, he also had to satisfy loyal and deserving Democrats who demanded a complete sweep. After all, the Democrats had been out of power for twenty-four years and were anxious for the spoils. "I have a hungry party behind me," the President remarked sadly. On another occasion he spoke more bluntly when he exclaimed, "the d——d everlasting clatter for office continues to some extent, and makes me feel like resigning, and Hell is to pay generally." The horde of eager office seekers annoyed and distracted Cleveland, so that he cried in anguish: "My God, what is there in this office that any man should ever want to get into it?"

At first Cleveland would not yield to the wants of the spoilsmen, a stand that won the applause of the Mugwumps. He maintained that no officeholder should be removed simply because he was a Republican unless there was evidence of incompetence or "pernicious partisanship." But the office-seekers continued to exert an unrelenting pressure upon Cleveland. They argued that the patronage belonged to them. It had been won and it must be distributed. Finally, faced with a revolt from within his own party, Cleveland yielded and Republican heads began to fall. In his first term Cleveland approved of the removal of two-thirds of the Federal employees under his immediate control. Adlai Stevenson, of Illinois, who had left Congress in 1881, became first assistant postmaster general, and had the task of making changes in the Post Office. By the summer of 1887, Stevenson had refilled 40,000 of the 52,609 fourth-class postmasterships and 2,000 of the 2,359 presidential postmasterships. Since a few Republicans did remain in appointive posts, the *Civil Service Record* could in all fairness conclude that it was "not altogether a clean sweep."

Still, Cleveland may be credited with expanding the number of classified civil servants. Only 16,000 (out of 126,000) were in the classified service when he first took office. He increased this number to 27,000 during his first administration. Yet, neither the Mugwumps nor the Democrats were satisfied, for Cleveland had antagonized the party workers by lengthening the civil service list, and he had offended the reformers by replacing Republican office-holders with "deserving Democrats.' As Carl Schurz, one of the leading Mugwumps, told Cleveland, "your attempt to please both reformers and spoilsmen has failed."

Cleveland helped to restore both the actual and symbolic powers of the chief executive. The office of the president was at a low ebb in power and prestige in the post–Civil War period. "The executive department of a republic like ours should be subordinate to the legislative department," wrote John Sherman of Ohio, one of the leading Republicans of these years. "The President should obey and enforce the laws, leaving to the people the duty of correcting any errors committed by their representatives in Congress." Though Cleveland never took issue with this viewpoint, he stood firmly on the doctrine of separation of powers. He believed that "the office of President is essentially executive in its nature. . . . to compel the members of the legislative branch to see that they have responsibilities of their own."

For nearly twenty years Republican senators had dominated the national political scene. Reluctant to relinquish their control to a Democratic chief executive, they attempted to curb Cleveland's appointive power by resorting to the Tenure of Office Act. To be sure, that infamous act (passed specifically to hamstring Andrew Johnson), had been modified by Congress when Grant became president. The original enactment had provided that no civil officer appointed with the consent of the Senate could be removed except with senatorial acquiescence. The change of 1869 took the teeth out of the Act by lifting the obligation of the president to report the evidence and reasons for suspension to the Senate. The suspended officer could not return to his old place even if the Senate refused to concur in his removal. Instead, it allowed the president to continue to make nominations for his successor until one was approved. The Senate retained its recognized authority to advise and consent to a successor nominee, but lost its power to compel the retention of a man whom the president disliked. Yet, Republican senators boldly used the Tenure of Office Act to threaten and to humiliate Cleveland. They demanded that he give them full information not only about his new nominations (which was customary procedure), but also about his dismissals. Cleveland flatly refused to supply the information for removals. Instead, in an important state paper, he set forth the constitutional role of the president on the matter of appointments and dismissals. Cleveland's exposition was an emphatic defense of the constitutional right of the executive branch to withhold from Congress all information of a private or confidential nature and to determine which material was to be classified. Presidential power was enhanced.

An open battle commenced, and the public had its first opportunity in two decades to watch a fight between a Democratic president and a Republican Senate. The Senate threatened to block all appointments, but Cleveland held most of the winning cards in his hands. He realized that the Republicans lacked real power. He knew that public opinion supported his position. Most important, if the Senate rejected one of his nominations, Cleveland could simply wait until the end of the congressional session, reappoint the official, and keep him in office until the Senate reconvened. So crucial was this issue to Cleveland—for he was defending a fundamental prerogative of the presidency—that in March, 1886, he appealed directly to the people. Within a few weeks the Republican Senators broke ranks and gave up the fight. In June, 1886, the Tenure of Office Act was repealed. "Thus," wrote Cleveland, long after the event, "was an unpleasant controversy happily followed by an expurgation of the last pretense of statutory sanction to an encroachment upon constitutional Executive prerogatives, and thus was a time-honored interpretation of the Constitution restored to us." In this spectacular contest Cleveland had gained both a personal and political victory.

Meanwhile, another controversy had broken out between Cleveland and the Republicans, much more acrimonious since it revived the bitter feelings of the Civil War. When Cleveland took office he expressed the hope that Americans would "cheerfully and honestly abandon all sectional prejudice and distrust." But he stirred up the Union veterans by placing two Southerners in his

Cabinet, by proposing to return to the South the captured Confederate battle flags, and above all by his pension policy. The Civil War pension system had been established in 1862, and by the time Cleveland became president, nearly 900,000 pension claims had been filed, some 325,000 of which had been approved. If claims were turned down, congressmen could introduce private pension bills and secure pensions for claimants in this fashion. On one particular day Congress passed four hundred such bills. Instead of investigating each bill with care, in many cases the senators merely turned them over to their secretaries and clerks. The passage of private pension bills was by general consent. There was no quorum present on "pension day," and the proceedings were ordinarily perfunctory and swift.

This type of raid on the public treasury had disgusted many thoughtful Americans. It was common knowledge that the wounds of some claimants were simulated or imaginary; others were real enough, the result perhaps of falling into canals or open cellars while intoxicated. As Charles Francis Adams noted: "We had seen every dead beat, and malingerer, every bummer, bounty-jumper, and suspected deserter . . . rush to the front as the greedy claimant of public bounty." The situation was scandalous, but until Cleveland came along, no president had ever vetoed a private pension bill. Cleveland actually signed more of these private pension bills (1,453) than any previous president, but he vetoed hundreds. As a further example of his tremendous energy, he read and returned these bills to Congress, sometimes accompanied by satirically written veto messages. The Grand Army of the Republic, one of the most powerful pressure groups in the country, lashed out at these vetoes, and Congress responded by passing the Dependent Pensions bill in 1887. This monumental largesse would have given a pension to any veteran (who had served honorably for at least ninety days and who was dependent upon his own efforts for support) who suffered from any disability, regardless of when or how it was received. Also included were dependent parents of soldiers who had died in service. Cleveland vetoed this measure, though he knew it might and did contribute to his defeat in the election of 1888.

Cleveland's handling of the pension bills is revealing of his political leadership. It was a tedious and laborious job to examine these bills and to veto them whenever there were irregularities. To solve this problem Cleveland recommended "The most generous treatment of the disabled, aged, and needy among the veterans" by general laws. But when the Pension Committee of the House, attempting to carry into effect this proposal, drew up a general pension bill that passed both houses, Cleveland immediately vetoed it with the charge that it was "so ambiguous that it would put a further premium on dishonesty and mendacity," and restated his approval of a general measure. The puzzled Pension Committee then asserted "their hearty accord with these views of the President, and largely in accordance with his suggestions, they framed the bill which they thought and still continue to think will best accomplish the ends proposed." "Such a fiasco," wrote Henry Jones Ford in *The Cleveland Era,* "amounted to a demonstration of the lack of intelligent leadership. If the President and his party were cooperating for the furtherance of the same objects, as they both averred, it was discreditable all around that there should have been such a complete misunderstanding as to procedure."

Perhaps the most emphatic move toward reform in Cleveland's first administration came in his decision to push for a lowering of the tariff. He was motivated by several considerations. First, the protective tariff not only contributed to an increase in the price of consumers' goods, but to the development of trusts. Second, there was the embarrassing matter of a consistent surplus in the Treasury of almost one hundred million dollars annually. Third, Cleveland believed it was wrong for the Government so obviously to favor one portion of the business community. Fourth, the elections of 1886 showed Republican gains, and the Democrats realized that a live issue had to be exploited in order to win in the next presidential campaign.

Unlike many of his associates, Cleveland had paid little attention to the tariff. Carl Schurz relates that shortly after his election, Cleveland had asked him what big questions he ought to consider when he entered the White House. When Schurz recommended taking up the tariff, Cleveland confessed: "I am ashamed to say it, but the truth is I know nothing about the tariff. . . . Will you tell me how to go about it to learn?"

By 1887 public and political attention focused on the large and rapidly growing surplus in the Treasury. Numerous proposals for spending the money had been made, but they were either unorthodox or too remindful of the pork barrel. Tariff reduction impressed Cleveland as the only acceptable solution and he proceeded to move for it. Once he had decided to attack the tariff he displayed his trait of stubbornness. When advised to soft-pedal the tariff Cleveland replied in his blunt manner: "What is the use of being elected or re-elected if you don't stand for something?"

In 1887 he devoted his entire third annual message to an assault upon the high tariff rates. He especially emphasized the injustices of such a policy affecting the cost of necessities. This was the first time that a president had given over his whole State of the Union message to one topic. Such strategy centered nation-wide attention on the tariff and accented the President's leadership. Unfortunately, though, after committing himself and his party to tariff reform, Cleveland fumbled his chance to shape an effective bill. After instructing House leaders to pass a new tariff, he permitted them to frame one that was unsatisfactory. The Mills bill, passed by the House in July, 1888, made only moderate changes in rates, and it was soon evident that the projected reductions would not cause any substantial lowering of the Treasury surplus. Cleveland was not happy about this measure, but he had waited too long to prevent its introduction and passage. In the meantime the parties had begun to prepare for the election of 1888. With the tariff shaping up as a key issue in this contest, the Republicans introduced a protectionist measure in the Senate. When it proved impossible to work out a satisfactory compromise bill, the movement for tariff reduction ended with nothing accomplished.

The most significant lesson that Cleveland should have learned in the tariff episode was that he failed to lead. It was necessary for him to do more than make pronouncements and issue orders. He also lacked a sense of timing as to raising the issue. Against the unanimous advice of veteran politicians he had devoted his entire message to a demand for tariff revision. The feeling is that such action demoralized his party and delivered the Government into the hands of the protectionists without benefit to the presidency. And even after the harm had been done and he and his party defeated in the election of 1888, Cleveland showed no sign that he had changed his mind. "They told me it would hurt the party," he said, "that without it I was sure to be reelected, but that if I sent in the message to Congress it would, in all probability, defeat me. . . . Perhaps I made a mistake from the party standpoint; but damn it I was right."

In the four-year interval between his two administrations, Cleveland remained almost silent or straddled the various economic questions confronting the country. For the most part he shunned conspicuous political activity. While he was unhappy about the measures of the Harrison administration dealing with the tariff, currency, and surplus, he refrained from speaking out publicly until after the 1890 election. To him it seemed improper for a former president to do otherwise. As a private citizen Cleveland practiced law with a Wall Street firm. Here he had no opportunity to discover the agrarian discontents that were to stir up the West and South with Populism in the 1890's.

Only once in these four years did Cleveland speak out on a public issue. This occurred in February, 1891, when he challenged the growing silver movement in a public letter. A month earlier the Senate had passed a free-coinage-of-silver bill. Cleveland became aroused, because only one Democratic senator had voted against the measure, and because the newspapers had been circulating the story that the former President had become converted to free silver. With free-silver sentiment mounting in the country and looming up as a key issue in the 1892 campaign, Cleveland felt obligated to deal with the matter. The opportunity came when the Reform Club in New York City invited him to a dinner meeting to express opposition to free silver. Cleveland replied to the invitation in a letter released to the press in which he agreed "with those who believe that the greatest peril would be initiated by . . . the unlimited coinage of silver at our mints."

The Democratic machine politicians tried to prevent the nomination of Cleveland in 1892, but he won it on the first ballot. The Republicans again chose Harrison, but there was little enthusiasm for the President even within his own party. Cleveland gained the most decisive presidential election victory since 1872, and the Democrats won control of both houses of Congress. For the third time Cleveland had secured a majority of the popular vote over a Republican opponent and on each occasion by a wider margin.

One of the most severe panics in American history inaugurated Cleveland's second term. In 1893 alone, more than 600 banks closed their doors and over 15,000 businesses failed. Within a year there were four million unemployed out of a population of about sixty-five million. But the worst would come with the hard times of the next four years. There would be acute personal hardships and a deterioration in the Government's financial position. Cleveland's real testing time came during his second term which was entirely taken up by this depression. This was the climax of his public career, and two contemporary views about his leadership during this economic storm reveal how his actions gratified some Americans and angered others. Senator William B. Allison, Republican leader from Iowa, said, "It was God's mercy to this country that Grover Cleveland and not Harrison was elected President." But Democratic Governor John P. Altgeld of Illinois declared, "To laud Clevelandism on Jefferson's birthday is to sing a Te Deum in honor of Judas Iscariot on a Christmas morning."

Cleveland believed that the Sherman Silver Purchase Act and the McKinley Tariff had caused the panic and the subsequent depression. Whatever else was wrong in our national economy resulted from the folly or misfortune of individuals and thus was not the concern of the Federal government. In the face of the all-pervading social unrest, Cleveland concentrated his first efforts on repealing the Silver Purchase Act in order to prevent the Treasury's gold reserve from falling below the established minimum of $100,000,000. He summoned Congress into special session in August, 1893, and after two months' debate (during part of which Cleveland had been absent from Washington because of an operation for cancer in the roof of his mouth), a combination of Gold Democrats and Republicans produced enough votes to bring about repeal. Here Cleveland gave one of his few instances of leadership by withholding patronage from senators and congressmen until the contest was decided, by putting enormous pressure on wavering Representatives, and by purchasing the support of a lifelong inflationist, Senator Daniel Vorhees of Indiana, by giving him control of all the patronage in his state.

Cleveland's leadership, however, fell short of the accomplishment of positive legislation to meet the Treasury crisis. Though he had said that "the administration must be ready with some excellent substitute for the Sherman Law," he failed to offer any constructive alternative. Many business leaders, as well as many Democrats who favored repeal, had advocated the enactment of a substitute measure to provide for currency expansion and flexibility. Most of the Democrats, being practical politicians, feared that unconditional repeal might destroy their party, which was already sharply divided on the currency issue. But Cleveland insisted on unconditional repeal. At a Cabinet meeting on the matter he smote the table with his fist and asserted he would not yield an inch, and the compromise movement collapsed.

Unfortunately the repeal did not restore prosperity, or have any noticeable effect on the depression. The Treasury's gold reserve continued to fall, and in order to maintain an amount sufficient to remain on the gold standard, Cleveland had the Treasury sell United States Government bonds for gold. A group of bankers, headed by J. P. Morgan, absorbed three bond issues in 1894 and 1895, but it was not until 1897, when the depression had finally run its course, that the Treasury crisis ended. The gold purchases had enabled the Treasury to meet its obligations, but the decision to sell bonds to New York bankers proved to be one of the most unpopular ones that Cleveland ever made. Many Americans became alarmed over the dependence of the Government upon a syndicate of bankers in Wall Street.

As in his first administration Cleveland also faced the problem of the tariff. The Democrats, fulfilling their campaign promises, had passed a tariff bill in the House drawn up by William L. Wilson, of West Virginia, which provided for a modest reduction in rates. When the measure reached the Senate, a group of protectionists from both parties, led by Senator Arthur Gorman, influential Democrat from Maryland, attacked the bill with more than six hundred amendments and restored most of the cuts that had been made in the House. The bill, now known as the Wilson-Gorman Tariff of 1894, was a far cry from genuine reform. Bitterly disappointed by this result, Cleveland allowed the measure to become law without his signature.

But Cleveland had contributed to this failure. He had played no effective part in framing the tariff. Then, too, the bitterness in his own party that he had aroused by the fight over the repeal of the silver act had made agreement nearly impossible. Discipline and party loyalty no longer existed, and Cleveland had already used his ace political card—patronage—in getting the Senate to repeal the Sherman Act. It was only when the Senate had completely mutilated the Wilson Tariff that Cleveland took some kind of action. Through a letter read on the floor of the House, he declared, "Every true Democrat knows that this bill in its present form . . . falls far short of the consummation for which we have long labored. . . . Our abandonment of the cause or the principle upon which it rests means party perfidy and party dishonor."

While this blast relieved the President of his anger, it further antagonized the Senate and failed to accomplish the ends sought. Democratic senators savagely attacked Cleveland and defied him. While he refused to sign the bill he also declined to veto it. Cleveland's crusade for a lower tariff, which he had launched in 1887, had come to a sad conclusion. The reform phase of his public career had also ended. For the remainder of his presidency, Cleveland reduced his role to that of a protector of the *status quo*. In this he was more successful than he had been as a crusader for change, for he could play his usual, and many times effective, role of a righteous chief executive. He vetoed the Seigniorage bill which would have increased the supply of the currency. Through subordinate officials, he rudely rejected the petitions of angry wage earners, such as those who marched with Coxey's Army in 1894, and he sent Federal troops to crush the Pullman strike that same year.

The Pullman Company had reduced wages as much as 25 per cent by 1894, but there had been no reduction in rents in the town of Pullman, Illinois, completely owned by the company. When their requests for lower rents or higher wages were refused and their spokesmen discharged, the Pullman employees went on strike in May, 1894. In June the American Railway Union, headed by Eugene V. Debs, came to the assistance of the Pullman workers by voting to boycott all Pullman cars, and the General Managers' Association, made up of officials from twenty-four railroads, joined forces with the Pullman Company. The strike spread rapidly, and the President received numerous appeals from railroad officials, shippers, and business leaders to intervene.

Under these pressures from the business community and urgings from his attorney general, Richard Olney, a former important railroad lawyer, and a foe of labor unions, Cleveland decided to end the boycott. Olney had the Federal circuit court in Chicago serve an injunction on the officers of the American Railway Union against obstructing the railroads or interfering with the mails. This was based in part on the Sherman Anti-Trust Act of 1890. When the union ignored the injunction, Cleveland exploded, "If it takes the entire army and navy of the United States to deliver a post card in Chicago, that card will be delivered." He dispatched a regiment of regulars to Chicago to "restore law and order," and a short time later the strike collapsed.

Historians have been very critical of Cleveland's action in the Pullman strike. He had sent the troops to Chicago over the protests of John P. Altgeld, Democratic Governor of Illinois, and there was an angry exchange between the two men. Altgeld challenged the right of the President to order soldiers to the scene, and he gave detailed information to show that local and state officials had the situation completely under control. "To absolutely ignore a local government," the Governor charged, "not only insults the people . . . but is in violation of a basic principle of our institutions." Cleveland answered that the troops had been sent "in strict accordance with the Constitution and laws of the United States, upon the demands of the Post Office Department that obstructions of the mails should be removed, and upon representations of the judicial officers of the United States that the process of the Federal Court could not be executed through the ordinary means, and upon competent proof that conspiracies existed against commerce between the States." There was no intention on the part of the Federal government of "interfering with the plain duty of the local authorities to preserve the peace of the city."

Cleveland's solution of this labor dispute was costly. The friends of labor were determined to oust Cleveland from control of the Democratic party. Yet, others supported the President on this issue. James J. Hill, the financier and great railroad builder, reported that "the public, without reference to party lines, are unanimous in approving and supporting the action of the President." But the continuance of the depression coupled with Cleveland's failure to do much about it caused a steady deterioration of his popularity among the voters and the politicians of his own party. Democrats, who did not like Cleveland, felt that his attitude on the depression and free silver would ruin the party and their own political fortunes. In a letter to his former secretary of state in 1895, Cleveland remarked, "Think of it! Not a man in the Senate with whom I can be on terms of absolute confidence."

Grover Cleveland, for all his faults and limitations, appeared as a symbol of civic staunchness in his own day. Few men regarded him as a great constructive force in public affairs. Yet, they looked to him to lead the reform movement as expressed in honesty, economy, and efficient government. Cleveland performed his task so well that for his generation and later ones he became the embodiment of this type of reform. While historians have praised Cleveland for being strong enough to resist popular pressures that not many other men could have withstood in the Gilded Age, they have also wondered at his ability to turn his back upon the most acute distress the country had yet suffered. Yet for all his shortcomings, writes Professor Hofstadter, "He was the flower of American political culture in the Gilded Age."

Theodore Roosevelt

by RICHARD LOWITT

E ntering the White House in 1901 following the assassination
of William McKinley, Theodore Roosevelt became America's youngest—and many would say most popular—president. William Allen White aptly described him as a "gorgeous, fighting, laughing, loving, hating, robust man." He had a strong and handsome face, a bristling mustache, the fire of youth, and an air of sincerity. As president he quickly excited the interest and the admiration of the majority of American people. A set of glistening teeth, quickly revealed when he burst into his well-known grin and uttered his famous "dee-lighted" or when he soberly discussed the issues of the day, soon became a trademark of which cartoonists quickly took advantage. In 1904 Roosevelt was irked by the "outrageous lies" that he had been kissing babies during the campaign. Thereupon the American sage, Mr. Dooley, the creation of Chicago newspaperman Finley Peter Dunne, quipped that a baby kissed by the President knew it had been kissed and probably would bear the honorable scars for life.

Indeed, throughout his tenure of office, Americans chuckled or listened in amazement to their president when he ventured opinions that seemed strange for a political leader. His remarks on such diverse topics as divorce, birth control versus the "full baby carriage," the novels of Zola and Dickens, the poetry of Edwin Arlington Robinson, the private life of Maxim Gorki, simplified spelling and nature-faking, were discussed and debated but never ignored, for as he once said, "The White House is a bully pulpit." Well satisfied with their energetic and brilliant president and his toothy grin, people adopted the "Teddy-bear" as a symbol of his ferocious playfulness.

Born into a prominent family of inherited mercantile wealth, he was given the best training and education that his society could offer, though he broke with family tradition by going to Harvard instead of Columbia College. By overcoming poor health (asthma, defective vision, poor hearing, abscesses on his thighs and legs, plus most childhood diseases) in his early years, Roosevelt disciplined himself physically and found renewed vigor in the great outdoors. Though he lived an incredibly active life, his keen and intelligent mind roamed over a wide range of subjects which in varying degrees continually held his interest.

Roosevelt felt ill at ease in a nation devoted to the pursuit of material gain based on the exploitation of human and natural resources. There seemed to be little consideration for the moral and ethical values of the older mercantile community in which he was reared. These values included a belief in a fundamental law and in progress predicated upon individual responsibility. In 1910, when he received the Nobel Peace Prize, he summarized his position by insisting "that the great end in view is righteousness, justice as between man and man, nation and nation, the chance to lead our lives on a somewhat higher level, with a broader spirit of brotherly love for one another." In revolt against the deterministic views that bound many Americans to a general acquiescence in the *status quo*, Roosevelt believed that an individual, with the cooperation of his fellow men, might improve his lot and make America a better place in which to live. Thus Roosevelt, with the advantage of an assured income, rejected a business career and turned instead to one of public service, where he might help restore to American life the values of individual responsibility and his inherited code of morality. These, he believed, were being degraded if not destroyed in an America that was rapidly transformed in the decades following Appomattox from a relatively isolated, individualistic, agrarian nation into an urbanized, industrialized, and integrated economy with a growing international focus.

Politics broadened Theodore Roosevelt. His career in New York and in Washington prior to his election as vice president in 1900 brought him into contact with a maze of issues and problems on all levels and in all areas. The miseries of the poor and the intimate relationship between business and corrupt politics, early led him to support social welfare legislation and to champion civil service reform. As governor of New York State, Roosevelt was able to work with politicians with whom he rarely was in full accord to obtain goals he desired. And he came to appreciate fully that it was in the legislative mill and in the administration of a great office that ideas and programs might be translated into realities. Admittedly, compromise was and is the essence of politics, and Roosevelt operated on this premise. William Henry Harbaugh, Roosevelt's most recent biographer, has noted that by the end of his governorship, "Roosevelt was committed by deed and by thought to conserving the moral potential of the masses by meliorating their conditions of life, to preserving the capitalistic structure by eradicating the corporations' more flagrant abuses, and to reinforcing the democratic system by appointing men of integrity and ability to public office."

Furthermore, as governor, Roosevelt had learned that to carry out a program he would have to make his party the instrument of its fulfillment neither by reforming the Republican party nor by fighting the bosses. Rather it would have to be achieved by recognizing their existence, by inciting and marshalling public opinion and, if possible, by out-maneuvering the politicians at their own game.

Service as assistant secretary of the Navy and as colonel of the famed Rough Riders in the war with Spain confirmed his expansionist views. Military experience strengthened his belief that war was sometimes a necessity in a world where power politics and responsible politics were not always equated. Roosevelt, throughout his life, was an ardent nationalist, at times almost a jingoist. He believed in a strong balance of power, an attitude which proved to be a motivating force in his presidential direction of foreign affairs. In brief, few men entered the White House better prepared in terms of experience, training, and understanding for the responsibilities of the presidential office than did Theodore Roosevelt.

Nevertheless, it must be remembered that he was an "accidental president." The controlling interests in the Republican party were hardly in agreement with his political or economic views. Though Roosevelt had campaigned vigorously for McKinley, both in 1896 and 1900, he did so because he feared Bryan's emotionalism as well as his monetary and pacifist views more than he disliked the Republican party's support and concern for the *status quo*. He feared "Bryanism" more than he disliked high tariffs and ineffective legislation that rarely came to grips with crucial economic issues. He feared Bryan more than he did the politicians who cemented the notorious alliance between the Republican party and big business leaders.

Thomas C. Platt, Republican boss of the Empire State, recognized in Governor Roosevelt a threat to his control of state patronage. Platt also realized that the Governor's policies were too radical for the conservative contributors to Republican party coffers in New York. Therefore in 1900 at the Philadelphia convention, Platt joined forces with Matthew Quay of Pennsylvania in successfully selling Roosevelt's candidacy as vice-presidential running mate for William McKinley. When Mark Hanna, McKinley's chief political mentor, learned of Roosevelt's nomination he is alleged to have exclaimed, "Don't any of you realize that there's only one life between this madman and the White House?" In 1901 an assassin in Buffalo, New York, snuffed out this life and the "madman," not quite forty-three years old, became the twenty-sixth president of the United States. One of the abiding realities of his tenure of office was the persistent and nagging opposition of the Republican Old Guard firmly entrenched in powerful positions in both houses of Congress.

It was Henry Adams who had characterized William McKinley as an able political strategist who "undertook to pool interests in a general trust into which every interest should be taken, more or less at its own valuation, and whose mass should, under his management, create efficiency." Roosevelt, like his predecessor, undertook to carry out this task without offending (at the outset at least) Mark Hanna and other Republican leaders. He announced, properly enough under the circumstances, that he would continue McKinley's policies and maintain his Cabinet. Initially, Roosevelt proceeded cautiously, feeling his way, neither issuing statements nor launching policies that went counter to the wishes of the Old Guard and their powerful financial and business allies. His first message to Congress in December, 1901, had been prepared in consultation with President A. J. Cassatt of the Pennsylvania Railroad, Senators Mark Hanna and Nelson W. Aldrich, Secretary of War Elihu Root, and two Morgan partners, George W. Perkins and Robert Bacon.

But it was not long before Roosevelt assumed the reins of government and initiated policies that raised him to a level well above that of all previous presidents in the post–Civil War period. First, he centered his attention on a vigorous foreign policy, which soon projected the United States to a major position in international affairs—a national power whose interest and influence all foreign ministries needed to consider when contemplating the prevailing balance of power. In the Far East Roosevelt sought to maintain the Open Door in China and to extend American financial and commercial investments. With America's newly-acquired stake in the Philippine Islands, Roosevelt assumed the United States had become a dominant power in the Pacific along with Great Britain, Japan, and Russia. Hoping to preserve this balance, he early became concerned over the rising industrial and military power of Japan. Thus he sought to negotiate peace in the Russo-Japanese War of 1905. Both belligerents accepted Roosevelt's offer to arbitrate, and the Treaty of Portsmouth (New Hampshire) ended the war. Neither the Russians nor Japanese were wholly satisfied with the final settlement, but Roosevelt's endeavors were regarded highly enough to win him the Nobel Peace Prize. Before he left the White House, Roosevelt was convinced that Japan represented a threat to America's newly-defined interests in the Far East as well as to the Open Door in China.

In the Caribbean area Roosevelt pursued an even more vigorous program in his determination to promote American interests. Accepting the Monroe Doctrine as the basis of Latin-American policy, he added his own unique corollary. If any nation were unable to meets its financial obligations, thereby inviting foreign intervention, then the United States would be justified in interfering to untangle the affairs of the distressed American republic. Roosevelt announced in his message to Congress on December 6, 1904: "Chronic wrongdoing . . . may force the United States, however reluctantly . . . to the exercise of an international police power." The President applied this corollary reluctantly and in a limited way. Its primary purpose was to prevent disturbances that might threaten the United States' newly-acquired rights in the construction of a Panama canal. Under this policy American troops were sent to Santo Domingo. And the Platt amendment, incorporated into the Cuban constitution, gave the United States the power to interfere in the affairs of that newly-created nation.

189

During his tenure of office Roosevelt found it necessary to station marines in Cuba to safeguard American interests and to aid in the island's rehabilitation.

Roosevelt's opponents and critics have usually been severe in their denunciation of his expansionist policies in Latin America. Therefore, it is interesting to note that William Jennings Bryan, a bitter foe of American imperialism, after his service as secretary of state during the first Wilson administration, came to approve of Roosevelt's policies. Bryan confessed:

> My experience with the Latin-American countries has convinced me that the most important service that we can render to them (except the underwriting of their loans) is like that we rendered to Cuba under the Platt amendment. The fact that we stand ready to assist in the preserving of order will usually make it unnecessary for us to take any action. We are like the "big Brother" whose presence is a silent protection to the "little brother."

The most notable achievement of the President in this area was the acquisition of a small strip of land, the Isthmus of Panama. To acquire this territory, Roosevelt, by rather dubious means, encouraged a revolution against the Republic of Columbia. That nation's parliament had refused to ratify the Hay-Herran Treaty (1903) by which the United States agreed to pay 10 million dollars down and 250,000 dollars annually after nine years, for a perpetual lease on a canal zone. The President and his advisers in the Department of State were outraged. Understanding Roosevelt's anxiety in this matter, and capitalizing on the fear of the people of Panama that they might lose the benefits of a canal, Philippe Bunau-Varilla, aided by members of the prominent New York law firm of Sullivan and Cromwell, planned and financed an uprising against the Columbian government. Bunau-Varilla discussed his plans with several officials of the Roosevelt administration and possibly with the President himself. On November 2, 1903, the day *before* the revolution was scheduled to occur, the commander of the U.S.S. *Nashville* at Colon received orders to "prevent landing of armed force, either government or insurgent with hostile intent." The next day the American consul at Panama received a wire from Washington: "Uprising on isthmus reported. Keep Depart [of State] promptly and fully informed." Whereupon he answered, "no uprising yet. Reported will be in the night. Situation is critical." As the consul suggested, the uprising occurred that very night. Its success was practically guaranteed by orders issued to American forces to prevent the Columbian government from putting down the rebellion.

Within a fortnight following the Panamanian revolution, the United States officially recognized the new nation; received its minister (Bunau-Varilla); and signed a treaty, similar to the rejected Hay-Herran Convention, by which the United States received a perpetual lease of a ten mile zone across the Isthmus. In his January, 1904, message to Congress, the President claimed that "no one connected with this Government had any part in preparing, inciting or encouraging the late revolution on the Isthmus of Panama." However, seven years later, Roosevelt more accurately revealed his role. Addressing an audience in Berkeley, California, he said:

I am interested in the Panama Canal because I started it. If I had followed traditional conservative methods I would have submitted a dignified state paper of probably two hundred pages to the Congress and the debate would be going on yet, but I took the Canal Zone and let the Congress debate, and while the debate goes on, the canal does also.

Though Roosevelt's ethics in this matter are open to censure, the efficiency and dispatch with which his objectives were obtained command attention. Though his means were certainly not justified, few criticisms were leveled at the time against our acquisition of this territory. Within ten years, at a cost of approximately 600 million dollars, the Canal was completed.

Since Roosevelt believed the Canal would become America's economic and naval lifeline to the Pacific, no threats against it could be permitted. He regarded the Caribbean as an American sea. Stability, which the United States alone could insure in this part of the world, was a necessity, along with the removal of all possibilities of foreign intervention. In this policy Roosevelt was signally successful though the citizens of many independent American republics resented paternalism. And Latin-American affairs have been gravely affected by it well on into the twentieth century.

In dealing with Europe, Roosevelt was on less certain ground.

The political balance was in a state of flux, with Germany gradually emerging as a disrupting factor. Meanwhile Russia, with her poor performance in the war against Japan and her abortive revolution of 1905, caused world leaders to doubt her effectiveness as a major power. Moreover, Russian pogroms had aroused vocal and influential segments of the American people against her policy of religious persecution. Viewing the fluid situation in Europe, Roosevelt worked to strengthen Anglo-American good will as a potential force against the rising naval might of Germany. However, it is clear from his negotiations in helping to solve a boundary dispute in 1903 between Canada and Alaska favorable to the American claim, that Roosevelt regarded the United States as a senior partner in this relationship. In short, Roosevelt desired that the United States play a dominant role in international affairs. And given the transitory situation in Europe, during his tenure of office he influenced these affairs to some extent.

For example, Roosevelt tried to solve the crisis in Morocco. This crisis had arisen over German activities in an area which France regarded as her own particular sphere of interest. War over the Moroccan problem was a distinct possibility. But Roosevelt was instrumental in calling the Algeciras Conference in 1906 to attempt a solution of this question by peaceful means. Through the American representative, Henry White, Roosevelt believed he had negotiated a settlement which thwarted German penetration, thus preventing an overthrow of the prevailing Anglo-French supremacy which he favored in western Europe. This conference, however, did not achieve any permanent abeyance of the German threat to the balance of power in Europe; though it probably helped to delay until 1914 the outbreak of the First World War.

Roosevelt made use of personal relationships wherever possible in his dealings with other nations. Formal diplomatic channels were utilized only when no other means were available. The Kaiser shrewdly capitalized on this knowledge by sending Speck von Sternberg, whom Roosevelt personally admired, to Washington. Only the British Foreign Office refused to cater to Roosevelt's wish that Cecil Spring Rice be sent to represent Great Britain in the United States. Similarly, those American ambassadors whom Roosevelt liked and admired, such as George von Lengerke Meyer, were entrusted with personal missions and rewarded with promotions while other officials of the foreign service were bypassed.

Theodore Roosevelt believed that a nation had to expand its influence—by peaceful means if possible, by war if necessary—or lose place, power, and prestige. He realized that this required strength, determination, and sacrifice. Though he did not regard the race among individuals as invariably going to the swift, Roosevelt believed that among nations it was almost always so. Cognizant of the risks involved, he was, nevertheless, determined that the United States should assume a dominant position in the family of nations. In an age when foreign relations still did not directly influence the lives of the majority of American people, Roosevelt launched the nation into an enlarged sphere of operations and proclaimed, for better or worse, the end of American isolation.

Though Roosevelt talked in terms of power politics, critics based their opposition on traditional arguments in favor of isolation, pacifism, and historic policies. They started from the premise that the United States had come into existence committed to the concept that no man should be governed without his consent. They based their essential appeal on political principle and the ideas of the Declaration of Independence. It was the role of Woodrow Wilson to proclaim, at the end of the First World War, the only feasible challenge to Roosevelt's views; namely, collective security as an effective answer to power politics. But Roosevelt's importance lies in the fact that it was he who showed the nation, possibly with a touch of braggadocio, that with great wealth and power comes great governmental responsibility both abroad and at home.

While pursuing a forceful foreign policy which aroused little opposition from the dominant interests in the Republican party, Roosevelt soon launched into domestic programs that did. In February of 1902 he ordered Attorney General Philander Knox to institute a suit for violation of the Sherman Act against the Northern Securities Company. Created by James J. Hill and E. H. Harriman and their banking associates, the purpose of the company was to manage more effectively western railroads. In 1904 the Supreme Court decided in favor of the Government, and the Northern Securities Company was forced to dissolve. This was the first time that a corporation was found guilty of violating the Sherman Anti-Trust Act of 1890. In all, Roosevelt's attorney generals initiated over forty anti-trust suits, more in number than all previous attorney generals had instituted.

Roosevelt should be credited as the first post–Civil War president who recognized the threat of monopoly to the nation's economic life. Nevertheless, he did not favor crushing all large businesses in an effort to return to a competitive economy based on small economic units. Rather, Roosevelt accepted "bigness" as a reality of American economic life and was concerned only that the Government have power to scrutinize and regulate these huge corporate entities. Toward this end he organized a Bureau of Corporations in the newly-created Department of Commerce and Labor. This bureau could provide the President with requisite information; and if the facts indicated any unscrupulous or illegal activities, Roosevelt was willing for his attorney general to institute proceedings under the anti-trust laws. In short, Roosevelt made a distinction between "good" and "bad" trusts, a moral distinction which the Supreme Court accepted by 1911. Indeed, the first great wave of business consolidation, directed primarily by investment bankers, reached its climax during the years Roosevelt was in the White House pursuing a policy of attacking only "bad" or "evil" trusts.

Yet the fact that some corporations were prosecuted was enough to arouse the enmity of the business community. For example, after the suit against the Northern Securities Company was launched, the Detroit *Free Press* commented caustically: "Wall Street is paralyzed at the thought that a President of the United States would sink so low as to try to enforce the law." On the other hand, reformers pointed out that by utilizing the machinery of government and asserting the majesty of the law, Roosevelt is entitled to great credit. Joseph Pulitzer, editor of the distinguished *New York World*, echoed these sentiments when he wrote in 1907: "The greatest breeder of discontent and socialism is lack of confidence in the justice of the law, popular belief that the law is one thing for the rich and another for the poor." Thus by challenging the power of corporate wealth and other vested interests, albeit on a moral rather than a knowledgeable economic base, Roosevelt won the support of vast segments of public opinion. Aided by growing prosperity, he helped to alleviate discontent in many quarters.

Many writers, then and since, have criticized Roosevelt for his failure to seek the enactment of a lower tariff law. The belief that a high protective tariff was "the mother of trusts" was prevalent at the time; and it has been alleged that Roosevelt entered into an agreement with leading senators not to tamper with the tariff in exchange for their support of other aspects of his legislative program. In Roosevelt's defense it should be pointed out that he did seek tariff adjustments in the case of Cuba, where he was successful, and in the case of the Philippine Islands, where he failed. Furthermore, Roosevelt knew that over-all tariff legislation was usually unsatisfactory because every special interest would be represented in Washington by lobbyists seeking consideration for their clients. He also knew that what was needed was a more rational method of preparing tariffs—one which would take into account the differences between the cost of production at home and abroad.

Thus, if a president wished to hazard the risk of obtaining a sensible tariff from Congress, the best time to push for such legislation was immediately after a presidential election, preferably in a special session. Then members of Congress, fresh from the hustings with the next campaign at least two years away, might feel less bound to the controlling economic views of their more influential constituents. Roosevelt had his opportunity to sponsor tariff reform immediately after his overwhelming victory in the election of 1904. Instead, he chose to concentrate on another issue, effective railroad regulation, which was as significant as tariff reform and for which there was greater popular demand.

It was in the fight over the Railroad Rate bill of 1906 that Roosevelt revealed his consummate skill in securing legislation he thought necessary. Senate leader Nelson W. Aldrich of Rhode Island, a champion of railroad interests, was determined to prevent its passage. Employing his vast talents for political legerdemain against the measure, Aldrich continually sought to embarrass the President by offering crippling amendments. Further, he placed the direction of the bill in the hands of the one person in Congress whose behavior Roosevelt found so distasteful that he would not speak to him, Senator Benjamin R. Tillman of South Carolina. Yet Roosevelt was able to out-maneuver Aldrich by securing a compromise which gave the President what he most desired (power for the Interstate Commerce Commission to lower railroad rates) along with a concession granting district courts the power to issue injunctions against these decisions. This compromise Roosevelt found palatable because the law also provided for speedy appeals to higher federal courts.

While not attempting to achieve general tariff legislation,

Roosevelt threatened to do so in order to force other items of legislation from a recalcitrant Congress. More than any previous president, Roosevelt revealed a positive genius for coaxing from a critical Congress, particularly a Senate where supporters of special interests were most powerfully entrenched, measures that he wanted and which were usually contrary to its desires.

One of the most important laws in recent American history— the Reclamation Act—was signed by President Roosevelt in June, 1902. This bipartisan measure, sponsored by Congressman Francis E. Newlands, Democrat of Nevada, received strong support from the President. Under its terms citizens in the arid regions who manifested a desire to obtain Federal aid in irrigating their lands, would be assisted by the Government's construction, when feasible, of dams for irrigation and other purposes. The farmers who received the benefits of the impounded water agreed to pay to the Federal treasury, over a period of years, the cost of the dam's construction. Involved in this law was an expansion of the democratic process whereby interested citizens could band together to meet a common problem—lack of water in an arid region—with the help of the Federal government. Since the farmers involved in the project would reimburse the Government, in no sense could they be considered as receivers of charity or a bonus in the way, for example, various manufacturers benefited from a high protective tariff. Roosevelt favored this law for two reasons. First, it attempted to solve a crucial Western problem. Second, it contained the germ of an equally important concept, comprehensive multiple-purpose river valley development, which Roosevelt envisioned as a sensible solution to the problems of underdeveloped American regions.

With these measures, as with most other legislation he desired, Roosevelt rarely ran into difficulty in the House of Representatives. Speaker Joseph G. Cannon of Illinois was a leading member of the Republican Old Guard and personally had little regard for the President or his policies. Yet Roosevelt, until the very end of his administration, was able to work well with Cannon. He frequently consulted the Speaker, sought his advice and respected his judgment. Their association was formal and polite, never cordial, yet each man came to have a begrudging respect for the other. Once this relationship was established, most legislation Roosevelt favored and the Speaker thought feasible, quickly passed the lower house which Cannon ruled with an iron hand. Opposition and compromising amendments were encountered in the Senate where Old Guard leaders, Democrats and a handful of progressive Republicans, sought for their own purposes to modify most bills. So effective was the political cooperation between the President and the Speaker, that Congressman George W. Norris of Nebraska (who in 1910 was primarily responsible for curbing part of what he then considered the tyrannical power of Speaker Cannon) could proclaim in 1904 that he was for Cannon and Roosevelt, and saw nothing incongruous in the remark.

Besides railroad and reclamation legislation, Congress enacted significant measures calling for Federal meat inspection, a pure food and drug law, and welfare laws for residents of the District of Columbia. These latter measures, while of no transcendent national consequence by themselves, were of enormous importance to America's future. Even in Theodore Roosevelt's day critics denounced them as indicative of growing paternalism—as policies which stressed stronger and more centralized government than had existed previously. Technically trained experts and regulatory agencies supervising sectors of the economy, under the direction of the chief executive, were already evident early in the twentieth century. Congress also provided for a new Cabinet post, a Department of Commerce and Labor, and approved the setting aside of vast areas of the public domain for wilderness preservations and other conservation purposes. Land laws were realistically modified allowing homesteaders to utilize larger tracts in accord with actual conditions in different areas.

In all, the list of Roosevelt's legislative achievements is not lengthy or startling, yet with the possible exception of Cleveland's first administration, more important enactments were passed during his term of office than during that of any president since Lincoln. And, equally important, the way was prepared for the outstanding record of Taft's and especially Wilson's administrations. Furthermore, through vigorous executive action, Roosevelt was able to accomplish deeds which he believed to be in accord with his over-all purpose of promoting the progress and prosperity of the American people.

In October, 1902, at the end of his first year in the White House (a name which he preferred to Executive Mansion), Roosevelt won wide public acclaim by interfering in a long and bitter strike in the anthracite coal fields of Pennsylvania. The strikers, led by John Mitchell of the United Mine Workers, were willing to submit their grievances to arbitration, but the operators refused to consider any terms. One of their spokesmen, George F. Baer, President of the Reading Railroad, went so far as to explain that the miners' interests would be protected "not by the labor agitators, but by Christian men to whom God in His infinite wisdom, has given control of the property interests of the country."

With winter approaching and coal prices steadily rising, many Eastern cities faced a public health crisis. Roosevelt ascertained that the mine owners would not arbitrate, and reached the conclusion that they were solely responsible for the strike and its continuation. The prime consideration, however, was that the public safety was imperilled, and Roosevelt then took forceful action. He issued secret orders directing the Army to move troops into the area and to seize and administer the mines as receiver for the Government. Meanwhile, Secretary of War Elihu Root, acting in his capacity as a private citizen (though he had the President's approval) went to see J. P. Morgan in New York City. Morgan, who was critical of the way the mine operators were antagonizing public opinion by their extreme pronouncements, listened carefully as Root fully explained the situation. Morgan then exerted pressure on the operators. After further negotiations with the President, the operators soon capitulated and agreed to abide by the decision of a commission of prominent experts. Most of the miners' demands were found to be neither unjust nor unreasonable. As a result of the commission's work, an Anthracite Board of Conciliation was created to settle further grievances in the industry.

Roosevelt's interference in this dispute marked the first time in the history of organized labor that the Federal government had intervened without automatically siding with management. For the first time since the Civil War an American president in effect proclaimed that working people had rights which could not be ignored by the Government of the United States. Roosevelt, a president who opposed any group in power which, by virtue of its wealth, unjustly oppressed any other group, had public opinion on his side. He became the champion of a "square deal." An editorial in the *Springfield Republican* went to the core of the matter when it noted that "the most formidable attempt ever made in this country to crush labor-unionism has ended in defeat." As a result certain segments of organized labor, while generally hostile to the Republican party, nevertheless came to have some regard for Theodore Roosevelt. Later in his administration he became openly critical of the widespread issuance of injunctions by Federal judges against labor unions. Indeed, Roosevelt sought and obtained a plank in the 1908 Republican platform condemning such indiscriminate practice.

Actually, Roosevelt was no champion of the trade-union movement. He was critical of some labor leaders just as he was critical of the mine owners and other capitalists who exercised power without a sense of stewardship and concern for the public interest. On the one hand, he challenged the misuse of power by capitalists and, as a rule, thought they knew little outside their own business. On the other hand, he agreed with them that the collective force of labor constituted a potentially grave menace. However, owing to his experience in the anthracite coal strike, Roosevelt's appreciation of the plight of labor became more perceptive. But it never quite downed the memory of violence in the Haymarket affair, the Homestead, the Pullman, and other strikes which had engendered in him a distrust or fear of labor on the march. In short, accepting Lincoln's dictum that the rights of labor deserved priority over those of capital, Roosevelt somewhat reluctantly supported labor's right to organize and advocated Government supervision of big business. The way to curb the power of both groups, if necessary, was for the executive to be prepared to exercise authority to protect the public interest. Fundamentally he believed that no group in the United States was to be deprived of its basic rights. As chief executive, Roosevelt sought, in several instances that came to his attention, to secure these rights. This point of view was at the core of the phrase "Square Deal" which he made so popular.

In the case of minority groups, Roosevelt was anxious to extend them the rights and privileges of all citizens. Never did he prejudge an individual merely because he was not a member of a dominant American group. Indeed he was the first president to have all major American religious faiths represented in his Cabinet. With the aid of Booker T. Washington, an advisor on patronage problems, Roosevelt appointed Negroes to the most important Federal jobs members of that race had held since the days of Reconstruction.

In the Brownsville (Texas) affair, however, where Negro soldiers were charged with rioting and shooting, Roosevelt made what was possibly the most egregious blunder of his entire career.

On November 5, 1906, he ordered the men of the companies allegedly involved in the fracas "discharged without honor . . . and forever barred from reenlistment in the Army or Navy of the United States." With the President's authority, the troops were informed that if the guilty were not discovered, all would be discharged. Thus, when the offenders were not revealed, the penalty was applied and one hundred and sixty soldiers, six of whom held the Congressional Medal of Honor, were summarily discharged. Criticism was leveled against Roosevelt; a congressional investigation revealed the undue pressures Negro troops had been subjected to in the community and stressed the arbitrary handling of the entire proceeding. Yet Roosevelt remained adamant in his decision.

Aside from this important instance, Roosevelt's actions as they affected minorities were quite impressive. In the process of negotiating the so-called Gentlemen's Agreement with Japan (to curtail emigration to the United States by peasants and laborers), Roosevelt managed to lessen domestic discrimination. He was able to exert enough pressure on the city authorities of San Francisco to obtain their revocation of a 1906 segregation order against all Oriental school children. Temporarily at least, Roosevelt thus helped to reduce the mounting tension against the Japanese in the Pacific coast states. Unfortunately, discrimination soon reasserted itself in legislation enacted by the California legislature, which later embarrassed the Wilson administration in its relations with Japan.

In other areas as well, Roosevelt displayed, through executive action, his dynamic concept of the presidency. For example, while not neglecting political appointments, he advanced the cause of civil service to its greatest extent since the enactment of the Pendleton Act. Qualified men of high calibre were brought into the Government's employ on all levels, and the consular service was reorganized and placed on a professional basis. Technically trained men in various fields found that Government officials did not frown upon their advice and that their services were in demand. Furthermore, Roosevelt ferreted out graft and corruption; negligent officials were discharged and some of the corrupt ones were convicted. Frauds were discovered, for example, in the Post Office Department and in the management of public lands; the perpetrators were quickly prosecuted. Finally, Roosevelt was able to attract into Government service able and high-minded officials of impeccable integrity, many of whom shared some of his enthusiasms. The President was a good listener and on numerous occasions showed his willingness to accept the advice of subordinates. Under Theodore Roosevelt, a career in government offered to men of ability attractive and exciting possibilities for public service. Lord Bryce, British Ambassador to the United States and author of the classic, *The American Commonwealth*, commenting on the quality of men serving under Theodore Roosevelt, stated he had never "in any country seen a more eager, highminded, and efficient set of public servants—men more useful and creditable to their country—than the men doing the work of the American Government in Washington and in the field." Democracy during Roosevelt's administration was learning to become efficient as well as effective.

One particular device that has played a significant role in making democracy more efficient and effective was first put into operation under Roosevelt's administration—the government corporation. Building the Panama Canal represented, as one writer has recently noted, a "triumph over Panama mountains, mosquitoes and sliding mud," a triumph comparable to the victories obtained on some of the nation's historic battlefields. The Panama Railroad Company, a government corporation, made its initial appearance in this tropical zone and played a role in organizing the masses of men, machinery, and energy so necessary for the construction of the Canal.

The advantages of a government corporation are many. On-the-spot decisions can be quickly made, and the necessity of referring important matters to Washington for approval is thereby obviated. It represents a notable attempt to operate the Federal government on a practical rather than a theoretical level, at the place where it is at work rather than at the place where the seat of government is situated. Managerial responsibility is concentrated, by this device, in the hands of competent people who have been given free rein in finance and management to achieve the desired results. Since the concept was introduced in 1904, almost one hundred government corporations have been created. Both Republican and Democratic administrations have utilized them, and even foreign governments have adopted the idea.

It was in the field of conservation, however, that Roosevelt achieved an outstanding victory by making the nation dramatically aware of this most important issue. With the help of Gifford

Pinchot, W J McGee, James R. Garfield, and others, he did much to conserve natural resources for intelligent use according to the best principles of scientific management, or for permanent preservation in their natural state. By establishing an Inland Waterways Commission, Roosevelt showed concern for the comprehensive development of the nation's internal waterways. Opposed to considering rivers as subjects of pork-barrel legislation, he thought the United States should establish a policy for an entire river in a single piece of legislation. Roosevelt's summation of the findings of this commission is one of the most significant documents in the history of this crucial topic. He said, in part:

> . . . It is poor business to develop a river for navigation in such a way as to prevent its use for power, when by a little foresight it could be made to serve both purposes. We cannot afford needlessly to sacrifice power to irrigation, or irrigation to domestic water supply, when by taking thought we may have all three. Every stream should be used to the utmost. No stream can be so used unless such use is planned for in advance. When such plans are made we shall find that, instead of interfering, one use can often be made to assist another. Each river system, from its headwaters in the forest to its mouth on the coast, is a single unit and should be treated as such. Navigation of the lower reaches of a stream cannot be fully developed without the control of floods and low waters by storage and drainage. Navigable channels are directly concerned with the protection of source waters and soil erosion, which takes the materials for bars and shoals from the richest portions of our farms. The uses of a stream for domestic and municipal water supply, for power, and in many cases for irrigation, must also be taken into full account. . . .

Furthermore, by vetoing various measures, Roosevelt helped establish the principle that the Government should lease rather than sell or grant power sites, mineral and forest lands, etc., to private interests. But during his last year in office, as the Old Guard recognized Roosevelt's growing impotency as a political leader, he met many rebuffs from Congress. Some members ignored him altogether. Nevertheless, Roosevelt fought hard for his policies; he bombarded Congress with messages calling for an extension of public authority over vast accumulations of private and corporate wealth. State action was obtained by holding (with all possible fanfare and publicity) White House conferences or by presenting reports on such issues as conservation, inland waterways, or child welfare. Incidentally, by asking all of the state governors to one of these meetings, Roosevelt inaugurated the custom of an annual governors' conference. When he failed to invite John Muir, one of the grand old men of the movement, to the conference on conservation, Roosevelt helped to alienate those individuals who favored wilderness preservation to the exclusion of all other aspects of conservation. Yet, as the American people in the twentieth century become more concerned about the protection and preservation of their priceless natural sites and resources, the stature of Theodore Roosevelt as the first great leader in this movement grows ever more notable.

American presidents serve a double role—chief spokesmen of the nation and titular (if not real) heads of their party. Not for one moment did Roosevelt forget his position as party leader. In 1904, of course, he was primarily concerned with politics and the presidential election. When Mark Hanna died, shortly before the Republican convention convened in Chicago that year, opposition to Roosevelt's candidacy disappeared as the Old Guard was unable to focus on any suitable candidate. America's "Teddy-bear" easily won the nomination—and the election. The Democrats rejected Bryan and chose as their standard bearer Alton B. Parker, a conservative New York judge. Though Parker charged (with some validity) that the Republican campaign chest had obtained funds from leading financiers, Roosevelt won the election by a two million plurality, the greatest landslide in American history to that time.

It was in this election that many Bryanites and former Populists returned to the Republican party, where they became ardent Roosevelt supporters. The fusion between Democrats and Populists in the Western farm states was irrevocably destroyed. Not only did the returns reveal Theodore Roosevelt at the apex of his popularity and able to assume control of the Republican party organization for the first time, but also as a result of the election he emerged as master of his party's destiny.

After this resounding victory Roosevelt made the serious political mistake of announcing that he would not seek another term in the White House. He thereby assured his Old Guard opponents in the Republican party that by the spring of 1909 they would be rid of him. As his second term of office drew to an end, however, Roosevelt was determined to choose a successor who would pursue the policies he had inaugurated. That successor was to be William Howard Taft.

As secretary of war, Taft had been a devoted supporter of the President and a reliable "trouble-shooter." Roosevelt had assigned Taft difficult problems and sent him on delicate missions knowing full well that they would be skilfully handled. Taft had broad experience as a Federal judge, governor general of the Philippines, and as a Cabinet member. Though the presidency would be his first elective office, Roosevelt felt that Taft was politically acceptable to the American people and best fitted to continue his policies. Through his tremendous prestige, his control of patronage, and his maneuvering with powerful politicians, the President was able to extinguish the hopes of other presidential aspirants. Indeed the only thing he had to fear was the possibility that the delegates, despite their pledges to Taft, might insist upon his own renomination.

When the Republican convention met, however, Taft's nomination was secured on the first ballot. Though Roosevelt did not participate actively in the 1908 campaign, he exerted considerable influence in other ways to assure Taft's easily-won victory over the Democratic candidate, William Jennings Bryan. With Taft's election seemingly assuring the advancement of his policies, Roosevelt completed plans for an African game-hunting expedition and an extended tour of Europe. When he departed on this jaunt some of his bitter opponents expressed the hope that every lion would fulfill its duty to Theodore Roosevelt.

Roosevelt, it turned out, erred in choosing Taft. While a capable man, Taft lacked the broad executive capacity of his predecessor. He could carry out plans, obey orders, and ably administer a department or a territory; yet he lacked the ability to formulate over-all policy and to work effectively with a recalcitrant Congress without compromising the essence of his program. The magnitude of Roosevelt's mistake became all too evident during the following four years as the Republican party, wracked by internal dissension, disintegrated into opposing factions.

Taft had made a splendid Cabinet member, and indeed, most of Roosevelt's Cabinet appointments or carry-overs from the Mc-

Kinley administration were excellent men. Elihu Root, whose previous corporate connections made him unavailable as a successor to Roosevelt, was probably the ablest of the group. As secretary of war from 1899 to 1904, Root had reorganized the War Department. By helping to create the staff system of command and the National Guard, which replaced the state militia as the basis of a military reserve force, he had advanced the military efficiency of the United States. Most other Cabinet members, though not of Root's stature, ably administered their departments and promptly brought before the President all matters of national or international policy for decision, usually accompanied by a clear-cut recommendation of their own.

Roosevelt believed in shifting Cabinet members and other appointed officers if he noticed signs that the official was beginning to enjoy any ease and comfort in his post. In this way he hoped the official would utilize the ability and energy, which made him valuable in the first place, in some other department or post that needed bolstering. If, on the other hand, Roosevelt found him inefficient, he was quickly dropped. "It is so easy to put one's personal affections for men above the public service," said Roosevelt, yet rarely if ever did the President allow himself this luxury.

In most instances this policy worked well enough; the Government reached new heights in efficiency and intelligent administration under Roosevelt. But in one important area the effect was to hinder and obstruct any real progress. The Navy Department which was close to the President's heart had half a dozen secretaries while Roosevelt was chief executive. It is true that the Navy was efficient and fully staffed; appropriations for additions to the fleet were forthcoming from Congress; and, in Roosevelt's last year in office, the fleet was sent around the world on a good-will tour which also was designed to impress upon foreign rulers the naval strength of the United States. The numerous changes in the Department found the secretaries unwilling or unable to make recommendations or decisions, however, on technical and crucial matters of size, speed, and armament of naval vessels. Thus, while the British and German navies were being modernized, that of the United States was becoming antiquated.

As president, Roosevelt accepted the premise that continued industrialization would modify but not radically change the stable social and economic institutions of nineteenth-century America.

"Hence," notes Elting E. Morison, "he used his authority with restraint in those areas where evolutionary modification should properly take place and did not try to impose arbitrary solutions of his own for immediate problems." The one notable exception that could be cited to disprove this valid generalization as it applies to domestic problems was his handling of the Brownsville affair. In all, his presidential actions—both legislative and administrative—on the domestic scene marked the noticeable beginning of the concept of the democratic welfare state. Roosevelt was the first American president to attempt to face the task of adjusting individual freedom to industrialization. On the other hand, in the realm of foreign policy, where Roosevelt knew the evolutionary process could not be relied upon to ward off threats to the national interest, he acted with much less restraint. The world beyond the American coastline he regarded in good part as a moral jungle where power was the natural arbiter and ethical behavior might be understood as a sign of weakness. His foreign policies signalized the emergence of the United States as a world power with specific commitments and responsibilities.

The middle-class citizens of America understood, accepted, and in most instances applauded Roosevelt's approach to problems. They lived in a world whose leading rulers could still understand (if not accept) the dimensions of moral behavior. As the twentieth century unfolded, however, this force gradually declined in favor of more relative values based on self-interest, which fragmented the country into coteries of diverse social, ethnic, and economic groups. Meanwhile, instruments of government, originally forged to reconcile the realities of an industrialized economy with individual liberty, were greatly expanded. And the purposes or goals of reform, which men expounded but never precisely defined, became confused, ignored, or rejected, while the mechanisms and the state itself tended to become ends in themselves. Though Theodore Roosevelt's type of political morality has largely disappeared, it still can serve as a guide to attract those who believe that the maintenance of civil order based on fundamental moral values should take primacy above all other social urges.

Woodrow Wilson

by E. DAVID CRONON

Shortly before noon on March 4, 1921, a black limousine left
the White House and headed up Pennsylvania Avenue toward
the Capitol. For one of its two occupants, genial Warren G.
Harding, the short trip was in the nature of a triumphal march.
Passing along the flag-draped streets, Harding smiled and waved
happily to the holiday crowds come to cheer his inauguration as the
twenty-ninth president of the United States. With the easy assurance and limited vision of a small-town Rotarian, he was confident
he knew what the American people expected of him—no idealistic
reforms, no emotional crusades; simply "normalcy."

In contrast, the mood of his companion, retiring President
Woodrow Wilson, was serious, even a trifle grim. Ailing in body,
deeply discouraged over the rejection of his dream of American
leadership in a League of Nations, for Wilson the ride was a painful duty, to be endured rather than enjoyed. Wilson, if not Harding, was keenly aware that these were the final moments of an administration more vigorous and constructive, more challenged and
tested, yet also more bitterly controversial, than any since that of
Abraham Lincoln.

To most of those who watched the presidential limousine pass
that day on its way to the Capitol, the event symbolized merely
the end of an administration. Only a scattered few perceived that
they were also witnessing the end of a notable era in American life.

207

Thomas Woodrow Wilson (he stopped using the first name after graduating from college) is remembered by history as a great reforming president, an imaginative statesman who exercised skillful direction over Congress, greatly strengthened the powers of his office, and left for his successors an enviable example of responsible and vigorous presidential leadership. With his administration came the climax of the Progressive Movement—that remarkable burst of reform energy which sought to transform large areas of American life in the early years of the twentieth century. Yet ironically, up to the time Wilson entered political life—only a scant two years before he was elected president—he was an avowed conservative, who distrusted governmental regulation, feared the power of organized labor and the agrarian radicals in his party, and considered the office of the presidency almost hopelessly weak for really efficient government.

Wilson was the first Southerner since Zachary Taylor to occupy the White House, though he reached it via an unlikely northern route. Born at Staunton, Virginia, on December 28, 1856, he grew up in Georgia amidst the physical wounds of Civil War and the psychological scars of Reconstruction. Yet somehow he escaped the bitterness of spirit that afflicted so many Southerners of his generation. As a young man he could confess frankly, "*because* I love the South, I rejoice in the failure of the Confederacy." In other respects, however, Wilson showed the distinctive influence of his Southern upbringing. He was characteristically Southern in his love of family and his chivalrous attitude toward women; he inherited the upperclass Southerner's paternalistic view of the Negro; he tended to romanticize Southern history. Wilson's preacher father, the Rev. Dr. Joseph Ruggles Wilson, instilled in his children a lasting faith in the fundamentals of the Presbyterian creed. On a daily diet of prayers and Bible reading, young Tommy Wilson grew up never doubting the existence of an unalterable moral law or the ultimate triumph of God's will. In later life he would undertake a reformer's role with almost messianic zeal, supremely confident that what he did was morally right, and thus by definition must in the end prevail. But Dr. Wilson also taught his children humor and tolerance and shared with them his love of books and his lively interest in politics. He was a stickler for precision in thought and speech. "Learn to think on your feet," he would insist. "Shoot your words straight at the target. Don't mumble and fumble." Good training, this, for a future president.

Wilson's undergraduate years at Princeton (where, incidentally, he heard *The Star Spangled Banner* for the first time) marked an important turning point in his life. He found the work hard but exciting, and quickly became fascinated by the study of government and politics. He read *The Federalist*, and discovered Aristotle, Burke, Bright, Macaulay, and Bagehot. His reading of the British political theorists, especially Bagehot, left Wilson ever after convinced of the superiority of British parliamentary government. Many years later, as president, he would attempt with considerable success to adapt some features of the British system to American conditions—by assuming more active leadership of Congress, by developing the caucus to promote party regularity, and by taking his case on major issues directly to the people.

While still an undergraduate, Wilson managed to publish several essays; one, an article on "Cabinet Government in the United States," appeared in the *International Review* after having duly impressed that august journal's associate editor, a young Boston intellectual named Henry Cabot Lodge. At the same time Wilson gained a measure of student fame as a debater. He dreamed of going into politics, and in the privacy of his room wrote out a number of calling cards: "Thomas Woodrow Wilson, Senator from Virginia."

After graduating from Princeton in 1879, Wilson had to break the unwelcome news to his family that he felt no call to the ministry. Instead, law seemed the logical path to a desired political career, but at the University of Virginia Law School he found that he was "most terribly bored" studying it. An unremunerative year of legal practice in Atlanta further convinced him that his future lay outside the courtroom. He resolved to become a professor, even though this would probably mean the end of any hope for an active political career. For the requisite graduate training, he went to the new Johns Hopkins University in Baltimore to study history and political science under the noted Herbert Baxter Adams. In 1885, even before receiving his degree, Wilson published his Ph.D. thesis, *Congressional Government*, a brilliant and widely-acclaimed analysis of the Federal government. As the title implies, Wilson argued that the real federal power lay with Congress, which he judged inefficient and irresponsible as compared with the British cabinet system. Strangely, in the light of his own later career, he wrote off the president as weak and unimportant, a virtual nonentity.

Wilson's elation over the book's success was, characteristically, tempered with a measure of doubt and disappointment. To his future wife, Ellen Axson, he confessed that he felt "shut out from my heart's *first*—primary—ambition and purpose, . . . a statesmen's career."

> I have a strong instinct of leadership, an unmistakably oratorical temperament, and the keenest possible delight in affairs; and it has required very constant and stringent schooling to content me with the sober methods of the scholar and the man of letters. I have no patience for the tedious toil of what is known as "research"; I have a passion for interpreting great thoughts to the world; I should be complete if I could inspire a great movement of opinion, if I could read the experiences of the past into the practical life of the men of today and so communicate the thought to the minds of the great mass of the people as to impel them to great political achievements.

Whatever his doubts, Wilson quickly embarked upon a distinguished academic career: three years at the brand new Bryn Mawr College, where he was the entire department of history; two years at Wesleyan University, where he published probably his best scholarly book, *The State*; and then, in 1890, the return to Princeton as professor of jurisprudence and political economy. Back amidst the familiar haunts of his alma mater, he soon became the most popular lecturer on the campus and spoke increasingly to public groups around the country. Nor did he slacken his scholarly pursuits; over the next twelve years he published nine books and thirty-five articles. His prestige was such that he was offered and declined the presidency of a number of colleges and universities. Thus when the time came to choose a new president of Princeton in 1902, it was not surprising that the trustees considered only one name. Unanimously they voted to offer the post to Woodrow Wilson.

As the first lay president in Princeton's history, Wilson experienced both impressive success and humiliating defeat. Energetically he set about revising the curriculum and overhauling the antiquated administrative structure of the university; eloquently he persuaded the trustees to approve the expensive preceptorial method of teaching undergraduates in small groups; with contagious enthusiasm he invigorated both the faculty and the student body to a new sense of dedication. Within a remarkably short time his educational reforms had made Princeton a model for other institutions and had marked Wilson as one of the outstanding educators of his time. But several of Wilson's later proposals provoked mounting opposition from influential members of the faculty, the trustees, and a vocal segment of the alumni. The critics, it might be said, objected not so much to his goals as to what they regarded as his evasive tactics and his proud and unbending stubbornness. The details of the internecine battles during Wilson's last years at Princeton are less important than the serious defects they revealed in his character. In the face of defeat he showed himself curiously unable to compromise, unduly sensitive to criticism, willing to break completely with old friends who dared to oppose him. Honest differences over issues became bitter personal quarrels in which Wilson revealed a characteristic trait of viewing his own behavior in terms of a high moral crusade. Thus his largely personal feud with Dean Andrew F. West of the Graduate School became for Wilson a great battle for democratic education against the evil forces of privilege. By 1910 he had so alienated a majority of the trustees, as well as a sizable element of the faculty and alumni, that all concerned were relieved when he resigned to run for governor of New Jersey.

Wilson's foray into the political arena at the age of fifty-three, though spurred by his difficulties at Princeton, was not a sudden or completely unexpected development. He had never lost his early interest in government, and for some time past his generally orthodox views and his growing national reputation had brought him to the attention of a group of conservative politicians anxious to rehabilitate the shattered fortunes of the Democratic party. These men were impressed both by Wilson's forensic eloquence and by his thoroughly conservative approach to the great economic issues of the day: his defense of big business, his attacks on trade unions, his denunciation of government control, and his antipathy to radicalism in any form. As early as 1906, Colonel George Harvey, the editor of the conservative *Harper's Weekly*, had begun to groom Wilson as a potential Democratic presidential

211

nominee. Few except perhaps Wilson took the idea seriously, however, and even Harvey realized that it would first be necessary to give his candidate some political experience, and get him more in the public eye. To this end, in 1910 Harvey persuaded the Democratic bosses in New Jersey that the scholarly and principled president of Princeton was the only candidate who could win the governorship for the somewhat tarnished state Democracy. Wilson received the nomination from a well-controlled convention on the first ballot, but only over the angry protests of the reformers in the party, who quite naturally assumed that he was to be only a respectable front for continued boss rule. Two months later he was governor by an impressive fifty thousand majority, after a brilliant campaign in which he had cut loose from his early conservative and boss support and had convinced suspicious New Jersey progressives that he was heart and soul one of them.

How to account for Wilson's rather abrupt conversion to progressivism at this time is a matter that has troubled observers then and since. Undoubtedly there was an element of expediency involved, for Wilson rightly saw that without the votes of the independents and progressives of the state he could not be elected. Yet for a personality as complex as Woodrow Wilson's, expediency is by no means the entire answer. Though he had received the nomination from the bosses, no one knew better than they that Wilson was no ordinary machine candidate. In fact he had stipulated that there must be no strings attached to his candidacy. A good share of Wilson's previous conservatism stemmed from sheer ignorance; he simply had not bothered to study carefully the issues that had been agitating the progressives for the past decade and more. As he struggled to formulate his position during the campaign in response to pointed queries from the reformers, he gradually and quite sincerely found himself agreeing with them. "We are not in the same America as we were ten years ago," he explained in one campaign speech. And another time: "I'll agree not to change my mind if someone with power to do so will guarantee that if I go to bed at night I will get up in the morning and see the world in the same way." By the end of the campaign he was excoriating in the bluntest terms the very boss system to which he owed his nomination.

Wilson's acts as governor soon captured the attention of much of the nation. He swiftly beat down the bosses and established his own leadership of the Democratic party in the state, and then proceeded to cajole or coerce a reluctant legislature into enacting a whole parcel of progressive reforms: a direct primary, corrupt-practices legislation, strict regulation of railroads and public utilities, and a workmen's compensation law. In less than a year progressives in the Democratic party were rallying to Wilson as the outstanding contender for the presidential nomination in 1912, and Wilson on his part was campaigning actively throughout the country, demanding stricter control of the trusts, tariff and banking reform, and an end to special privilege. His early conservative supporters now rapidly lost interest in Wilson's presidential prospects, with George Harvey, the original Wilson man, departing with an aggrieved public blast.

The details of the political infighting at the Democratic national convention in Baltimore in June, 1912, need not concern us here. It is enough to note that Wilson, after a slow and discouraging start against Speaker Champ Clark of the House of Representatives, finally managed to win the nomination on the forty-sixth ballot. As a result the Democrats could face the country with control of the party firmly in the hand of its progressive wing. Wilson's chances were immeasurably helped, moreover, by a deep split within the Republican party. The Republican Old Guard proceeded ruthlessly to renominate William Howard Taft over the anguished howls of the party's progressive faction, led by former President Theodore Roosevelt. Roosevelt and his partisans thereupon took to the field under the banner of a new Progressive party, pledged to enact a remarkably broad and advanced program of reform. Taft was hopelessly out of the running; his candidacy seemed designed chiefly to defeat Roosevelt. This, at any event, was its effect. For when the ballots were counted, Wilson had garnered a sweeping total of 435 electoral votes to Roosevelt's 88 and Taft's 8. The popular vote told another story, however. Wilson had managed to win only a little over six million out of nearly fifteen million cast. The vote was an emphatic mandate for progressivism, but it could hardly be construed as an unrestrained endorsement of Wilson's own program of reform, his call for a New Freedom.

Few presidents have entered office better able to serve the public interest than Woodrow Wilson. His previous political experience was limited, but already he had shown himself a leader

213

of rare ability, imagination, and boldness. His equipment was first-class: a keen analytical mind, superb oratorical and literary skill, and a thorough understanding of history and the nature of government. Neither at the Democratic convention nor during the campaign had he been forced to make any embarrassing commitments to special interests that would limit his freedom of action. His stern Presbyterian conscience demanded that he serve *all* the American people, with understanding and justice. Wilson closed his inaugural address on a note of solemn consecration:

> This is not a day of triumph; it is a day of dedication. Here muster, not the forces of party, but the forces of humanity. Men's hearts wait upon us; men's lives hang in the balance; men's hopes call upon us to say what we will do. Who shall live up to the great trust? Who dares fail to try? I summon all honest men, all patriotic, all forward-looking men, to my side. God helping me, I will not fail them, if they will but counsel and sustain me!

During the campaign Wilson and his chief rival, Theodore Roosevelt, had given the country a spirited and enlightening debate over the nature and future course of progressivism. Roosevelt's program, known as the New Nationalism, called for vigorous action by the Federal government to regulate the national economy in the interest of the many rather than the few. He demanded a variety of laws to protect the less-favored classes in American life, especially workers and farmers. Roosevelt did not condemn big business as such, for he thought it often more efficient than small business, but he proposed to control it to whatever extent was necessary to protect the public interest. Even private monopoly—suitably regulated—might in some instances be desirable, or in any event inevitable, he conceded.

Wilson, on the other hand, was in 1912 still fundamentally a states' rights Democrat who feared excessive governmental power. Though he, too, was committed to the progressive ideal of social justice, he considered laws to aid farmers and workers as wrong in principle as tariffs and other subsidies for business. Roosevelt's proposal to regulate big business through a powerful trade commission seemed to Wilson merely a move to legalize and perpetuate monopoly. Aided by the counsel of Louis D. Brandeis, a leading progressive lawyer and student of the trust problem, Wilson

214

argued that monopoly and special privilege must be destroyed if the nation were to prosper. There could be no effective political democracy without economic democracy, he warned; the situation required not Roosevelt's paternalism, but a return to truly free enterprise, a New Freedom. "I am fighting," Wilson asserted, "not for the man who has made good, but for the man who is going to make good—the man who is knocking and fighting at the closed doors of opportunity. There is no group of men big enough or wise enough to take care of a free people."

Once in the White House, Wilson moved energetically to translate the New Freedom into reality. No sooner was he inaugurated than he called a special session of Congress, and when the lawmakers assembled he went dramatically before them to urge an end to the system of high tariff protection for "infant" industries long since grown fat and sluggish with age. Not since John Adams had a president addressed Congress in person, but Wilson, well aware of the pitfalls of tariff reform, wanted from the first to achieve a close working relationship with the legislative branch, as well as to emphasize to the country his seriousness of purpose. Afterward, driving home, Mrs. Wilson remarked that his decision to break the old precedent was the sort of thing Theodore Roosevelt would have liked to do, had he only thought of it. "Yes," chuckled her husband, "I think I put one over on Teddy."

Wilson followed up his tariff message with a series of personal conferences with congressional leaders, both at the White House and in the hitherto rarely used President's Room at the Capitol. He even had a special telephone line installed so that he could reach wavering members quickly and directly. When the protection-minded Senate, buttressed by a swarm of lobbyists, threatened to sabotage the low tariff bill passed by the House, Wilson lashed out hard. "It is of serious interest to the country," he warned in a public statement, "that the people at large should have no lobby and be voiceless in these matters, while great bodies of astute men seek to create an artificial opinion and to overcome the interests of the public for their private profit." In the end the Senate gave in before the incessant presidential pressure and actually reduced the general level of rates of the House bill, chiefly by adding certain agricultural products to the free list. Though the Underwood-Simmons Tariff of 1913 was no free trade measure (it gave an average *ad valorem* protection of about 25 per cent as opposed to the more than 40 per cent average of the Payne-Aldrich Tariff of 1909), it was nevertheless the first significant tariff reform since the Civil War and was designed to put American industry into genuine competition with European manufactures. It contained, moreover, another important progressive reform, the first graduated income tax under the new Sixteenth Amendment. Rates were low and exemptions high, but a first step had been taken to democratize the nation's tax structure.

Even while he was guiding the tariff measure through Congress, Wilson was hard at work on a much more difficult task, reform of the nation's banking and currency system. Conservatives and progressives alike agreed that it was urgently necessary to do away with the existing disorganized banking system with its immobile reserves and inelastic money supply. But they disagreed profoundly over the nature and extent of the changes to be made. The banking community favored the creation of a powerful central bank with some fifteen regional branches, able to issue currency, hold reserves, and set discount rates, with the entire system controlled by member banks on the basis of capitalization. Advanced progressives, on the other hand, insisted that the Federal government, not the bankers, must control the banking structure and that the issuance of currency must be an exclusive governmental function.

Wilson had not studied the matter carefully before his election and had no fixed opinions as to specific details, other than his general laissez faire outlook and his conviction that some reform was badly needed. Accordingly, he was at first inclined to accept a plan presented by Representative Carter Glass of Virginia, a leading member of the House Banking Committee, for the establishment of a thoroughly decentralized system of reserve banks. Glass thought the system should be run by the bankers; Wilson suggested that it should at least be supervised by a Government board. The more advanced progressives in the party were aghast at the Glass plan, which they considered hardly a reform at all. They demanded instead that the Government control both the reserve banks and the issuance of currency. The dispute became so critical that for a time it threatened to wreck party unity and thus block any banking reform whatever. After seeking Brandeis' advice, Wilson decided that the Government must control the Federal Reserve Board and must alone issue currency, and thereafter he refused to retreat in the face of outraged cries from the bankers that this was rank socialism. When a group of prominent bankers came to the White House to argue for banker representation on the Federal Reserve Board Wilson asked bluntly: "Will one of you gentlemen tell me in what civilized country of the earth there are important government boards of control on which private interests are represented? Which of you gentlemen thinks the railroads should select members of the Interstate Commerce Commission?" To this the bankers prudently made no reply.

The passage of the Federal Reserve Act on December 23, 1913, was by all odds the most important domestic achievement of the Wilson administration, and it was due largely to Wilson's great skill in holding intact his party's ranks in Congress. The measure gave the United States a banking structure well geared to modern needs, combining private operation at the local level with suitable public control. The act also pioneered in providing the first significant national economic stabilizers: an elastic currency, flexible bank reserves, and centralized control over discount rates. Subsequent experience would suggest ways to improve the Federal Reserve system, but it would remain the heart of the nation's banking structure.

Tariff and banking reform constituted a major part of the New Freedom's drive to destroy monopoly and restore competition, by removing, as Wilson told Congress, "the trammels of the protective tariff" and requiring the banks to be "the instruments, and not the masters, of business and individual enterprise." Yet there remained the job of strengthening the anti-trust laws. Wilson had argued during the campaign that since most businessmen were honest and well-meaning all that was needed was to define and proscribe by law those evil practices that led to unfair competition and monopoly. He therefore threw his influence behind a number of proposals, which were soon combined in the Clayton bill in the House of Representatives. The measure prohibited a long list of unfair trade practices, forbade interlocking directorates and stock ownership, and, to satisfy organized labor, restricted the use of injunctions in labor disputes and declared that farm and labor organizations should not be considered as illegal combinations in restraint of trade when pursuing lawful objectives.

Many progressives, however, especially Roosevelt's followers but also some Democrats, protested that this approach was both inadequate and naive, that it was impossible to foresee and spell out in precise detail all the possible roads to monopoly. In time, their criticism had an effect on the President. Not long after the

217

Clayton bill passed the House, Wilson reversed his campaign stand and swung over to the idea of a strong trade commission with the power to inquire into business practices and issue cease and desist orders against unfair conduct. Once converted, he worked zealously to overcome the opposition, with the result that in the fall of 1914 Congress passed both measures, the Federal Trade Commission Act and a somewhat weakened Clayton Act. The President's remarkable success in securing the adoption of his domestic program led a conservative Republican, Chauncey M. Depew, to observe with wonderment: "This man who was regarded as a pedagogue, a theorist, is accomplishing the most astounding practical results."

Wilson's decision to insist upon government control over the Federal Reserve system and his acceptance of a strong trade commission showed that the line between the New Freedom and the New Nationalism was becoming blurred. By the end of his first administration it had disappeared altogether. No doubt partly because it was politically expedient, but also because he sincerely came to believe in more advanced reforms, Wilson by the summer of 1916 had taken over and shepherded through Congress the major part of the Progressive party's platform of 1912. The list was impressive: a law improving maritime safety requirements and the working conditions of seamen; a system of Federal farm loan banks to provide farmers with cheap credit; larger self-government for the Philippines; a model workmen's compensation act for Federal employees; a law prohibiting child labor; the eight-hour day for railroad employees, long a primary labor objective; and a tariff commission to review tariff rates. And although his more conservative advisers had originally talked Wilson out of offering a Cabinet post to the militant reformer Louis D. Brandeis, Wilson in 1916 overjoyed progressives by naming Brandeis to the Supreme Court and then grimly stood by him while outraged conservatives and business spokesmen tried unsuccessfully to block his confirmation.

By the time of the presidential campaign of 1916 Wilson had succeeded not only in enacting the most significant progressive legislation the country had yet known, but in the process had also managed to remake the Democratic party into a vital, unified instrument of reform, with far-reaching consequences for American politics that would extend through the New Deal and the Fair Deal a generation later. The election of 1916 demonstrated how nearly the two major parties were divided on a progressive-conservative basis. Though Wilson also benefited from the peace issue, he attracted a substantial number of the progressive Republicans who in 1912 had followed Roosevelt, along with most of the labor and farm vote. His margin over the Republican candidate, Charles Evans Hughes, was narrow—9,129,606 popular votes to 8,538,221, and a majority of only 23 electoral votes—but it was significant that the President had gained nearly three million votes over his total in 1912.

"It would be the irony of fate," Wilson had remarked to a friend shortly before his inauguration in 1913, "if my administration had to deal chiefly with foreign affairs." Grim irony, indeed! For from the very beginning of his administration the new President had to contend with a succession of urgent and critical foreign problems the like of which the nation had never before experienced.

Wilson, like most Americans, had not paid much attention to foreign affairs before entering the White House; he much preferred to apply what he sometimes jokingly described as his single track mind to domestic problems. He had traveled abroad several times, but only to vacation in the quiet English countryside. Like most of his countrymen he scarcely comprehended the profound implications of the recent emergence of the United States as a full-fledged great power. But both Wilson and his first secretary of state, William Jennings Bryan, shared certain deeply held convictions that gave a distinctive character to their diplomacy. Both were moralists who were guided by what they thought was right rather than by what was merely expedient; both had a strong sense of an American mission to civilize and uplift the world; both regarded war with horror.

The evangelistic quality of Wilson's and Bryan's diplomacy was manifested in a number of ways: the negotiation of a treaty of apology with an indemnity of 25 million dollars to Colombia for Theodore Roosevelt's aggressive role in obtaining the Panama Canal Zone in 1903 (Roosevelt's friends in the Senate blocked ratification); repeal of the tolls exemption for American ships using the Canal because it violated British rights under the Hay-Pauncefote Treaty; Bryan's great effort to arrange "cooling off" treaties with some thirty nations for the conciliation of disputes; the well-meant attempts to look out for the interests of small Latin-American states. Bryan, for example, advised the Cuban government not to accept a Wall Street loan that was not in Cuba's long range interest, and turned down an offer from Haiti of exclusive American concession rights on the ground that this might lead to the exploitation of the Haitian people.

Unfortunately, there was another, much less happy, side to the Wilson administration's moralistic diplomacy. Old-fashioned imperialism and dollar diplomacy gave way before what might be described as a new "moral" imperialism, which seemed to have the same tools and results, if different objectives and rationale. In their zeal to help spread the American ideals of freedom and democracy, Wilson and Bryan intervened on an unprecedented scale in the internal affairs of the nations of Central America and the Caribbean. Their actions were partly motivated, it is true, by the need to protect the American interest in the nearly completed Panama Canal. But equally important was their fervent belief that the United States ought to help the people of these small countries achieve stability and democracy, to protect them both from foreign dangers and themselves. By 1916 Wilson's moral impulses had led him to meddle repeatedly and disastrously in Mexican affairs, to make Nicaragua into a virtual American protectorate, and to clamp full-scale military occupations on Haiti and the Dominican Republic. Latin Americans might be pardoned for failing to distinguish between gunboats sent to help them elect good men and gunboats sent to protect foreign concessions; but Wilson, for one, was satisfied that his intervention was guided by a high moral purpose. In a sense his Mobile address in 1913 renouncing any future American territorial ambitions and his vision of a Pan-American pact guaranteeing the political independence and territorial integrity of the nations of the Western Hemisphere foreshadowed the Good Neighbor Policy of a later president. In practice, however, Wilson's Latin-American diplomacy left a legacy of distrust and bitterness that would fester for years.

Wilson's difficulties with Latin America were only a preliminary to larger and more ominous problems. While Mrs. Wilson lay dying in the White House in the summer of 1914, a Serbian student assassinated the Austrian Archduke, and one by one the great nations of Europe drifted into war. From his wife's bedside on August 4, only two days before her death, the distraught President issued an official proclamation of neutrality, and followed it with an appeal to Americans to be impartial in thought as well as in deed. This, as it turned out, proved to be an unattainable goal. Although the vast majority of Americans were strongly opposed to any active involvement in the war before 1917, this did not prevent them from hoping, in some cases quite loudly and belligerently, for the victory of one or the other of the opposing sides. As the conflict progressed probably a majority of the American people came to favor an Anglo-French victory, though there remained a substantial hard core of German sympathizers right down to the time the United States entered the war. There were a number of reasons for this preponderance of support for the Allies. Perhaps most important, many Americans, and this included the President and most of his advisers, were horrified at Germany's callous violation of Belgian neutrality and her ruthless submarine attacks against defenseless passenger ships. Consequently they were ready even without the stimulus of Allied propaganda to believe that the British and the French were fighting to preserve Western civilization. Germany, aggressive and expansive, seemed a potential threat to American interests and security, whereas the Allies did not. Moreover, as the United States gradually became an important arsenal of the Allies, providing both needed loans and vital war supplies, the American stake in an Allied victory grew accordingly. Before 1917, however, Americans from President Wilson down overwhelmingly hoped to stay out of the war and use their influence toward a just peace.

How, then, did the United States come to enter the war? The answer lies in Wilson's fight to protect some, but not all, American neutral rights. Like Jefferson and Madison before him, Wilson found himself caught between two powerful belligerents, neither of which was willing to permit legal abstractions to stand in the way of victory. Because he was at heart sympathetic to the Allies, Wilson protested but in the end acquiesced in the various British violations of American neutral rights at sea, restrictions that effectively choked off American trade with the Central Powers. At the same time he permitted the sale of raw materials and war supplies to the Allies, on the theory that such trade was open to all belligerents even though in practice British control of the sea denied Germany access to the American market. And although the Administration at first frowned on loans by American bankers to the belligerents, in 1915, when the Allies began to run out of ready cash to continue their profitable purchases in the United

States, Wilson reversed himself and allowed the bankers to extend large credits. On the other hand, when the Germans sought to check the increasingly dangerous flow of war materiel from the United States to the Allies, using the only weapon available, the submarine, Wilson reacted angrily in defense of the right of Americans and American ships to travel in safety on the high seas. The compelling difference, in the eyes of the President and many Americans, was that British actions, while oppressive and illegal, did not involve loss of life or the destruction of property, while German torpedoes accomplished both with deadly effect.

The inauguration of the German submarine blockade of the British Isles in February, 1915, faced Wilson with a painful dilemma. On the one hand, he could tacitly accept this new violation of neutral rights just as he had acquiesced in the British blockade of the Central Powers, though this might in the end insure Germany's triumph. Or he could insist that Germany respect American rights to freedom of the seas, and risk having to fight for those right if Germany refused. Either course would favor one or the other of the belligerents. The sinking without warning of the British liner *Lusitania* on May 7, 1915, with the loss of more than 1200 lives, including 128 Americans, shocked the President and led him to take a strong stand on behalf of the right of American citizens to travel in safety in the war zones. This in turn brought the first serious rift within the Administration, for Secretary of State Bryan resigned rather than sign the second strong *Lusitania* note. Bryan argued that Americans should be warned that they traveled on belligerent ships only at their own risk, and that Wilson's firm policy toward Germany would ultimately lead to war. The President and his new secretary of state, Robert Lansing, rejected this counsel, however, determined to force a change in German policy or else break diplomatic relations. In the end the Berlin government capitulated, agreeing to sink no more passenger ships without warning and without provision for the safety of crew and passengers.

Unhappily, this diplomatic victory proved to be short-lived. In the long run, as Bryan had predicted, Wilson found it impossible to protect American neutral rights from German violation without resorting to war, for the Germans ultimately refused to abandon the use of their most effective weapon against the ever-increasing flow of American war supplies to the Allies. Early in

1917 after Germany resumed unrestricted submarine warfare against all merchant shipping in the war zone, the President saw no alternative but to fight—ironically, for the right to be neutral. Meanwhile, Wilson had prudently begun to strengthen the nation's defenses, winning reluctant congressional approval to reorganize and enlarge the Army and greatly expand the size and strength of the Navy. At the same time he made a number of attempts to end the conflict in Europe, for he wisely saw that the best hope of an enduring peace was to gain a settlement before either side succeeded in crushing the other. Twice the President sent his trusted adviser and confidant, Colonel Edward M. House, on a round of the belligerent capitals in Europe to explore the possibility of American mediation, but House found the European leaders unwilling to give up the thought of all-out victory. On both sides the interest in Wilson's proposals varied inversely with the fortunes of the armies in the field. Shortly after his reelection in 1916, the President made one last effort at a negotiated settlement, outlining in his famous "peace without victory" speech to the Senate the kind of settlement the United States favored. It must be, he declared, a peace of justice between equals, without indemnities or annexations, a peace that would insure freedom of the seas, limitation of armaments, and the right of freedom and self-government for captive peoples.

Germany's answer came a few days later when Berlin announced the resumption of unrestricted submarine warfare. The Germans, it was clear, still hoped to enjoy the spoils of a victor's peace, and were confident that their submarines could bring Britain to her knees before any effective American intervention. Reluctantly, Wilson severed diplomatic relations, still hoping desperately that war might be averted. But events were rapidly passing out of his control. Finally, after several American ships had been sunk with heavy loss of life and the intercepted Zimmermann note had revealed German plans for an anti-American alliance with Mexico, the President on April 2, 1917, went before a special session of Congress to request a declaration of war. Sadly but with moving eloquence he concluded:

It is a fearful thing to lead this great peaceful people into war, into the most terrible and disastrous of all wars, civilization itself seeming to be in the balance. But the right

223

is more precious than peace, and we shall fight for the things which we have always carried nearest our hearts,—for democracy, for the right of those who submit to authority to have a voice in their own Governments, for the rights and liberties of small nations, for a universal dominion of right by such a concert of free peoples as shall bring peace and safety to all nations and make the world itself at last free. To such a task we can dedicate our lives and our fortunes, everything that we are and everything that we have, with the pride of those who know that the day has come when America is privileged to spend her blood and her might for the principles that gave her birth and happiness and the peace which she has treasured. God helping her, she can do no other.

Wilson's modest preparedness program had unfortunately sufficed neither to impress the Germans nor to equip the nation to fight a major war in 1917. Yet with remarkably few failures and false starts the Administration managed to mobilize men, ships, and supplies at a rate that astonished both friend and foe alike and proved to be the decisive factor in the Allied victory in 1918. For this much of the credit was due to Wilson himself. To meet the emergency he asked for and received from Congress vastly increased presidential powers, thereby leaving for his successors both the precedents and tools necessary for strong executive leadership in time of crisis. To help pay the astronomical war cost, for example, the Wilson administration demonstrated the enormous revenue potentials of steeply graduated income, inheritance, and excess profits taxes, as well as the direct popular sale of government bonds. A selective service law raised nearly three million men for the Army with none of the confusion, riots, or scandal that had marred the operation of a similar draft measure under Lincoln. To coordinate the domestic war effort, Wilson developed a variety of controls and new administrative machinery: powerful agencies to control industrial production and conserve scarce supplies of food and raw materials, temporary nationalization of the railroads and the telegraph lines, Government operation of shipyards and a large fleet of merchant ships, boards to settle labor disputes and help place workers in vital industries, and an ambitious propaganda effort to popularize American war aims and make Americans war-conscious. Future presidents, faced with the challenge of paralyz-

Wilson's wartime experience and governmental innovations.

Even before the full force of American arms had been felt on
the battlefields of Europe—before, indeed, an Allied victory was
assured—Wilson was hard at work on a peace settlement. The
United States, he was convinced, must play the leading role in the
struggle for a just and enduring peace. The other belligerents
were too cynical, too embittered, too bound by tradition and
previous commitments to approach the peace table with the necessary magnanimity and tolerance. Just as American military might
was essential to win the war, so American morality was vital to the
building of a stable world order. There were Fourteen Points in
the bold peace program the President outlined before a joint session of Congress on January 8, 1918: including open diplomacy,
freedom of the seas and of trade, reduction of armaments, impartial adjustment of colonial claims, self-determination for subject nationalities, and, as a capstone, a League of Nations "afford-
ing mutual guarantees of political independence and territorial integrity to great and small states alike." The Fourteen Points became at once one of the great weapons of the war, bolstering the
flagging morale of the Allied peoples and seriously weakening the
resolve of the enemy. As word of his liberal peace aims spread,
Wilson became a great popular hero abroad. Allied leaders were
skeptical, but to millions of war-weary Europeans the American
President seemed to offer the best hope of a new and better world
order. Nine months later when a beaten Germany sued for an
armistice, its leaders appealed directly to Wilson for a peace based
on his Fourteen Points.
Yet although Wilson approached the problems of peace with
great intelligence and vision, he himself was partly responsible for
some of the formidable obstacles in his path. In the final analysis
it was, of course, his decision to take the United States into the war
that made possible a dictated, rather than a negotiated, peace. Like
Lincoln, Wilson's very idealism led him to underestimate the force
of wartime hatred and vengeance, which ironically his own
war propagandists had helped to intensify. Of even greater importance was the fact that his severe Presbyterian conscience forbade
any sharp bargaining with Allied leaders over peace terms at a
time when his cards were the strongest, before America's entry

225

into the war. This would have been the ideal time to nail down Allied approval of American peace aims, not after Germany was beaten. But because Wilson tended to think of the war as a great crusade, he simply could not bring himself to demand even a high-minded *quid pro quo* as the price of American participation. Moreover, when he subsequently learned of some of the secret Allied agreements proposing to divide the spoils of victory in a manner scarcely in the spirit of the Fourteen Points, he declined to jeopardize the war effort by wielding the club of American military and economic power, trusting that the force of world public opinion would enable him to override these selfish commitments at the peace conference.

Wilson blundered, too, in failing to keep his political fences mended at home, though surely the onetime professor of government ought to have remembered that the president shares responsibility for foreign policy with a jealous Senate. Anxious to aid his party in the off-year elections of November, 1918, he called for the return of a Democratic Congress, terming the poll a personal vote of confidence in his leadership. His ill-advised appeal probably had little effect on the electorate one way or the other, but when the Republicans won control of both houses of Congress Wilson's political enemies were able to assert that by his own admission he stood repudiated by the American people. Even more serious was Wilson's failure to include any senators or prominent Republicans as members of the American delegation he took with him to the Paris Peace Conference. No doubt he ignored the Senate because he would have been obliged to invite one of his bitterest critics, Republican majority leader Henry Cabot Lodge—the same who forty years earlier had published the essay of an unknown Princeton undergraduate. Lodge had developed a consuming hatred for Wilson which was heartily reciprocated, but the President might well have avoided needless offense to the great body of moderate Republicans by including among his advisers such able and distinguished men as former President William H. Taft, Elihu Root, or Charles Evans Hughes. Wilson took with him to Paris hundreds of experts to assist in the political, economic, and ethnographical work of the conference—"Tell me what's right and I'll fight for it," he told them earnestly—yet by failing to make the undertaking truly bipartisan he greatly reduced the chances that his handiwork would survive the pitfalls of domestic politics upon his return.

Wilson has been strongly criticized for the shortcomings of the Versailles Peace Treaty, for its many failures to live up to the bright promise of his Fourteen Points. "It is incomprehensible," protested the president of the German National Assembly when the terms of the treaty were revealed, "that a man who had promised the world a peace of justice, upon which a society of nations would be founded, has been able to assist in framing this project dictated by hate." Yet the critics tend to overlook the fact that Wilson was in no position to dictate the peace terms. Inevitably he had to compromise with the less enlightened views of his chief colleagues, the shrewd, ambitious David Lloyd George of Great Britain, the cynical and vindictive Georges Clemenceau of France, and the covetous Vittorio Orlando of Italy. The wonder is not that the treaty violated some of Wilson's lofty principles but that he was able to achieve so much of his program in the face of skillful and determined opposition. Certainly Wilson's presence at the peace table was the main reason why the treaty was neither so harsh as the other Allied leaders would have liked nor indeed so ruthless as a victorious Germany would have imposed.

Wilson in fact managed to block most of the more extreme demands of his colleagues at the peace conference. For example, he set himself firmly against Clemenceau's drastic proposal to create a series of small buffer states under French control in western Germany, mollifying the French premier by agreeing to a joint Anglo-French-American defensive alliance against future German aggression. Had this defense agreement been maintained subsequently it might well have preserved the peace of Europe in the next generation. In the face of inflexible Allied demands that Germany must not regain her former overseas colonies, Wilson won an important concession that the colonies be mandates of the new League of Nations. He prevented France from annexing Germany's Saar Basin outright—which would have been a clear violation of the principle of self-determination—substituting instead temporary French control under a League mandate. He insisted that Fiume go to the new state of Yugoslavia rather than to Italy, though this action caused Orlando to withdraw for a brief sulk. In general Wilson's vigilance successfully protected the principle of self-determination in what turned out to be the most drastic reshuffling of European boundaries in over a century. Wilson made probably his most damaging concessions in the matter of reparations. Earlier he had declared that punitive damages had no place in a proper peace settlement, but at Paris he reluctantly acceded to Allied demands that Germany be saddled with a potentially astronomical reparations bill. Along with the companion war guilt clause, the heavy reparations burden insured the rise of vengeful German nationalism under a demagogue like Adolf Hitler and contributed heavily to the dangerously unstable world financial structure of the 1920's.

No one knew better than Wilson that the peace treaty fell far short of his ideals—he remarked at one point that if he were a German he thought he would never sign it—yet he was willing to accept an imperfect settlement in order to obtain what was nearest his heart, an international organization to preserve the peace. The League of Nations he felt was the heart of the post-war peace structure; it would provide the machinery through which defects in the peace settlement could gradually be remedied as wartime passions cooled. It was upon Wilson's insistence that the Covenant of the League was made an integral part of the treaty and the League entrusted with the execution of the treaty. "A living thing is born," he solemnly told the peace conference delegates when he presented the Covenant for their formal approval. "There is a compulsion of conscience throughout it. It is practical, and yet it is intended to purify, to rectify, to elevate." Yet the success of the League would be dependent upon the wholehearted support of the great powers, especially the United States. And tragically, Wilson himself would in the end bear a heavy responsibility for the American failure to join the League of Nations.

When Wilson returned with the peace treaty early in July, 1919, he faced the most difficult and most important fight of his life. The Republican majority in the Senate, led by his archenemy Senator Lodge, were bitterly resentful of what they regarded as the President's attempt to maintain a Democratic monopoly of peacemaking. Lodge, indeed, was contemptuous of even the phraseology of Wilson's cherished League Covenant. "It might get by at Princeton," he sneered, "but certainly not at Harvard." He determined to delay the vote on ratification to give time for the opposition to build up, and then to humiliate the President and win partisan advantage by attaching unacceptable reservations. Still, only twelve to fifteen bitter-end isolationist senators—the so-called "irreconcilables"—were set against any United States participation in an international organization. At all times during the

debate over ratification of the treaty more than three-fourths of
the Senate and the overwhelming majority of the press and articu-
late public opinion of the country favored joining the League
with some reservations to protect American interests. The task of
true statesmanship was to create a bipartisan majority for ratification without crippling amendments or reservations.

But Wilson, his Scotch stubbornness no less inflexible than the
obstinacy of the irreconcilables, was temperamentally incapable
of compromise with the Republican opposition. He refused to
accept any but the mildest interpretive reservations, arguing that
the rest would violate the nation's solemn word and reopen the
treaty to wholesale amendment by other signatories. As he had
done so often in the past with spectacular success, he resolved to
take his case directly to the people. Surely if they understood
what was at stake they would not permit the Senate to nullify
his labors. His never robust health had begun to give way at
Paris; his doctors protested that a strenuous speaking tour might
cost him his life. "I must go," he replied earnestly. "I promised
our soldiers, when I asked them to take up arms, that it was a
war to end wars; and if I do not do all in my power to put the
Treaty in effect, I will be a slacker and never be able to look
those boys in the eye."

And so, for three weeks in September he traveled eight thousand miles through the West delivering with passionate eloquence
and conviction some thirty-seven speeches to ever larger and
more enthusiastic crowds. With tears in his eyes he told an audience at Pueblo, Colorado, on September 25:

> Nothing less depends upon this decision, nothing less than
> the liberation and salvation of the world. Now that the great
> mists of this question have cleared away, I believe that men
> will see the truth, eye to eye and face to face. There is one
> thing that the American people always rise to and extend
> their hand to, and that is the truth of justice and of liberty
> and of peace. We have accepted that truth and we are going
> to be led by it, and it is going to lead us, and through us
> the world, out into pastures of quietness and peace such as
> the world never dreamed of before.

That night, as the presidential train sped toward Wichita, Wilson's frail body gave way; his doctor cancelled the remaining

speeches and ordered an immediate return to Washington. There on October 2 the President suffered a stroke that nearly killed him and left him paralyzed on the left side of his face and body.

With Wilson's physical collapse came the collapse of his brave new world as well. His meager strength jealously guarded by his physician and his devoted second wife, the ailing President was isolated and unable effectively to command the forces favoring ratification. Nor would he listen to suggestions that he compromise with his enemies. Twice the Senate voted on the treaty; twice Wilson sent word from his sickbed that his followers must not accept the Lodge reservations. After the second adverse vote had killed the treaty and with it American participation in the League of Nations, Senator Brandegee, one of the irreconcilables, remarked gratefully to Lodge: "We can always depend on Mr. Wilson. He has never failed us."

Like Abraham Lincoln, Woodrow Wilson is a great but tragic figure among American presidents—great in his imaginative and forthright leadership, tragic in his inability to persuade his countrymen to adopt a noble dream. Wilson's—and the nation's—supreme tragedy was that his own stubbornness was at least partly responsible for his most costly defeat, the failure of the United States to take the lead in making the League of Nations a vital instrument of peace. Yet the failure should not blind us to Wilson's very real contributions. It was Wilson who demonstrated beyond question that the United States was a major world power with responsibility for mature leadership in world affairs. It was his League of Nations that pioneered in providing collective security for all countries, large and small. A later generation, after suffering the horrors of another world war, would pay tribute to Wilson's ideals by creating the United Nations, and this time only a scattered few would question the wisdom of wholehearted American participation. In other respects, too, Wilson left a tangible and living legacy: the first national economic stabilizers, democratization of the tax structure, stronger anti-trust protection, and a host of other domestic reforms. No other chief executive before him so systematically and successfully made use of the legislative powers of his office. Indeed, it might be said that he largely established the modern pattern of the president as both the leader of his party and of Congress. He greatly extended the war powers of the presidency and showed his successors how these powers might be used boldly in emergency. He accomplished an unprecedented mobilization of the nation's military and economic resources without a major scandal touching his administration. In sum, Wilson's achievements were many and spectacular. If on occasion he also failed spectacularly, it was because, being human, he was not always capable of transforming noble dreams into reality.

Franklin Roosevelt

by PAUL L. MURPHY

The United States which Franklin D. Roosevelt inherited on a cold March day in 1933 was a nation of confused, disillusioned, pessimistic and often bitter people. The United States which he left to his successor on a warm April day in 1945 was a nation of vigorous, purposeful, optimistic and generally hopeful people. That such a change could be produced in the collective psyches of one hundred and thirty million human beings in a period marked by depression, dictatorship, war and destruction is testimony to the ability of a talented leader both to instruct his people in the ways of meeting the crises of a twentieth-century world, and to convince them that by meeting such crises they and their children, and their neighbors and their children, could not only expect but count on a better tomorrow. "This generation of Americans," the President once predicted, "has a rendezvous with destiny." What he did not add was that he himself had had a hand in arranging that rendezvous and fully intended to play a role in shaping that destiny. And the passage of time has brought a growing appreciation of that role. Thirteen years after his death, when a national magazine queried its readers—"Which great historical figure do you believe would be most capable of dealing with the present world crisis, based both on his ability to understand the nature of the problem and his ability to inspire a following for his leadership?"—the name most mentioned was that of Franklin D. Roosevelt.

The American people in the dozen or so years prior to Roosevelt's ascension to power had had a peculiar existence. Life in the 1920's and early thirties had departed from most prior norms. Further, the pace it demanded left little time for introspection, even if people had wished to analyze their new world, which most did not. At least this was true until the depression of 1929 shocked many into the realization that it was high time for a thorough and critical assessment of American society. If what they saw puzzled them, the problem of finding a way to do something remedial and constructive overwhelmed them. The reasons for such a state of affairs are complicated, yet an accurate understanding of them is essential if one is to appreciate the success of the presidency of Franklin D. Roosevelt.

The 1920's was a decade not far removed in point of time from the Progressive period. Yet the changes which took place in America in the years between 1914, the height of that period, and 1927, the height of the frenetic jazz age, were so great as to produce almost a new civilization, even though great numbers of the same Americans lived in both eras. The America of 1914, although in reality highly complex, was still sufficiently uncomplicated in the public eye that people felt well able to cope with it. One knew one's neighbors, read a newspaper written in a personal vein, set and enforced the moral code for one's children, and recognized and respected certain families and individuals in the community who exerted leadership so as to preserve fundamental American values of thrift, decency and personal respectability. The evils of society could be handled, and responsible citizens had a moral duty to pitch in and support their leaders in this task. The seedy side of political life could be eliminated by proper institutional changes— the direct primary, the short ballot, the recall. Through reason, goodness, and an aggressive local organization, responsible people could crusade successfully against the city machine, the sweatshop employer, the traction magnate, or the real corruptor of the community, the saloon-keeper. If certain local problems seemed to have their roots in some larger and less manageable national situation, the influential local citizens could sit down with the national politician when he came through town and make it clear to him what action they expected to come from Washington.

By the 1920's the comfortable small-town life was disappearing before the impact of the apartment-house-studded metropolis. Parents were no longer sure they knew how to raise their children and the children were fairly convinced of it. The respected family, who had been looked to for leadership, was being discredited in an era in which impersonal newspapers made it clear that the businessman was the person to whom Americans should look for direction. Financial success should be the real American goal. "The business of America is business," said President Calvin Coolidge, as the national administration fell in line, and many nodded approvingly at his wisdom.

Yet even before the great crash of 1929 many other Americans slept uneasily. Where was all this leading? Was not the United States being swept along in a wave of crass materialism which seemed to be destroying all the old values and leaving fairly brittle ones in their place? Were the business leaders the sort of people who could be trusted to rule the nation in such a way as to provide a decent life for all? By the late 1920's these questions were being asked more and more by the man in the street. In fact, a profound discontent with the monopoly of power and prestige by a single class and the resulting indifference of the national government to deeper tensions was becoming more evident. Many Americans were finding that the greatly advertised benefits of the new business civilization were somehow not managing to reach them. The small businessman, far from the salubrious climate of Wall Street, found himself very much an outsider and severely handicapped by the nation's tightly-controlled money market. Farmers discovered that the natural laws of economics which worked so well for the corporations did little to stimulate agricultural prosperity. Elements in the labor movement were growingly aware of their second-class citizenship. Although these groups tended to be sullenly inarticulate, they had little trouble in finding a wave of fairly eloquent protest to substantiate their discontent coming from the pens of writers such as H. L. Mencken and Sinclair Lewis, educators like John Dewey, and academicians like Charles A. Beard and Robert and Helen Lynd.

Dissatisfaction in the 1920's, however, had other causes. Not only was nothing being done to remedy unsatisfactory conditions but the normal avenues of approach toward solutions seemed to be disappearing. The evils of machine-age life no longer seemed susceptible to correction by righteous campaigns of public-minded citizens. Curbing the city boss or the traction magnate was no longer sufficient. The former sense of confidence was no longer present and in fact men were not always even sure what evil was, or how to recognize their enemies. The politician offered little help, for he seldom came through town any more, and preferred to speak to large invisible audiences on the radio. And the very impersonality of this approach left people feeling that he not only failed to understand their problems but did not want to. Both parties seemed anxious to underwrite the *status quo*. In fact, as Walter Lippman was to point out in 1927: ". . . our political leaders are greatly occupied in dampening down interest, in obscuring issues, and in attempting to distract attention from the realities of American life." Some people took this as an indication that possibly America's political leadership had things fairly well under control and saw no use for lengthy discussion. Others, however, had an ominous suspicion that the politicians were as perplexed about how to cope with the increasing dislocations of an impersonal society as they were.

The collapse of the whole hollow structure of prosperity in 1929 left a nation that had previously begun to feel awkwardly left-footed, frankly helpless. If it had been virtually impossible to deal with serious problems when times were supposedly good, how did one go about confronting an economic depression unparalleled in American history? Certainly the much vaunted and supposedly infallible business leadership which most people felt had gotten them into this mess could hardly be looked to to lead them out. The reigning politicians seemed at most to offer the dubious hope that in time the depression would run its course and that there was really nothing wrong with the nation's basic economic and political system. But neither claim eased many minds. As the depression seemed to worsen instead of improve, loud and seemingly authoritative voices chanted with regularity that there were many things wrong with the system. In fact, these analysts stated that a whole new system would have to be turned to for the old one had run out of energy, it had exhausted its intellectual and moral resources, its bag of tricks was played out.

But if they disagreed on means, there was one thing certain of the most vocal and outspoken politicians and critics did agree upon. The United States had reached a point in its history where it had to choose between one of two definite alternatives. Stated Secretary of the Treasury Ogden Mills: "We can have a free country or a socialistic one. We cannot have both. Our economic system cannot be half free and half socialistic. There is no middle ground between governing and being governed, between absolute sovereignty and liberty, between tyranny and freedom." At the same time Winston Churchill in England was doubting "whether institutions based on adult suffrage could possibly arrive at the right decisions upon the intricate propositions of modern business and finance. . . . You cannot cure cancer by a majority." The only solution lay, felt Churchill and many others, in a managed economy, controlled by the state with representative democracy sacrificed for economic stability. Neither the far Right nor the far Left could accept as practical or possible a mixed system of socially directed and managed capitalism which might give the state enough power to assure economic and social security, but still not so much as to create dictatorship. If Americans felt hopeless about their own inability to shape their future, this presenting of two unattractive but dogmatically inflexible alternatives by supposedly enlightened leaders plunged them into a deeper gloom.

When Franklin D. Roosevelt entered the White House in 1933, he was well aware of the problems confronting the American people. But more important, he shared neither the hopelessness of the average citizen, nor the intransigent dogmatism of the Right and the Left. If he had no specific, well-conceived, long-range master plan ready to put into action, he nevertheless had definite goals which he hoped to attain and he lost no time in setting out to attain them. From the days of his own unsuccessful campaign for the vice-presidency in 1920, Roosevelt had become more and more discontented with the Democratic party. The majority of its Southern wing stood for reactionary racism, intolerant Protestantism, extreme laissez faire, and the feudalistic ideology of the South, while in many Northern cities it was associated with the graft, corruption, and racketeering of the city machines. Roosevelt not only conceived of the party as an agency for good, but hoped to reshape it by making it attractive to such groups as farmers, union members, small entrepreneurs, Negroes, immigrant groups and intellectuals. Once in office, he hoped to elicit from these elements strength and leadership which would further the development of new programs beneficial to all citizens. The party would thus be purged of the dominant influence of its undesirable membership; more importantly, it would gain strength less because of patronage than for progressive leadership.

The president, as party leader, would also be strengthened by such a process. But Roosevelt was far less concerned about the power of the presidency than what its real functions should be and for that matter what the functions of government should be.

To Roosevelt, government should become the positive agency for the control and molding of society. "That nation or state which is unwilling by government action to tackle new problems caused by the immense increase of population and the astonishing strides of modern science is headed for a decline and ultimate death from inaction." He rejected the previously well-accepted concept of the negative character of government. He felt strongly that the essential democracy of the nation and the safety of the people should not depend upon the absence of power. Rather it should be lodged with those whom the people could change or continue at stated intervals through an honest and free system of elections, especially those who would exert positive leadership while in office. Such a position was startling both because it seemed to depart from old ways and because it could easily be interpreted as a theory leading to statism. Roosevelt went out of his way to make clear he was calling for nothing revolutionary, however. The reason for governmental authority, he was fond of saying, was to help make the system of free enterprise work and provide that minimum security without which the competitive system could not function. Granted this might seem to threaten restrictions on individual freedom, but actually it would only limit the kind of individual action which in the past had been harmful to the community. Capitalism worked well enough, but unfortunately it had been perverted by a group of grafters and chiselers who fouled up the engine of private enterprise. A minor overhauling was in order.

But the long-range purpose of positive government was to be more than the abstract one of refurbishing the capitalistic system. Government should exist to serve the best interests and provide for the general welfare of all the people. As Roosevelt stated in the 1932 campaign: "Our government, formal and informal, political and economic, owes to everyone an avenue to possess himself of a portion of that plenty [from our industrial society] sufficient for his needs through his own work." Along with opening avenues, was an equal duty of aiding the depressed: "Those suffering hardship from no fault of their own have a right to call upon the government for aid, and a government worthy of its name must make fitting response." Thus human resources should be revitalized as a part of the general task of rebuilding. Further, broadening social and economic opportunity for the individual, channeling his energies into useful pursuits, would also serve to breathe life back into the ailing machinery of democracy.

If this was to be the general role of the Government, the president's role was to be that of translating these broad objectives into positive programs. But Roosevelt, the democrat, knew that this could not be done unilaterally. "Any system which tries to provide for security for everyone from above only calls for an impossible task and a regimentation utterly uncongenial to the spirit of our people." Public opinion had to be enlisted into the process, and this would prove a ticklish task, especially since public opinion in 1933 tended to be fragmented, negative, and unconstructive. As important as the mere enlisting of public opinion was the job of channeling it into desirable paths of action. Too many Americans looked to the past, especially to the days when life was simpler and sweeter and easier to understand and hoped that some way might be found to return to that bygone era. This meant rejecting the civilization of which they were a part, blindly attacking bigness and impersonality; in other words, it meant refusing to cope with the present reality of America's system. Others manifested the familiar human emotion which is evoked when one is sure the shoe is on the other foot. "We are in now," they seemed to say. "We are, after years of being pushed around, in a position to push back." "We have been the have-nots and it is the Government's duty to see that we now become the haves."

Roosevelt's task then entailed education and salesmanship. He had to convince an unwieldy public of the acceptability and desirability of new and, in some instances, radical programs. This would mean both showing the people the practicality of such programs and making clear that they were in the American tradition and did not threaten to lead the country down dangerous paths. To do this he realized the value of making the people feel they were a part of the governing process, making them feel that by throwing their active support behind such programs, taking part in them willingly and working to make them succeed, they would be advancing their own interests and the community's as well. Here he sensed the personal frustrations Americans had experienced from being unable to fight impersonality and saw an immense opportunity to channel these frustrations into positive action. Roosevelt knew this would take patience. He could lead only so fast as his following would permit. He knew there were real limits to individual idealism and that he would have to continually emphasize practicality. He also knew that unless people saw quick results, immediately beneficial to themselves, they would rapidly become disillusioned and might not support more long-range programs. In this sense, Roosevelt would have to be a reflector of public desires as much as a leader. He would have to keep a sensitive finger on the public pulse to be sure the public felt that what was being done was actually translating their desires into proper policies and courses of action.

Although such a task seemed overwhelming, Roosevelt felt it was possible. Despite a very real appreciation of man's weaknesses and often selfish character, he had a fundamental faith in the goodness, decency, and rationality of mankind. Further he was convinced that rugged individualism was no more a part of the American character than was the more important element of communal effort. The history of America had been a history of pioneers and of individuals moving within a framework of civil responsibility. If Americans would once again be convinced of the wisdom of working together toward a common goal, they would come to realize that only as a member of a group can a citizen best realize his own potential, or can he create conditions in which his own abilities can be awarded their proper recognition and recompense. In this regard, Roosevelt was anxious to convince the American people that they could find, through an active participation in their government, the proper instrument with which the individual could confront the ever-rising problems of a complex civilization.

The pressure upon Roosevelt as president to begin implementing his policies was unmerciful at the time of his first inauguration in March, 1933. Most of the country's banks, especially the great metropolitan institutions, had managed to survive the first blows of the depression but as the economies of European nations began collapsing in 1931, American banking strength began to give way. By the summer of 1932 total bank resources had declined over 13 billion dollars from the previous year. As the public suspected the banking structure was collapsing they contributed by runs and heavy withdrawals to force growing failures. State governors then began declaring banking holidays and closing banks in an attempt to save what was left. But although people were assured banks would be reopened in due time, by March 4, 1933, banks were either closed or doing business under severe restrictions in forty-seven states.

"This nation asks for action, and action now. . . . We must act and act quickly," stated the new President on noon of March 4. That night the Cabinet was sworn in quietly at the White House.

The next day the President called a special session of Congress for March 9 and late in the evening proclaimed a nation-wide four-day bank holiday. Day-and-night conferences of administration officials, economists and the nation's leading bankers then followed at the White House, and an emergency banking bill was ready seventy-two virtually sleepless hours later. When Congress met, the two houses hastily organized and received a presidential message asking for the passage of the measure, and while some freshman House members were still looking for their seats, token debate was carried on and the bill was rushed into law in a record thirty-eight minutes. The Senate approved the measure in three hours and the President signed it into law at nine o'clock in the evening. The bill authorized Federal Reserve banks to issue currency against bank assets, empowered the Hoover-originated Reconstruction Finance Corporation to provide liquid funds to banks by buying their preferred stock and directed Treasury officials to investigate the financial status of individual banks and supervise their reopening at the first realistic opportunity.

If action, and seemingly sensible action was what people wanted, they certainly had gotten it in record time. But the new President was not ready to take the chance that people would automatically approve what had happened and jump on the bandwagon while he took a bow or two. He wanted this initial action stamped and approved. He realized all too well that like the first veteran returning to the home town from the wars, the first act of a new public official is the most important and draws the most attention. On March 12, at the end of his first week in office, he set out to establish direct contact with the people in the first of what developed into a long series of "fireside chats." The necessity of the educational process had not been forgotten. "I want to talk for a few minutes with the people of the United States about banking," he began, and for twenty minutes he went on, explaining the banking situation in simple, but never condescending terms, pointing out what the Government had done and appealing for public confidence in the nation's banking system. Even while the speech was being made banks were being reopened. By March 15, over half the banks in the country, with 90 per cent of the deposits, had been given a clean bill of health by Treasury officials.

The public's response to the fact that "the President was both talking and delivering the goods," was overwhelming. By the first week in April more than a billion dollars in currency had flowed back to the banks, hoarders had returned gold to the Federal Reserve banks, and Treasury officials had to issue only a small amount of new Federal Reserve currency. Almost as important was the simple response of millions of Americans in attempting someway to tell the President they were with him, that they understood what he was trying to do and wanted him to continue such "brave" and "decisive" action. In the week after the speech, over ten thousand telegrams swamped the White House. Up to March, 1933, one man had handled the entire presidential mail, but suddenly the mail clerk found himself with nearly half a million unopened letters stacked in his office, so demanded, and got a permanently enlarged staff in order to keep up. Even after this immediate crisis, Roosevelt averaged about ten times as much daily mail as his predecessor.

Sophisticated conservatives were partially surprised and greatly relieved at the action that had been taken. Given the magnitude of the crisis, the virtually blank-check he had, and the willingness of Congress to approve any program he might offer, the President had neither moved toward fascism, socialism, or communism, but had decided to restore and strengthen private ownership and management in the financial field. "The policies which vanquished the bank crisis," wrote Raymond Moley a few years later, "were thoroughly conservative policies. The sole departure from convention lay in the swiftness and boldness with which they were carried out."

But Roosevelt, although stimulated by the response to his initial action, was interested in doing far more than patching up past damage. The next step had to be revising and reforming the banking system so that it could not again get into such a state. And while agriculture, labor, business, and the masses of the unemployed were not quite in a condition to require immediate crash programs, all needed extensive assistance and this meant positive programs for them which could also combine immediate relief with long-range reform.

Thus Congress was kept in session for a hectic hundred days, one of the most remarkable legislative periods in American history. Committees met and studied or modified legislation. Hearings were held and laws pushed through. A host of presidential advisers were at work in a dozen agencies, in governmental buildings, hotel rooms, shabby Georgetown houses, anywhere they could find a desk, drafting, tearing up, redrafting, wrangling over further proposed bills. They in turn drew upon the abilities of a novel group of bright younger advisers whom they brought or attracted to the nation's capital from the academic world. These second line "New Dealers," for the term was already well implanted in the nation's vocabulary, were attracted both by the fact that the depression had closed the normal openings in business, industry, and law-firms, and by the intriguing prospect of having a part in the challenging process of rebuilding America. Again an atmosphere which invited the people to take part in the direction of their government had brought constructive results, and although there was to be some public scoffing at the "brains trust" and occasional annoyance at the vanity, arrogance, and starry-eyed idealism of these academic refugees, no one could deny that they were a vital part of the new spirit of activism and experimentation. Nor could anyone deny that their activities, added to those of their chiefs, plus the continuous pouring forth of advice and suggestions from private citizens representing practically every special interest in the United States, created a welter of confusions which staid Washington had never before witnessed. However, as Arthur M. Schlesinger, Jr., has written:

> Somewhere the commotion had a center. Perhaps it was the President's bedroom, where every morning Moley, [Lewis] Douglas and one or two other reigning favorites discussed the urgencies of the next twenty-four hours. Somehow Roosevelt kept all the balls in the air. He cracked jokes, stroked egos, mixed politics and professors, and came out with a policy. He saw agitated Congressmen, frightened businessmen, jealous bureaucrats, and had energy left over for arguments into the night. His press conferences crystallized the excitement for the reporters. And on occasion, the whirl would come to full stop, and that confident, mellow, friendly voice would explain necessities to the common people across the land.

The results of the "Hundred Days" left Americans occasionally gasping, at times a bit alarmed, but never bored. Those who lived through the period can still recall the electric excitement, the surging vitality, the mounting hope, the exhilaration that came over the American people after years of futility and frustration. In the financial area, legislation was passed designed to prevent another debacle such as the one in 1929 from ever happening again. The Glass-Steagall Banking Act of 1933 forbade commercial banks from speculating with their depositors' money, and also established the Federal Deposit Insurance Corporation to insure the deposits of banking customers in case a day of future bank failures ever came. The Truth-in-Securities Act, augmented a year later by the Securities Exchange Act of 1934, left the operation of stock exchanges in private hands, but compelled all underwriters and brokers to furnish complete information regarding the true value of securities being offered for sale and the arrangements under which the sale was being made.

For agriculture, after consultation with leaders of all the big farm organizations, the President recommended a bill designed to raise farmers' purchasing power, relieve the pressure of farm mortgages, and increase the value of farm loans made by banks. The measure, geared to the idea that the root of the farmers' problems was overproduction, set up a program of acreage controls on major crops with a system of benefit payments to secure necessary compliance. Farmers, by participating in the program, would receive immediate cash relief, and it was anticipated that through the program of curtailed production, prices on major agricultural commodities would gradually rise. The long-range goal was to re-establish prices of farm commodities at a level which would give the farmers a purchasing power equal to that which they enjoyed in the plush period, 1909 to 1914. Congress quickly pushed through legislation formalizing the program in the Agricultural Adjustment Act of 1933 and created a Farm Credit Administration to consolidate all Federal agricultural credit agencies and extend credit for the refinancing of farm mortgages.

For industry, after consultation with business leaders and such organizations as the United States Chamber of Commerce, the New Dealers came up with a National Industrial Recovery Act. The measure was designed both to stimulate economic recovery and bring some order into the chaotic, survival-of-the-fittest competitive system of the business community. It sought to provide for controls on production and prices, agreements on wages and hours of labor, and the regulation of advertising and of sales areas in an industry. The terms of the program were to be set by its participants. It was expected that industrial trade associations would convene to draw up codes which its members thought were fair for their particular industry. The codes were then taken to the National Recovery Administration in Washington where they were reviewed to decide whether they fitted in with the over-all policies of the program. If a code did not meet with approval, the bureau suggested amendments which would make the code acceptable. If an industry neglected to draw up a code for itself, the NRA was permitted to impose upon the industry a code of its own writing. Once a code was imposed, all individual companies within that industry were forced to abide by it upon pain of prosecution, whether or not they had signed it. In return for its cooperation with the NRA, industry was freed from the anti-trust laws.

Labor's reward for cooperation in forming the program—labor leaders as well as businessmen had been called in to help plan the codes—was Section 7(a). This guaranteed labor's right to bargain collectively through representatives of its own choosing, outlawed the yellow-dog contract, and declared that workers should not be required to join a company union as a condition of employment.

It was fondly hoped that given time to operate, this body of agriculture, business and labor legislation would start the wheels of recovery in motion. However, in the meantime people could not be left to starve. Harry Hopkins once responded to a proposed relief plan which he was told would work out in the long run: ". . . people don't eat in the long run—they eat every day." Relief legislation for the unemployed was rushed through, although in two instances an attempt was made to channel it into programs of positive service to the nation. The Civilian Conservation Corps was organized to put a quarter of a million young men to work building dams, draining marsh-lands, fighting forest fires, planting trees and generally extending the conservation goals of the early Progressives. The Tennessee Valley Authority sought to create work by rebuilding an entire region of the country through a program of power development, flood control, soil erosion control, reforestation, retirement of marginal lands, and industrial distribution and diversification. When Congress adjourned in June, 1933, scarcely a segment of the nation or its people had failed to be brought under one of the New Deal's various programs. Even the President admitted fatigue, but certainly no disappointment.

In the retrospect of the 1960's, it was a good thing for Roosevelt that he had built up as solid a reservoir of good-will and public support as he had in the initial banking crisis. For if his actions then were conservative, the later programs represented the largest step toward a state-run economy ever attempted in the United States. Both the NRA and the AAA, although geared to aid conservative businessmen and farmers, represented decided attempts toward doing so through national economic planning. If they had not eventually either failed or been declared unconstitutional by the Supreme Court, the later New Deal might not have returned to the more orthodox approaches to recovery and reform that it did. At the time, however, and despite radical theory, the President's popular support did not wane. The man in the street spent little time questioning the philosophy of the legislation Congress was passing. He was far more impressed that the various measures all seemed to set up programs through which he, as a private citizen, was given a concrete chance to do something very real and constructive to improve his own immediate conditions. At the same time, with emphasis upon group action, he was also able to feel that by cooperating with the programs, he was doing his part to save the nation. Given an opportunity to express his sentiments at the polls in 1934, he brought about the almost unprecedented phenomenon for an off-year election, an increase in the strength of the party in power in both houses of Congress and in state capitals throughout the country. Roosevelt had not only been able to capture the support and loyalty of the electorate; he had managed to invest his party with his own vote-getting power. The New Deal, wrote Arthur Krock in *The New York Times*, has won "the most overwhelming victory in the history of American politics. . . . There has been no such popular endorsement since the days of Thomas Jefferson and Andrew Jackson."

Yet even as the election returns were being counted, some early New Deal programs were beginning to sputter and break down. Enforcement of the various code provisions of the NRA had led to mountains of red tape, and as more bureaucrats were assigned to attempt to straighten them out, the situation became increasingly impossible. Further, business, by whom and for whom the program had been designed, ceased to feel the necessity for further cooperation as soon as conditions began to improve. The Ford Motor Company, for example, had refused to take part in the program, and after it became apparent that nothing was being done to force it to do so, other companies and industries quickly began to follow suit. In turn, labor and liberal groups, while they had been impressed with what initially seemed to be an intelligent program of economic planning, quickly saw that its operation led toward an accelerated tendency of concentrating wealth and economic power in the hands of the business community. Labor especially was annoyed by the apparent reluctance on the part of the Administration to enforce the supposedly advantageous provisions of Section 7(a) as industry successfully evaded them at every turn. Similarly, although they denounced the AAA, it was the large commercial farmers of the country who drew the most benefits from the program. The ill-conceived acreage restriction provisions were of little use to the small farmer who could ill afford to take much land out of cultivation. The large land owner, on the other hand, could retire great portions of land, cut his costs by dispensing with tenant farmers and field hands and use his Government checks to buy tractors and other equipment to farm the remaining land. For many small farmers, especially in the South and Southwest this meant more and more an active contemplation of the long trek to California, so aptly described by John Steinbeck in his famous novel *The Grapes of Wrath.*

Roosevelt, although disappointed as large elements of his former following seemed on the verge of desertion, generally responded by a renewed determination to try a new approach, or a series of approaches to deal with the nation's ills. He had earlier likened himself to a quarterback in a football game, waiting to call the second play after seeing how the first one worked. And great portions of the public, conscious that while the first play might result in a fifteen-yard loss, the second might result in a touchdown, awaited the call, with little or no disillusionment that the quarterback's strategy had once backfired.

The second play, it quickly developed, was to be quite different from the first. The experiment in business self-government had failed and the failure produced a growing bitterness in the White House toward business. Further, bankers and industrialists, who had often benefited strongly from the New Deal, were rapidly becoming more anti-Roosevelt than any other group in the nation. They had been uneasy with the Administration from the first, especially as it had continually attempted to dissociate the concept of wealth from the concept of virtue and thus undermine their position of superiority in American society. Now, with money once again in their pockets, they set up a cry for a return to the 1920's and the laissez faire economic system in which they had been kings. It was this group, for example, that in August, 1934, formed the Liberty League, a well-financed organization actively interested in bringing a halt to any further New Deal action and attacking Roosevelt openly and often ruthlessly.

Deserted by business, the President then set out to concentrate on individual programs to benefit labor, the small farmer, the small taxpayer, the consumer and the "forgotten man." This meant a general abandonment of any policy of a rigidly planned economy and a new focus on piecemeal reforms. Taken together, it was hoped these reforms would result in the realization of the same long-range goals which had been the object of the earlier programs. The very shift in technique was once again testimony to the absence of any philosophic commitment on the part of Roosevelt toward any preconceived theory or any master program for dealing with the problems of faltering capitalism.

The "second New Deal" as some historians have called it, was, however, no fundamental rejection of the first. No NRA codes or acreage restrictions were included, but neither were programs like the banking legislation, the CCC or the TVA scrapped. New Deal leaders in Congress moved to salvage Section 7(a) of the initial NRA legislation and expanded it into a far broader labor law, with a National Labor Relations Board established to enforce its various pro-labor provisions. This act served notice that the government would actively participate in securing the unionization of the American worker and make it possible for him thereby to develop effective bargaining and negotiating machinery by which he could improve his own status. Remnants of the earlier agriculture program were salvaged through the passage of a farm-mortgage moratorium measure in 1935 providing for a three-year grace period on foreclosures, and a Soil Conservation and Domestic Allotment Act early the following year. The latter measure enabled the continued restriction of agricultural output, not by contracts with farmers for acreage restrictions, but by benefit payments to growers who actively practiced soil conservation in cooperation with the Government. Farmers participating in the program through their county agricultural association leased to the Government land formerly planted in soil-depleting crops, and in return received compensation for their efforts to check wastage of fertility and erosion. Payments depended upon acreage withdrawn from soil-depleting crop production and turned over to soil-conserving crops. Provision was made whereby sharecroppers and tenants received part of the payments.

New programs, however, showed the desirability and practicality of avoiding such all-engrossing approaches as the NRA and concentrating more upon individuals and individual needs. The demand for unique legislation for the coal industry and for railroad employees was met with specific laws applying to each. The citizen now wishing to buy a home found lending agencies ready to extend money both for long terms and at low interest since a Federal Housing Administration was now insuring mortgages and thus breaking the credit log-jam. A Social Security program was adopted reminiscent of that established in Germany in the 1880's and in England and France in the early years of the twentieth century. Under it the Federal government, either by direct action or by cooperation with the states, set up programs of unemployment compensation, old-age and survivor's insurance, and old-age pensions, and authorized money grants for state-administered relief programs for the destitute blind, for homeless, crippled, dependent and delinquent children, and for services such as public health work, vocational rehabilitation, and maternity and infant care. The employed citizen, by registering with the program, submitting to payroll deductions for its support and generally cooperating with it was made to feel that he was participating in a program to underpin his future security and that of millions of his fellow Americans.

A new approach to relief, encompassed in the Works Progress Administration, also gave great numbers of unemployed Americans a new feeling of usefulness and constructive endeavor. Instead of direct handouts to individuals, or to individuals through the states, projects were created which would use the particular skills of many different occupational groups. Actors and playwrights worked in the Federal Theatre Project, musicians were hired to give symphony concerts in parks and schools, artists decorated public buildings with murals, biologists were assigned to assist in the public health program, skilled craftsmen worked in adult education programs, athletes directed recreational programs, scholars worked on historical surveys, and librarians were given cataloguing and indexing work. A special portion of the

program made funds available to students trying to finance themselves through college. A generation of artists and intellectuals
came through a crisis period, feeling they had made some small
contribution to the public welfare. In turn they responded to
this opportunity for service by exhibiting an extreme loyalty and
devotion to the President, who, although actually functioning in
a near paternalistic capacity, seemed to stand as merely the warm
personal figure which had made the opportunity available.

If Roosevelt seemed an opportunity-maker to many Americans, he was anathema to much of the business community, which
felt he was ruthlessly destructive of its interests and a "traitor
to his class." The second New Deal included a radical new tax
policy designed to encourage a wider distribution of wealth in
the country. Higher tax rates were imposed on corporations, and
an excess-profits tax and an undistributed-profits tax were enacted.
Denounced by wealthier elements as a vengeful "soak-the-rich"
program with Roosevelt playing the role of a Robin Hood, it
was generally popular with the electorate since few people outside the Liberty League objected in the least to soaking the rich.

If Roosevelt and the New Deal had received approval in
the election of 1934, the overwhelming endorsement of 1936 made
such earlier approval seem mild by comparison. Running for
a second term, Roosevelt carried forty-six of the forty-eight
states. The voters gave him the biggest popular plurality in history; his 523 to 8 ratio of electoral votes was the largest since
1820. And again the President's appeal had rubbed off on his
party. The Democrats made substantial gains in both the Senate
and the House, and controlled them by overwhelming majorities.
Indeed, the President privately expressed concern that without
strong Republican opposition, splits might well develop within
the huge Democratic majorities as shifting factions fought with
one another.

Opponents charged that the New Deal bought the votes; that
by using relief jobs and public funds, millions of Americans were
bribed into support. These charges missed the secret of Roosevelt's popularity. The second New Deal, even more than the
first, had created the illusion of opening up channels by which
people could do something, and something very real and concrete
to improve their own status and generally have a role in their
own salvation. The demonstration of loyalty to the President
was no mendicant's dutiful expression of thanks to a generous

and impersonal benefactor. It was far more an enthusiastic demonstration of loyalty and admiration toward a friend and equal who had personally wrestled with the devil in their behalf and made life safe for them by his victory. But the Roosevelt triumph was also, to Roosevelt especially, a personal reply on the part of people to whom he had talked to warmly and confidently in his speeches. He had sought to express in simple language the hopes and aspirations of the average man and approval meant the people had apparently understood. He was convinced that he was appealing to the best in people, bringing out their decency, unselfishness and innate goodness, and was exhilarated when the result seemed favorable.

But the question of the day was where from here. Roosevelt had run on the New Deal record. Did the voters want a continuation of the present program, and enlargement, or a shift in new directions? Once again the job of leadership, if it were to be effective, required a mastery of the moods and impulses of American public opinion.

In his second inaugural address in early 1937, Roosevelt indicated that he read the election returns as a mandate for new and extended reform programs. He thus proposed a broad, coordinated plan of social, economic, and political reform to extend both to old and new areas of American life. The next two years proved a bitter disappointment to New Deal leadership. The record might seem to indicate that the pulse-taker had lost his touch.

A slum clearance and public housing program was instituted but not until real-estate interests had successfully pressured Congress to curtail it drastically. A Farm Security Administration was established to enhance the status of beleaguered farmers, but proved a disappointment in operation. Although a second AAA was set up in 1938 to extend the farm program of 1936, the projected extension of social security did not come until August, 1939. Then it resulted in only minor administrative changes in the original act, and offered little in the way of wider coverage or greater benefits. A Fair Labor Standards Act, to create a national maximum hour and minimum wage standard, squeaked through Congress by the narrowest majority in 1938 and then had to be revised two years after its passage to provide anything like the benefits the Administration had initially hoped it would produce. If the President had to be content with half a loaf in most of these instances, he had to resign himself to the complete rejection of other proposals. A hoped-for extension of the application of the principle of constructive regional planning, as embodied in the TVA, to seven other great river valleys got nowhere. Also turned down were proposals for reorganization of public-works programs to provide for long-term planning of community welfare, and complete reorganization of both the executive and judicial branches of the Government with an eye to eliminating bureaucratic overlapping and administrative red tape. Roosevelt, always a realist, took defeat gracefully, admitting to Congress in January, 1939: "We have now passed the period of internal conflict in the launching of our program of social reform. Our full energies may now be released to invigorate the process of recovery in order to preserve our reforms."

The President had apparently missed the cue in seeking to extend reform activities. Yet the reasons for the breakdown of the "third New Deal" go far deeper than mere misreading of the public opinion charts. Roosevelt had made a bad tactical error in converting what even conservative lawyers initially had felt was a sensible reform program for the judiciary into a politically-motivated attack on the conservative members of the Supreme Court. The error, however, proved most disastrous in providing a rallying point for conservative Democrats in Congress to begin openly opposing the Administration. With Democratic party following fragmented and the conservative bloc no longer cowed, any prior rubberstamping of legislation came to an abrupt end, every new measure had to be fought for, often over long periods of time. The President then committed a second tactical error in attempting personally, and as it turned out, unsuccessfully, to purge Congress of a number of the leaders of his conservative opposition. The net result was a further coagulation of his growing intraparty opponents. To add to these problems, New Dealers, encouraged by the rise of the general business index from 1935 to 1937 and hopeful of returning to a balanced budget, cut back some of the artificial supports which the Government had been keeping under the economy, only to find that the country was not ready for such action and that their optimism about the degree of recovery which had been attained was too great. The resulting recession discredited the New Deal in many eyes. Since the Administration had taken credit for the earlier upswing, it could hardly avoid criticism when depression returned. Even the most loyal Roosevelt admirer was forced to admit that although the New Deal had made many reforms, it had not apparently solved the basic economic problems of the nation.

Yet, less tangible and more general factors also played a part in the surprising collapse of the domestic reform program. Woodrow Wilson had observed: "It is only once in a generation that a people can be lifted above material things. That is why conservative government is in the saddle two-thirds of the time." In many respects, 1937 and 1938 saw a return of conservatism which undercut continued activism. Many Americans felt it was time to slow down and consolidate what had already been done; to see how the current programs were going to work out before further new ones were introduced. And if there were those who still felt liberal goals should be pursued, they found it harder and harder to plunge in and concentrate fully upon them while constantly looking over their shoulder at the increasingly more alarming developments in Europe and Asia where non-liberal leaders in Germany, Italy, and Japan were driving their people toward goals of world conquest.

The remarkable thing about the New Deal domestic program was not that it ended with its objectives half-accomplished or that it ended when its leadership seemed at the height of its strength, but that in roughly five short years it accomplished what it did. By the late 1930's Americans accepted as part of their way of life: the responsibility of their governmental representatives to regulate the economy, to support agriculture, to provide job security and social security; the right of workingmen to organize in unions of their choice; the prohibition of child labor; the development of hydroelectric power under Government auspices; the guarantee of bank deposits, the regulation of securities; slum clearance, and Federal aid to public health and social services. The majority of these programs, representing a whole new approach to government and government's role, were unthinkable in 1932. Roosevelt had shown a despondent generation of Americans the virtue and value of positive government, a fact made more clear as a Republican administration in the 1950's embraced and even expanded many of the New Deal reforms.

But fully as important, such welfare state approaches had been brought about by reasoned experiment within the framework of the existing social, political, and economic system. Roosevelt

FRANKLIN ROOSEVELT

had been able to accomplish what both the extreme Right and Left felt was impossible, to find a route by which free men could manage their own economic destiny, with no essential loss of their freedom. The fact that this was a middle road was further made clear by the reaction of both the Right and the Left to the program. For while the business world and conservatives generally were joining or applauding the Liberty League, radicals were also attacking Roosevelt for missing the golden opportunity to bring about the total socialist state and proclaiming that by his piecemeal approach he accomplished little more than patching up a system which was ripe for elimination. Recent writers have also criticized the President for his rank opportunism, his inconsistency of approach and his wavering principles. Yet the Roosevelt strategy of compromise and restraint, of working for realizable goals, of never getting too far ahead of public opinion, of speeding up here and slowing down there is undoubtedly a vital factor in explaining why the President accomplished as much as he did. To the criticism that he was delinquent both in results and acceptable methods, one cannot help being impressed with the modest defense of Frank Freidel: ". . . measured by what other possible presidents might have achieved in the 1930's—Baker, Garner, or Smith, for example—he might receive higher marks."

The total Roosevelt picture, however, must also include an assessment of the President as a national and world leader in a period when Western civilization was wavering on the precipice. Here his marks also should be higher than many critics are willing to acknowledge. One of the ironies regarding the two great Democratic leaders of the twentieth century is that both came to office pledged to concentrate on solving the nation's domestic ills, yet both wound up with the awesome task of leading the nation into and out of a world war. But unlike Woodrow Wilson, who can legitimately be criticized for failing to prepare the American people both physically and psychologically for the harsh realities of war, Roosevelt did everything reasonably possible toward that end. The odds against him were great. Rising dictatorship in Europe had made a mockery out of the earlier crusade to "make the world safe for democracy." If conservatives and liberals were at odds over approaches to domestic recovery in

253

the 1930's, both could agree on the folly of internationalism and the virtue of the United States never again becoming involved with straightening out the insoluble difficulties of the Old World. Liberals especially, on whom the President had come to depend to support his domestic program, continually argued that collective security and preparedness led to war, and that war, just as in 1917, would mean the end of reform, a stifling of civil liberties, and a peace that left the world no better than it had been before. Again the President had a task of shaping public opinion along desirable and constructive lines, and in this case lines vital to survival; and again the device of "playing it by ear" led eventually to desirable results.

Roosevelt himself was an internationalist by instinct and experience. As assistant secretary of the Navy in the First World War he had been intimately associated with the Wilson administration and had supported its peace program and proposed League of Nations. Upon this country's failure to enter the League, he supported United States' participation in the World Court. In his first inaugural address, he endorsed the Good Neighbor Policy as a basis for international harmony. However, upon entering the White House, Roosevelt promptly chose to emphasize that the first and primary objective of his administration was to be domestic recovery. Foreign problems would have to wait until the United States had put its own house in order, even if this meant adopting, immediately, a callous attitude toward European recovery.

At the same time, it is difficult to brand his early activities as president as flatly isolationist. The New Deal itself was a demonstration of Roosevelt's acute awareness of the implicit dangers of fascism, national socialism, and communism. Understanding, as he did, what such programs did to democracy, he was conscious of the necessity of rejecting their principles for the United States. This also meant keeping American democracy alive in order that other would-be saviors of America might not push them on the country as panaceas. Further he was convinced there were vital international reasons for making democracy work in the United States. The example might well inspire other democratic nations to renewed confidence in the desirability of the system. But most importantly Roosevelt saw a day not far off when the United States would have to take the lead, as the one strong democratic power still afloat, in halting the dictators in behalf of Western

civilization. While Roosevelt's public utterances of these sentiments were few in the early years of the New Deal, some important quiet actions were being taken.

In June, 1934, Congress passed a reciprocal trade agreements
act authorizing the president through the secretary of state to
negotiate favorable, low-tariff, trading arrangements with nations
who would in turn grant favorable concessions to American
goods. Secretary of State Cordell Hull lost no time in implementing the measure with a series of international arrangements, particularly with Latin-American countries. In the early frenzy of
the New Deal, Roosevelt quietly slipped in a program of naval
construction "as a means of furthering national recovery," and
while the Government was busily building dams in the Tennessee
valley, it was also constructing aircraft carriers such as the *Enterprise* and the *Yorktown*. In 1933 formal diplomatic recognition
was extended to Soviet Russia. In 1936 the President opened a
Pan-American Conference at Buenos Aires with a speech urging
mutual cooperation against any non-American state seeking to
commit acts of aggression against any state in the Western Hemisphere. This policy was extended at a meeting two years later at
Lima, Peru.

All these actions could be done with some ease if they were
undertaken in the name of recovery, reform, international trade,
and the building of solid peacetime fences. Unfortunately, to
Roosevelt's discredit, they were not accompanied by any aggressive educational program aimed at convincing advanced pacifists
and isolationists of the growing threat which dictatorial aggression
presented to American democracy. This was not because Roosevelt was unconcerned. Sumner Welles indicates that by 1936, he
was "obsessed" with the dangers confronting the United States.
As late as 1937 the President was still operating on the theory that
an unrecovered and unreformed America would have little chance
before mobilized dictatorship. Having the ox fairly well in harness
and doing a reasonable job of plowing, he did not want to risk
waving the red flag of interventionism at him until further domestic objectives were achieved.

But by late 1937 that risk had to be taken. Roosevelt faced the
bitter reality that although he was not the only American either
who understood the gravity of the European situation, or who
sensed that the United States would eventually be forced to enter
the war, yet he was the one man with the authority to do some-

thing concrete. He realized that he must accept the responsibility of acting so as to enable the United States to confront the situation realistically. The task was a tremendous one. To prepare the American people for war involved more than merely overcoming the normal human antipathy toward war. It meant, much as with the depression, convincing them of the necessity of following certain programs—in this case preparedness and mobilization—so that they could best serve their own ends and those of their nation. It meant doing so quickly in order to make up the great deficit in strength between the United States and the mobilized dictatorships. It meant doing so without either provoking Japan or Italy or Germany into an attack on the United States at an earlier date than we were ready for. It meant doing so without having the Democratic party labeled the war party and forcing it out of office to be replaced by an isolationist-led Republican party including the Liberty League as its hard core. But it also meant undertaking this crucial educational job when nearly three-fourths of the American people, sampled in public opinion polls, expressed the firm conviction that the United States' entry into the First World War had been a mistake and that America's business lay between the Atlantic coast on one side and the Pacific coast on the other. Politically this had to be done at a time when conservative Democrats in Congress were beginning successfully to reject party discipline and defy Administrative leadership.

The initial Rooseveltian attempt clearly demonstrated these problems. Speaking in Chicago in October, 1937, three months after Japan had renewed her conquest of China, the President appealed to the American people to see the facts of international life, and suggested that the peace-loving nations might have to quarantine aggressors to prevent the spread of international anarchy. Popular reaction was immediate and largely negative. "Stop War Mongering, Mr. President," shouted the *Wall Street Journal*, and the words were echoed nationally by apprehensive isolationists. Roosevelt realized quickly that he had moved ahead of public opinion and would have to continue resorting to quiet and sometimes personal means to instigate preparedness rather than by any shock technique. But regardless of approach, he realized it had to come quickly. In September, 1938, the Munich Conference agreed to Adolph Hitler's demands for the partition of Czechoslovakia. One year later Poland fell. By early June of 1940 the Netherlands and Belgium had been taken, and later in the month France was brought under Nazi domination. By August, 1940, England was the only free nation left in Europe capable of confronting the Axis might, and she was being subjected to virtually daily air raids by the 2,600-plane German Luftwaffe. In the Far East the Japanese conquest of China was progressing relentlessly and French Indo-China was next on the agenda, with the Philippines dangerously near and tempting when that was completed.

Ever since 1935, however, Congress, through a program of neutrality legislation, had virtually legislated the United States into helplessness as far as direct aid to allies was concerned. Roosevelt then had to find ways of extending aid through administrative maneuvering without running afoul of Congressional restrictions. Money was diverted from relief programs for a further enlargement of the Navy. When Congress did vote a Naval Expansion Act in 1938 calling for a ten-year building program, ways were found to reduce its long-term nature. With grudging but growing approval the President was authorized to begin accumulating stockpiles of strategic raw materials for use if war occurred. In September, 1939, the President called Congress into special session in order to revise the Neutrality Laws, and in November the arms embargo provisions were repealed. A program of cash-and-carry exports of arms and munitions to friendly belligerents was substituted. In 1940 the President began funneling aid to Britain, in one instance taking it upon himself, with questionable constitutional authority, to trade fifty "over-age" United States destroyers for defense bases in Newfoundland, Bermuda, and British Caribbean possessions.

Public opinion was gradually coming along. By the time the Lend-Lease Act was passed in March, 1941, nearly 70 per cent of the people polled indicated it was more important for the United States to help England than to keep out of war. Nearly 60 per cent indicated they were willing to risk war with Japan rather than let her continue her aggressions. As Roosevelt and Churchill met in the Atlantic, in August, 1941, to agree upon long-range democratic hopes in a peaceful post-war world, these percentages increased even more. Roosevelt may have felt moments of desperation for his thankless efforts in preparing the American people for accepting their essential role in a war for the survival of their way of life. But public reaction to the sneak attack on Pearl Harbor left him feeling fully rewarded for his efforts. Overnight, significant opposition to the United States' accepting her world responsibilities vanished. Never before did Americans go to war with such determination and unity as during the Second World War. "We'll blaze a trail to Berlin and come back by Tokyo," went the song of an infantry division. Simultaneously came the honest revelation that "the 'old man' had obviously been right all along." "We were fools not to realize it, we won't be fools again." And along with the determination went the very real feeling that the American way of life was worth saving, a sentiment not so frequently expressed nine years earlier before the "old man" had come into office.

For Roosevelt, however, vindication carried with it the awesome task of once again being the reflector of the will and wishes of a huge majority, a task which at times made the preceding one of moving the donkey with a carrot seem easy by comparison. There was no question the American people wanted the war won as quickly and with as little loss of life as possible so the boys could be brought home and normal conditions re-established. Their desires with regard to the post-war world were less clear. Yet Roosevelt, always believing in the rational capacity of man to learn and profit by his experiences, could not help but feel that there was a widespread, if largely negative, sentiment to avoid the fatal mistakes of Versailles. The question was how, and how long could such a sentiment be sustained.

As to the military struggle, Roosevelt lost no time in exerting firm leadership. After Pearl Harbor, he told a press conference that "Old Dr. New Deal" had to be replaced by "Dr. Win-the-War," and his exhortations to complete effort for total victory met with a dedicated response by the majority of Americans in uniform and out. His relations with military leaders showed both tact and a surprising knowledge of the details of general planning. Former Secretary of War Henry L. Stimson, writing to Justice William O. Douglas in 1950, described him as "always a charming friend" whose "function as a war leader on the big question of grand strategy was superb." Yet, for every Stimson there have been five critics who, in the ever great wisdom of hindsight, have found the President sadly deficient in his attempts to deal successfully with the Russians and shape the structure of the peace in an enlightened fashion.

If the President erred, his errors were in adhering too closely to what he considered the demands and desires of public opinion, not in disregarding it and charting any new and dangerous course. Roosevelt, just as he had understood the limits of practical idealism in the area of domestic reform, had a sensitivity for those limits in the area of international relations. Wilson's errors from 1918 to 1921 Roosevelt interpreted as acting upon convictions which the American people did not share, with the consequence that presidential policy outran the possibilities of national support. Perhaps Americans in the 1940's were more mature and ready to assume the positive responsibilities of world leadership. But the President was unwilling to accept that assumption with bland faith and operate upon it, especially in light of his four- or five-year struggle with the isolationists.

Rather, he accepted the less optimistic, but certainly more realistic position that it might well be possible to capitalize upon the average American's natural instinct to subordinate temporarily his isolationist tendencies to broad international cooperation for the purposes of wartime survival. Such immediate instincts might be channeled into a constructive program for the post-war period, before the natural let-down of post-war relaxation made this impossible. Roosevelt never expected, for example, to be able to commit an extensive number of American troops to occupation duty following the war. Nor did he feel any other form of direct American intervention in world affairs could be accomplished. He sensed that the likely temper of post-war public opinion would make this impossible. Consequently he hoped that what he could do was convince the American people of the value of converting the wartime coalition with Britain and Russia into a continuing agency for peace; turn it, in other words, into the nucleus of a post-war international organization, while the war was still in progress. Then when peace came, a structure for international cooperation would be in existence to resist normal and natural tendencies to return to narrow nationalism and personal materialism. For more than this, he scarcely hoped.

Wartime military cooperation, especially as national survival was involved, afforded opportunities through vital wartime conferences for discussion of the nature of maintaining the eventual peace. At Moscow, in October, 1943, general agreement was reached as to the necessity of establishing at the earliest practical date a general international organization for the maintenance of international peace and security. Widespread approval from the people of the United States accompanied the move. Yet Roosevelt neither fully trusted the Russians' noble expressions of desired cooperation nor was he totally eased at the seeming unity of American public opinion. For he realized that his own gnawing distrust of the U.S.S.R. was magnified many times in the minds of many Americans. Roosevelt feared that the first show of Russion intransigence, which he knew was bound to come as Russia's military position improved, could well sour American public opinion on the desirability of any international cooperation except that dictated by immediate military necessity.

The practical course then was a series of adjustments, as minor as possible, to the growing demands of Stalin. These settlements were not based on any naive assumption that the Russians were "swell fellows, let's be nice to them," but upon the desire to nail down Russian promises of post-war cooperation. This result, in turn, would prevent needless flare-ups which might scare Americans out of a post-war international organization as they had been disillusioned out of joining the League following the First World War. And if American's instinctive distrust of Russia was not aggravated into total negativism prior to the creation of the United Nations and agreement of full American participation, this was also partly due to skilled Presidential pulse-taking. By instigating the course of action which was followed, Roosevelt correctly sensed and underwrote other sentiments of the American mind which fondly hoped that a continued cooperation among the leading world powers would guarantee a permanent and lasting peace.

The question remains why Roosevelt felt a United Nations was so valuable that he used all of the flagging energies of his later years to move Americans into full acceptance of it and prevent disillusionments which might have side-tracked such acceptance. Possibly this was because he remembered how during the 1920's and 1930's the absence of an effective organization for peace and security had led to nothing but human frustration, dictatorship, and war. Possibly it was because of a general belief that if mankind could be afforded the machinery of cooperation, it would generally learn to use it in time of stress rather than resorting to techniques of annihilation. More probably it was because as activator of the atomic age he realized all too well that another war might be mankind's last. A way had to be found to make it impossible for anyone to lead men into war. The only way was by creating an organization which would institutionalize international decision-making; which, hopefully, would eliminate the possibilities of an individual leader ever gaining sufficient power to lead a nation in moves contrary to the general welfare of all nations; which would, in other words, establish the concept of democracy and legislative responsibility as the required political process in the world community.

Admirable as such a goal might be, there was subtle irony in it. Roosevelt, who had cultivated the political arts so successfully and had become so nearly an absolute decider for his nation, who had personally exerted a type of leadership which had brought the most powerful community of the Western world out of the depths of economic depression, shepherded it to a responsible maturity, and led it to victory and world supremacy in the greatest of modern wars, ended his career advocating a body to curtail the limits of such leadership. "The highest use of one man's political genius," Rex Tugwell has written, "was to be stringent limitation on the future function of political genius." Yet who better could have advocated such a move? The political greatness of Franklin D. Roosevelt in final analysis lay in the full understanding of a Greek philosopher's ancient admonition, "Know thyself."

Selected Reading List

GEORGE WASHINGTON

BASSETT, JOHN. *The Federalist System, 1789–1801.* New York: Harper, 1906.

BEMIS, SAMUEL F. "Washington's Farewell Address: A Foreign Policy of Independence," *American Historical Review,* XXXIX (1934). Pp. 250–68.

BOWERS, CLAUDE G. *Jefferson and Hamilton: The Struggle for Democracy in America.* Boston: Houghton, 1925.

CARROLL, J. A. AND ASHWORTH, MARY W. *George Washington: First in Peace.* New York: Scribner, 1957.

CHANNING, EDWARD. "Washington and Parties, 1789–1797," *Massachusetts Historical Society Proceedings,* XLVII (1914). Pp. 35–44.

DECONDE, ALEXANDER. *Entangling Alliance.* Durham: Duke, 1958.

FORD, HENRY J. *Washington and His Colleagues.* New Haven: Yale, 1918.

FREEMAN, DOUGLAS S. *George Washington: Patriot and President.* New York: Scribner, 1954.

KROUT, JOHN A. AND FOX, DIXON R. *The Completion of Independence, 1790–1830.* New York: Macmillan, 1944.

SCHACHNER, NATHAN. *The Founding Fathers.* New York: Putnam, 1954.

STEPHENSON, NATHANIEL W. AND DUNN, W. H. *George Washington.* Vol II. New York: Oxford, 1940.

WHITE, LEONARD D. *The Federalists: A Study in Administrative History.* New York: Macmillan, 1948.

JOHN ADAMS

ADAMS, JAMES T. *The Adams Family*. Boston: Little, 1932.
ADAMS, JOHN QUINCY AND ADAMS, CHARLES F. *The Life and Works of John Adams: Life of Adams*. Vol. I. Boston: Little, 1856.
BOWEN, CATHERINE D. *John Adams and the American Revolution*. Boston: Little, 1950.
CHINARD, GILBERT. *Honest John Adams*. Boston: Little, 1933.
DAUER, MANNING J. *The Adams Federalists*. Baltimore: Johns Hopkins, 1953.
HARASZTI, ZOLTAN. *John Adams and the Prophets of Progress*. Cambridge: Harvard, 1952.
IACUZZI, ALFRED. *John Adams, Scholar*. New York: Vanni, 1952.
KOCH, ADRIENNE AND PEDEN, WILLIAM, eds. *Selected Writings of John and John Quincy Adams*. New York: Knopf, 1946.
KURTZ, STEPHEN G. *The Presidency of John Adams*. Philadelphia: Pennsylvania, 1957.
WALSH, CORREA M. *The Political Science of John Adams*. New York: Putnam, 1915.

THOMAS JEFFERSON

ADAMS, HENRY. *History of the United States during the Administrations of Thomas Jefferson and James Madison*. 9 Vols. New York: Scribner, 1889–1891.
ADAMS, JAMES T. *The Living Jefferson*. New York: Scribner, 1936.
CAPPON, LESTER J., ed. *The Adams-Jefferson Letters*. 2 Vols. Chapel Hill: North Carolina, 1959.
CHANNING, EDWARD. *The Jeffersonian System, 1801–1811*. New York: Harper, 1906.
CHINARD, GILBERT. *Thomas Jefferson: Apostle of Americanism*. Boston: Little, 1929.
MALONE, DUMAS. *Jefferson and His Time*. 5 Vols. Boston: Little, 1948, 1951–.
NOCK, ALBERT J. *Jefferson*. New York: Harcourt, 1926.
PADOVER, SAUL K. *Jefferson*. New York: Harcourt, 1942.
SCHACHNER, NATHAN. *Thomas Jefferson*. 2 Vols. Toronto: Collins, 1951.

WHITE, LEONARD D. *The Jeffersonians, 1801–1829.* New York: Macmillan, 1951.

ANDREW JACKSON

BASSETT, JOHN S. *The Life of Andrew Jackson.* New York: Macmillan, 1925.
CHAMBERS, WILLIAM N. *Old Bullion Benton: Senator from the West, 1782–1858.* Boston: Little, 1956.
HOFSTADTER, RICHARD. *The American Political Tradition and the Men Who Made It.* New York: Knopf, 1948.
JAMES, MARQUIS. *The Life of Andrew Jackson.* Indianapolis: Bobbs, 1938.
MEYERS, MARVIN. *The Jacksonian Persuasion: Politics and Belief.* Stanford: Stanford, 1957.
REMINI, ROBERT V. *Martin Van Buren and the Making of the Democratic Party.* New York: Columbia, 1959.
SCHLESINGER, ARTHUR M., JR. *The Age of Jackson.* Boston: Little, 1945.
SELLERS, CHARLES G., JR. *James K. Polk: Jacksonian, 1795–1843.* Princeton: Princeton, 1957.
VAN DEUSEN, GLYNDON G. *The Jacksonian Era, 1828–1848.* New York: Harper, 1959.
WARD, JOHN W. *Andrew Jackson: Symbol for an Age.* New York: Oxford, 1955.

JAMES POLK

DEVOTO, BERNARD. *The Year of Decision: 1846.* Boston: Little, 1943.
GRAEBNER, NORMAN A. *Empire on the Pacific.* New York: Ronald, 1955.
HAMILTON, HOLMAN. *Zachary Taylor: Soldier of the Republic.* Indianapolis: Bobbs, 1941.
McCORMAC, EUGENE I. *James K. Polk: A Political Biography.* Berkeley: California, 1922.
PARKS, JOSEPH H. *John Bell of Tennessee.* Baton Rouge: Louisiana, 1950.

QUAIFE, MILO M., ed. *The Diary of James K. Polk during His Presidency, 1845–1849*. 4 Vols. Chicago: McLaughlin, 1910.

REEVES, JESSE S. *American Diplomacy under Tyler and Polk*. Baltimore: Johns Hopkins, 1907.

SELLERS, CHARLES G., JR. *James K. Polk: Jacksonian, 1795–1843*. Princeton: Princeton, 1957.

SMITH, JUSTIN H. *The War with Mexico*. 2 Vols. New York: Macmillan, 1919.

WILTSE, CHARLES M. *John C. Calhoun: Sectionalist, 1840–1850*. Indianapolis: Bobbs, 1951.

ABRAHAM LINCOLN

CURRENT, RICHARD N. *The Lincoln Nobody Knows*. New York: McGraw, 1958.

DONALD, DAVID. *Lincoln Reconsidered*. New York: Knopf, 1956.

HESSELTINE, WILLIAM B. *Lincoln and the War Governors*. New York: Knopf, 1948.

POTTER, DAVID M. *Lincoln and His Party in the Secession Crisis*. New Haven: Yale, 1942.

RANDALL, JAMES G. *Lincoln the President*. 4 Vols. New York: Dodd, 1945–1955.

SANDBURG, CARL. *Abraham Lincoln: The War Years*. 4 Vols. New York: Harcourt, 1939.

STAMPP, KENNETH M. *And the War Came*. Baton Rouge: Louisiana, 1950.

THOMAS, BENJAMIN P. *Abraham Lincoln*. New York: Knopf, 1952.

WILLIAMS, T. HARRY. *Lincoln and His Generals*. New York: Knopf, 1952.

WILLIAMS, T. HARRY. *Lincoln and the Radicals*. Madison: Wisconsin, 1941.

GROVER CLEVELAND

BARNES, JAMES A. *John G. Carlisle: Financial Statesman*. New York: Dodd, 1931.

CLEVELAND, GROVER. *Presidential Problems.* New York: Century, 1904.

FORD, HENRY J. *The Cleveland Era.* New Haven: Yale, 1919.

HIRSCH, MARK C. *William C. Whitney: Modern Warwick.* New York: Dodd, 1948.

McELROY, ROBERT M. *Grover Cleveland: The Man and the Statesman.* 2 Vols. New York: Harper, 1923.

MERRILL, HORACE S. *Bourbon Leader: Grover Cleveland and the Democratic Party.* Boston: Little, 1957.

NEVINS, ALLAN. *Grover Cleveland: A Study in Courage.* New York: Dodd, 1932.

NEVINS, ALLAN, ed. *Letters of Grover Cleveland, 1850–1908.* Boston: Houghton, 1933.

OLSON, JAMES C. *J. Sterling Morton.* Lincoln: Nebraska, 1942.

PARKER, GEORGE F., ed. *The Writings and Speeches of Grover Cleveland.* New York: Cassell, 1892.

THEODORE ROOSEVELT

BEALE, HOWARD K. *Theodore Roosevelt and the Rise of America to World Power.* Baltimore: Johns Hopkins, 1957.

BLUM, JOHN M. *The Republican Roosevelt.* Cambridge: Harvard, 1954.

HARBAUGH, WILLIAM H. *Power and Responsibility: The Life and Times of Theodore Roosevelt.* New York: Farrar, 1961.

HAYS, SAMUEL P. *Conservation and the Gospel of Efficiency.* Cambridge: Harvard, 1959.

HOFSTADTER, RICHARD. *The Age of Reform: From Bryan to F. D. R.* New York: Knopf, 1955.

MORISON, ELTING E. WITH BLUM, JOHN M., eds. *The Letters of Theodore Roosevelt.* 8 Vols. Cambridge: Harvard, 1951–1954.

MOWRY, GEORGE E. *The Era of Theodore Roosevelt, 1900–1912.* New York: Harper, 1958.

PINCHOT, GIFFORD. *Breaking New Ground.* New York: Harcourt, 1947.

PRINGLE, HENRY F. *Theodore Roosevelt: A Biography.* New York: Harcourt, 1931.

ROOSEVELT, THEODORE. *Theodore Roosevelt: An Autobiography.* New York: Scribner, 1920.

WOODROW WILSON

BAKER, RAY S. *Woodrow Wilson: Life and Letters.* 8 Vols. Garden City: Doubleday, Doran, 1927–1939.

BELL, HERBERT C. F. *Woodrow Wilson and the People.* Garden City: Doubleday, Doran, 1945.

DAVIDSON, JOHN W., ed. *A Crossroads of Freedom: The 1912 Campaign Speeches of Woodrow Wilson.* New Haven: Yale, 1956.

GARRATY, JOHN A. *Woodrow Wilson: A Great Life in Brief.* New York: Knopf, 1956.

LATHAM, EARL, ed. *The Philosophy and Politics of Woodrow Wilson.* Chicago: Chicago, 1958.

LINK, ARTHUR S. *Wilson the Diplomatist: A Look at His Major Foreign Policies.* Baltimore: Johns Hopkins, 1957.

LINK, ARTHUR S. *Wilson: The Road to the White House; The New Freedom.* 2 Vols. Princeton: Princeton, 1947, 1956.

LINK, ARTHUR S. *Woodrow Wilson and the Progressive Era, 1910–1917.* New York: Harper, 1954.

WALWORTH, ARTHUR. *Woodrow Wilson: American Prophet; World Prophet.* 2 Vols. New York: Longmans, 1958.

WILSON, EDITH B. *My Memoir.* Indianapolis: Bobbs, 1938.

FRANKLIN ROOSEVELT

BURNS, JAMES M. *Roosevelt: The Lion and the Fox.* New York: Harcourt, 1956.

EINAUDI, MARIO. *The Roosevelt Revolution.* New York: Harcourt, 1959.

FREIDEL, FRANK. *Franklin D. Roosevelt: The Apprenticeship; The Ordeal; The Triumph.* 3 Vols. Boston: Little, 1952, 1954, 1956.

HARRITY, RICHARD AND MARTIN, RALPH G. *The Human Side of F. D. R.* New York: Duell, 1960.

PERKINS, FRANCES. *The Roosevelt I Knew.* New York: Viking, 1946.

ROBINSON, EDGAR E. *The Roosevelt Leadership, 1933–1945.* Philadelphia: Lippincott, 1955.

ROSENMAN, SAMUEL, ed. *The Public Papers and Addresses of Franklin D. Roosevelt.* 13 Vols. New York: various pub., 1938–1950.

SCHLESINGER, ARTHUR M., JR. *The Age of Roosevelt: The Crisis of the Old Order; The Coming of the New Deal; The Politics of Upheaval.* 3 Vols. Boston: Houghton, 1957, 1958, 1960.

SHERWOOD, ROBERT. *Roosevelt and Hopkins.* New York: Harper, 1948.

TUGWELL, REXFORD G. *The Democratic Roosevelt.* New York: Doubleday, 1957.